WILEY FINANCE EDITIONS

TRADING FOR
A LIVING

TRADING FOR A LIVING

Psychology
TradingTactics
Money Management

Dr. Alexander Elder
Director
Financial Trading Seminars, Inc.

John Wiley & Sons, Inc.
New York • Chichester • Brisbane • Toronto • Singapore

In recognition of the importance of preserving what has been written, it is a policy of John Wiley & Sons, Inc., to have books of enduring value printed on acid-free paper, and we exert our best efforts to that end.

Copyright © 1993 by Dr. Alexander Elder
Published by John Wiley & Sons, Inc.

Library of Congress Cataloging-in-Publication Data

Elder, Alexander
    Trading for a living : psychology, trading tactics, money management / Alexander Elder.
        p.   cm.
    Includes bibliographical references and index.
    ISBN 0-471-59224-2
    1. Stocks.   2. Futures.   3. Options (Futures)   I. Title.
HG4661.E43   1992
32.64'5 — dc20   92-35165

Printed in the United States of America
10   9   8

To Lou Taylor —
a trader, a wise man, a true friend

Contents

TRADING FOR
A LIVING

Introduction

1. TRADING—THE LAST FRONTIER

You can be free. You can live and work anywhere in the world. You can be independent from routine and not answer to anybody.

This is the life of a successful trader.

Many aspire to this but few succeed. An amateur looks at a quote screen and sees millions of dollars sparkle in front of his face. He reaches for the money — and loses. He reaches again — and loses more. Traders lose because the game is hard, or out of ignorance, or lack of discipline. If any of these ail you, I wrote this book for you.

How I Began to Trade

In the summer of 1976, I drove from New York to California. I threw a few books on psychiatry (I was a first-year psychiatric resident), several histories, and a paperback copy of Engel's *How to Buy Stocks* into the trunk of my old Dodge. Little did I know that a dog-eared paperback, borrowed from a lawyer friend, would in due time change the course of my life. That friend, incidentally, had a perfect reverse golden touch — any investment he touched went under water. But that's another story.

I gulped down the Engel book in campgrounds across America, finishing it on a Pacific beach in La Jolla. I had known nothing about the stock market, and the idea of making money by thinking gripped me.

I had grown up in the Soviet Union in the days when it was, in the words of a former U.S. president, "an evil empire." I hated the Soviet system and wanted to get out, but emigration was forbidden. I entered college at 16, graduated medical school at 22, completed my residency, and then took a job as a ship's doctor. Now I could break free! I jumped the Soviet ship in Abidjan, Ivory Coast.

I ran to the U.S. Embassy through the clogged dusty streets of an African port city, chased by my ex-crewmates. The bureaucrats at the embassy fumbled and almost handed me back to the Soviets. I resisted, and they put me in a "safe house" and then on a plane to New York. I landed at Kennedy Airport in February 1974, arriving from Africa with summer clothes on my back and $25 in my pocket. I spoke some English, but did not know a soul in this country.

I had no idea what stocks, bonds, futures, or options were and sometimes got a queasy feeling just from looking at the American dollar bills in my wallet. In the old country, a handful of them could buy you three years in Siberia.

Reading *How to Buy Stocks* opened a whole new world for me. Returning to New York, I bought my first stock — it was KinderCare. Ever since then, I have avidly studied the markets and invested and traded stocks, options, and now mostly futures.

My professional career proceeded on a separate track. I completed a residency in psychiatry at a major university hospital, studied at the New York Psychoanalytic Institute, and served as book editor for the largest psychiatric newspaper in the United States. These days, I am busy trading and go to my psychiatric office, across the street from Carnegie Hall, only a few afternoons a week, after the markets close. I love practicing psychiatry, but I spend most of my time in the markets.

Learning to trade has been a long journey — with soaring highs and aching lows. In moving forward — or in circles — I repeatedly knocked my face against the wall and ran my trading account into the ground. Each time I returned to a hospital job, put a stake together, read, thought, did more testing, and then started trading again.

My trading slowly improved, but the breakthrough came when I realized that the key to winning was inside my head and not inside a computer. Psychiatry gave me the insight into trading that I will share with you.

Do You Really Want to Succeed?

For the past 17 years I've had a friend whose wife is fat. She is an elegant dresser, and she has been on a diet for as long as I have known her. She says she wants to lose weight and she does not eat cake or potatoes in front of people — but when I come into her kitchen, I often see her go at it with a big fork. She says she wants to be slim, but remains as fat today as the day we met. Why?

The short-term pleasure of eating is stronger for her than the delayed pleasure and health benefits of weight loss. My friend's wife reminds me of a great many traders who say they want to be successful but keep making impulsive trades — going for the short-term thrills of gambling in the markets.

People deceive themselves and play games with themselves. Lying to others is bad enough, but lying to yourself is hopeless. Bookstores are full of good books on dieting, but the world is full of overweight people.

This book will teach you how to analyze and trade the markets and how to deal with your own mind. I can give you the knowledge. Only you can supply the motivation.

2. PSYCHOLOGY IS THE KEY

You may base your trades on fundamental or technical analysis. You may trade because of hunches about economic and political trends, use "inside information," or simply hope.

Remember how you felt the last time you placed an order? Were you anxious to jump in or afraid of losing? Did you procrastinate before picking up the phone? When you closed out a trade, did you feel elated or humiliated? The feelings of thousands of traders merge into huge psychological tides that move the markets.

Getting Off the Roller Coaster

The majority of traders spend most of their time looking for good trades. Once they enter a trade, they lose control and either squirm from pain or grin from pleasure. They ride an emotional roller coaster and miss the essential element of winning — the management of their emotions. Their inability to manage themselves leads to poor money management of their accounts.

If your mind is not in gear with the markets, or if you ignore changes in mass psychology of crowds, then you have no chance of making money trading. All winning professionals know the enormous importance of psychology in trading. All losing amateurs ignore it.

Friends and clients who know that I am a psychiatrist often ask me whether this helps me as a trader. Good psychiatry and good trading have one important principle in common. Both focus on reality, on seeing the world the way it is. To live a healthy life, you have to live with your eyes open. To be a good trader, you need to trade with your eyes open, recognize real trends and turns, and not waste time or energy on regrets and wishful thinking.

A Man's Game?

Brokerage house records show that most traders are male. The files of my educational firm, Financial Trading Seminars, Inc., confirm that approximately 95 percent of traders are men. For this reason, you'll find that I commonly use the masculine pronoun (he) in the anecdotes and cases throughout this book. Of course, no disrespect is intended to the many successful women traders.

The percentage of women is higher among institutional traders — employees of banks, trading firms, and the like. In my experience, however, the few women who get involved in trading succeed more often than men. A woman needs exceptional drive to plunge into this male preserve.

Trading is similar to such thrilling and dangerous sports as sky-diving, rock-climbing, and scuba-diving. They also attract mostly men — fewer than 1 percent of hang gliders are female.

Men are drawn to risky sports in our increasingly regulated society. Dr. David Klein, a sociologist at the University of Michigan, was quoted in the *New York Times* as saying, "as work becomes more and more routinized . . . we turn to recreation for a sense of accomplishment. The safer and more routine we make work, the more we will push people into recreations where individual distinction and discretion, adventure and excitement play a part."

These sports provide intense pleasure but have a stigma of danger because many participants ignore the risks and take thoughtless chances. Dr. John Tongue, an orthopedic surgeon in Oregon who studied accidents among hang gliders, found that the chance of death rises among more experienced pilots because they take greater risks. An athlete who wants to enjoy risky sports has to follow safety rules. When you reduce risks, you gain an added sense of accomplishment and control. The same goes for trading.

You can succeed in trading only if you handle it as a serious intellectual pursuit. Emotional trading is lethal. To help ensure success, practice defensive money management. A good trader watches his capital as carefully as a professional scuba diver watches his air supply.

How This Book Is Organized

Successful trading stands on three pillars: psychology, market analysis and trading systems, and money management. This book will help you explore all three.

The first chapter of this book shows you a new approach to managing your emotions as a trader. I discovered this method while practicing psychiatry. It has greatly improved my trading, and it can help you, too.

The second chapter describes the crowd psychology of markets. Mass behavior is more primitive than individual behavior. If you understand how crowds behave, then you can profit from their mood swings and avoid being swept up in their emotions.

The third chapter of the book shows how chart patterns reveal crowd behavior. Classical technical analysis is applied social psychology, like poll-taking. Trendlines, gaps, and other chart patterns actually reflect crowd behavior.

The fourth chapter teaches modern methods of computerized technical analysis. Indicators provide a deeper insight into mass psychology than classical technical analysis. Trend-following indicators help identify market trends, while oscillators show when trends are ready to reverse.

Volume and open interest also reflect crowd behavior. The fifth chapter focuses on them as well as on the passage of time in the markets. Crowds have a very short attention span, and a trader who relates price changes to time gains a competitive advantage.

The sixth chapter focuses on the best techniques of stock market analysts. They can be especially helpful for stock index futures and options traders.

Sentiment indicators measuring the opinions of investors and traders are profiled in the seventh chapter. Crowds follow trends, and it often pays to join them when prices are moving. Sentiment indicators show when it is time to abandon the crowd—before it misses an important reversal.

The eighth chapter reveals two proprietary indicators. Elder-ray is a price-based indicator that measures the power of bulls and bears below the surface of the markets. Force Index measures prices and volume. It shows whether the dominant market group is becoming stronger or weaker.

The ninth chapter presents several trading systems. The Triple Screen trading system is my own method. I have used it for years. This and other systems show you how to select trades and find entry and exit points.

The tenth chapter focuses on money management. This essential aspect of successful trading is neglected by most amateurs. You can have a brilliant trading system, but if your money management is bad, then a short string of losses will destroy your account. Trading without proper money management is like trying to cross a desert barefoot.

You are about to spend many hours with this book. When you find ideas that seem valuable to you, test them in the one crucible that matters — your own experience. You can make this knowledge your own only by questioning it.

3. THE ODDS AGAINST YOU

Why do most traders lose and wash out of the markets? Emotional and thoughtless trading are two reasons, but there is another. Markets are actually set up so that most traders must lose money.

The trading industry kills traders with commissions and slippage. Most amateurs cannot believe this, just as medieval peasants could not believe that tiny invisible germs could kill them. If you ignore slippage and deal with a broker who charges high commissions, you are acting like a peasant who drinks from a communal pool during a cholera epidemic.

You pay commissions for entering and exiting trades. Slippage is the difference between the price at which you place your order and the price at which it gets filled. When you place a limit order, it is filled at your price or not at all. When you feel eager to enter or exit the market and give a market order, it is often filled at a worse price than prevailed when you placed it.

The trading industry keeps draining huge amounts of money from the markets. Exchanges, regulators, brokers, and advisors live off the markets while generations of traders keep washing out. Markets need a fresh supply of losers just as builders of the ancient pyramids of Egypt needed a fresh supply of slaves. Losers bring money into the markets, which is necessary for the prosperity of the trading industry.

A Minus-Sum Game

Brokers, exchanges, and advisors run marketing campaigns to attract more losers to the markets. Some mention that futures trading is a zero-sum game. They count on the fact that most people feel smarter than average and expect to win in a zero-sum game.

Winners in a zero-sum game make as much as losers lose. If you and I bet

$10 on the direction of the next 100-point move in the Dow, one of us will collect $10 and the other will lose $10. The person who is smarter should win this game over a period of time.

People buy the trading industry's propaganda about the zero-sum game, take the bait and open trading accounts. They do not realize that trading is a *minus*-sum game. Winners receive less than what losers lose because the industry drains money from the market.

For example, roulette in a casino is a minus-sum game because the casino sweeps away 3 percent to 6 percent of all bets. This makes roulette unwinnable in the long run. You and I can get into in a minus-sum game if we make the same $10 bet on the next 100-point move in the Dow but deal through brokers. When we settle, the loser is out $13 and the winner collects only $7, while two brokers smile all the way to the bank.

Commissions and slippage are to traders what death and taxes are to all of us. They take some fun out of life and ultimately bring it to an end. A trader must support his broker and the machinery of exchanges before he collects a dime. Being simply "better than average" is not good enough. You have to be head and shoulders above the crowd to win a minus-sum game.

Commissions

You can expect to pay a round-trip commission of anywhere from $12 to $100 for every futures contract you trade. Big traders who deal with discount houses pay less; small traders who deal with full-service brokers pay more. Amateurs ignore commissions while dreaming of fat profits. Brokers argue that commissions are tiny relative to the value of underlying contracts.

To understand the role of commissions, you need to compare them to your margin, not to the value of the contract. For example, you may pay $30 to trade a single contract of corn (5,000 bushels, worth approximately $10,000). A broker will say that the $30 commission is less than 1 percent of contract value. In reality, you have to deposit about $600 to trade a contract of corn. A $30 commission represents 5 percent of margin. This means you have to make 5 percent on the capital committed to the trade, simply to break even. If you trade corn four times a year, you will have to make a 20 percent annual profit to avoid losing money! Very few people can do this. Many money managers would give their eyeteeth for 20 percent annual returns. A "small commission" is not a nuisance–it is a major barrier to success!

Many amateurs generate 50 percent and more of their account size in commissions per year — if they last that long. Even discounted commissions raise a tall barrier to successful trading. I have heard brokers chuckle as they gossiped about clients who beat their brains out just to stay even with the game.

Shop for the lowest possible commissions. Do not be shy about bargaining for lower rates. I have heard many brokers complain about a shortage of customers — but not many customers complain about the shortage of brokers. Tell your broker it is in his best interest to charge you low commissions because you will survive and remain a client for a long time. Design a trading system that will trade less often.

Slippage

Slippage takes either piranha-sized or shark-sized bites out of your account whenever you enter and exit the markets. Slippage means having your orders filled at a different price than that which existed when you placed an order. It is like paying 30 cents for an apple in a grocery store even though the posted price is 29 cents.

There are three kinds of slippage: common, volatility-based, and criminal. Common slippage is due to a spread between buying and selling prices. Floor traders maintain two prices in the market — the bid and the ask.

For example, your broker may quote you 390.45 for June S&P 500. If you want to buy a contract at the market, you'll have to pay at least 390.50. If you want to sell at the market, you will receive 390.40 or less. Since each point is worth $5, the 10-point spread between bid and ask transfers $50 from your pocket to floor traders. They charge you for the privilege of entering or exiting a trade.

The spread between bid and ask is legal. It tends to be narrow in big, liquid markets such as the S&P 500 and bonds, and much wider in thinly traded markets such as orange juice and cocoa. The exchanges claim that the spread is the price you pay for liquidity — being able to trade whenever you wish. Electronic trading promises to cut slippage.

Slippage rises with market volatility. Floor traders can get away with more in fast-moving markets. When the market begins to run, slippage goes through the roof. When the S&P 500 rallies or drops, you can get hit with a 20 to 30 point slippage, and sometimes 100 points or more.

The third kind of slippage is caused by criminal activities of floor traders.

They have many ways of stealing money from customers. Some put their bad trades into your account and keep good trades for themselves. This kind of activity and other criminal games were recently described in a book, *Brokers, Bagmen and Moles*, by David Greising and Laurie Morse.

When a hundred men spend day after day standing shoulder to shoulder in a small pit, they develop a camaraderie — an "us against them" mentality. Floor traders have a nickname for outsiders which shows that they consider us less than human. They call us "paper" (as in "Is paper coming in today?"). That is why you have to take steps to protect yourself.

To reduce slippage, trade liquid markets and avoid thin and fast-moving markets. Go long or short when the market is quiet. Use limit orders. Buy or sell at a specified price. Keep a record of prices at the time when you placed your order and have your broker fight the floor on your behalf when necessary.

Total Damage

Slippage and commissions make trading similar to swimming in a shark-infested lagoon. Let us compare an example from a broker's sales pitch to what happens in the real world.

The "party line" goes like this: A contract of gold futures covers 100 ounces of gold. Five individuals buy a contract each from someone who sells five contracts short. Gold falls $4 and the buyers bail out, losing $4 per ounce or $400 per contract. The intelligent trader, who sold five contracts short, covers his position and makes $400 per contract, for a total of $2000.

In the real world, however, each loser has lost more than $400. He paid at least a $25 round-trip commission and was probably hit with $20 slippage coming and going. As a result, each loser lost $465 per contract and, as a group, they lost $2325. The winner, who sold 5 contracts short, probably paid a $15 round-trip commission and was hit with $10 slippage coming and going, reducing his gain by $35 per contract, or $175 for 5 contracts. He pocketed only $1825.

The winner thought he made $2000, but he received only $1825. The losers thought they lost $2000, but in fact they lost $2325. In total, fully $500 ($2325 − $1825) was siphoned from the table. The lion's share was pocketed by floor traders and brokers who took a much bigger cut than any casino or a racetrack would dare!

Other expenses also drain traders' money. The cost of computers and data, fees for advisory services and books — including the one you are reading now — all come out of your trading funds.

Look for a broker with the cheapest commissions and watch him like a hawk. Design a trading system that gives signals relatively infrequently and allows you to enter markets during quiet times.

I

Individual Psychology

4. WHY TRADE?

Trading appears deceptively easy. When a beginner wins, he feels brilliant and invincible. Then he takes wild risks and loses everything.

People trade for many reasons — some rational and many irrational. Trading offers an opportunity to make a lot of money in a hurry. Money symbolizes freedom to many people, even though they often do not know what to do with their freedom.

If you know how to trade, you can make your own hours, live and work wherever you please, and never answer to a boss. Trading is a fascinating intellectual pursuit: chess, poker, and a crossword rolled in one. Trading attracts people who love puzzles and brainteasers.

Trading attracts risk-takers and repels those who avoid risk. An average person gets up in the morning, goes to work, has a lunch break, returns home, has a beer and dinner, watches TV, and goes to sleep. If he makes a few extra dollars, he puts them into a savings account. A trader keeps odd hours and puts his capital at risk. Many traders are loners who abandon the certainty of the present and take a leap into the unknown.

Self-Fulfillment

Most people have an innate drive to achieve their personal best, to develop their abilities to the fullest. This drive, along with the pleasure of the game and the lure of money, propels traders to challenge the markets.

Good traders tend to be hardworking and shrewd men. They are open to new ideas. The goal of a good trader, paradoxically, is not to make money. His goal is to trade well. If he trades right, money follows almost as an afterthought. Successful traders keep honing their skills. Trying to reach their personal best is more important to them than making money.

A successful New York trader said to me: "If I become half a percent smarter each year, I'll be a genius by the time I die." His drive to improve himself is the hallmark of a successful trader.

A professional trader from Texas invited me to his office and said: "If you sit across the table from me while I day-trade, you won't be able to tell whether I am $2000 ahead or $2000 behind on that day." He has risen to a level where winning does not elate him and losing does not deflate him. He is so focused on trading right and improving his skills that money no longer influences his emotions.

The trouble with self-fulfillment is that many people have a self-destructive streak. Accident-prone drivers keep destroying their cars, and self-destructive traders keep destroying their accounts (see Section 7). Markets offer unlimited opportunities for self-sabotage, as well as for self-fulfillment. Acting out your internal conflicts in the marketplace is a very expensive proposition.

Traders who are not at peace with themselves often try to fulfill their contradictory wishes in the market. If you do not know where you are going, you will wind up somewhere you never wanted to be.

5. FANTASY VERSUS REALITY

If you hear from a friend with little farming experience that he plans to feed himself with food grown on a quarter-acre plot, you will expect him to go hungry. We all know that one can squeeze only so much blood from a turnip. The one field in which grown-ups let their fantasies soar is trading.

Just the other day, a friend told me that he expected to support himself trading his $6000 account. When I tried to show him the futility of his plan, he quickly changed our topic of conversation. He is a bright analyst, but he refuses to see that his "intensive farming" plan is suicidal. In his desperate effort to succeed, he must take on large positions—and the slightest wiggle of the market is sure to put him out of business.

A successful trader is a realist. He knows his abilities and limitations. He sees what is happening in the markets and knows how to react to them. He analyzes the markets without cutting corners, observes his own reactions, and makes realistic plans. A professional trader cannot afford illusions.

Once an amateur takes a few hits and gets a few margin calls, he becomes fearful instead of cocky and starts developing strange ideas about the markets. Losers buy, sell, or miss trades thanks to their fantastic ideas. They act like children who are afraid to pass a cemetery or look under their bed at night because they are afraid of ghosts. The unstructured environment of the market makes it is easy to develop fantasies.

Most people who have grown up in Western civilization have several similar fantasies. They are so widespread that when I studied at the New York Psychoanalytic Institute, there was a course called "Universal Fantasies." For example, most people have a fantasy in childhood that they were adopted rather than born to their parents. A fantasy seems to explain the unfriendly and impersonal world. It consoles a child but prevents him from seeing reality. Our fantasies influence our behavior, even if we are not consciously aware of them.

In talking to hundreds of traders, I keep hearing them express several universal fantasies. They distort reality and stand in the way of trading success. A successful trader must identify his fantasies and get rid of them.

The Brain Myth

Losers who suffer from the "brain myth" will tell you, "I lost because I didn't know trading secrets." Many losers have a fantasy that successful traders have some secret knowledge. This fantasy helps support a lively market in advisory services and ready-made trading systems.

A demoralized trader often whips out his checkbook and goes shopping for "trading secrets." He may send money to a charlatan for a $3000 "can't miss," backtested, computerized trading system. When that self-destructs, he sends another check for a "scientific manual" that explains how he can stop being a loser and become a true insider and a winner by contemplating the Moon, Saturn, or even Uranus.

The losers do not know that trading is intellectually fairly simple. It is less demanding than taking out an appendix, building a bridge, or trying a case in court. Good traders are often shrewd, but few of them are intellectuals. Many have not been to college, and some have even dropped out of high school.

Intelligent and hardworking people who have succeeded in their careers often feel drawn to trading. The average client of a brokerage firm is 50 years old, is married, and has a college education. Many have postgraduate degrees or own their businesses. The two largest professional groups among traders are engineers and farmers.

Why do these intelligent and hardworking people fail in trading? What separates winners from losers is neither intelligence nor secrets, and certainly not education.

The Undercapitalization Myth

Many losers think that they would be successful if they could trade a bigger account. All losers get knocked out of the game by a string of losses or a single abysmally bad trade. Often, after the amateur is sold out, the market reverses and moves in the direction he expected. The loser is ready to kick either himself or his broker: Had he survived another week, he might have made a small fortune!

Losers take this reversal as a confirmation of their methods. They earn, save, or borrow enough money to open another small account. The story repeats: The loser gets wiped out, the market reverses and "proves" the loser right, but only too late — he has been sold out again. That's when the fantasy is born: "If only I had a bigger account, I could have stayed in the market a little longer and won."

Some losers raise money from relatives and friends by showing them a paper track record. It seems to prove that they would have won big, if only they had had more money to work with. But if they raise more money, they lose that, too — it is as if the market were laughing at them!

A loser is not undercapitalized — his mind is underdeveloped. A loser can destroy a big account almost as quickly as a small one. He overtrades, and his money management is sloppy. He takes risks that are too big, whatever the size of his account. No matter how good his system is, a streak of bad trades is sure to put him out of business.

Traders often ask me how much money they need to begin trading. They want to be able to withstand a drawdown, a temporary drop in the account equity. They expect to lose a large amount of money before making any! They sound like an engineer who plans to build several bridges that collapse before erecting his masterpiece. Would a surgeon plan on killing several patients while becoming an expert at taking out an appendix?

A trader who wants to survive and prosper must control his losses. You do that by risking only a tiny fraction of your equity on any single trade (see Chapter 10, "Risk Management"). Give yourself several years to learn how to trade. Do not start with an account bigger than $20,000, and do not lose more than 2 percent of your equity on any single trade. Learn from cheap mistakes in a small account.

Amateurs neither expect to lose nor are in any way prepared for it. The notion of being undercapitalized is a cop-out that helps them avoid two painful truths: their lack of trading discipline, and their lack of a realistic money management plan.

The one advantage of a large trading account is that the price of equipment and services represents a smaller percentage of your money. A manager of a million-dollar fund who spends $10,000 on computers and seminars is only 1 percent behind the game. The same expenditure would represent 50 percent of the equity of a trader with a $20,000 account.

The Autopilot Myth

Imagine that a stranger walks into your driveway and tries to sell you an automatic system for driving your car. Just pay a few hundred dollars for a computer chip, install it in your car, and stop wasting energy on driving, he says. You can take a nap in the driver's seat while the "Easy Swing System" whisks you to work. You would probably laugh the salesman out of your driveway. But would you laugh if he tried to sell you an automatic trading system?

Traders who believe in the autopilot myth think that the pursuit of wealth can be automated. Some try to develop an automatic trading system, while others buy one from the experts. Men who have spent years honing their skills as lawyers, doctors, or businessmen plunk down thousands of dollars for canned competence. They are driven by greed, laziness, and mathematical illiteracy.

Systems used to be written on sheets of paper, but now they usually come on copy-protected diskettes. Some are primitive; others are elaborate, with built-in optimization and money management rules. Many traders spend thousands of dollars searching for magic that will turn a few pages of computer code into an endless stream of money. People who pay for automatic trading systems are like medieval knights who paid alchemists for the secret of turning base metals into gold.

Complex human activities do not lend themselves to automation. Computerized learning systems have not replaced teachers, and programs for doing taxes have not created unemployment among accountants. Most human activities call for an exercise of judgment; machines and systems can help but not replace humans. So many system buyers have been burned that they have formed an organization, Club 3000, named after the price of many systems.

If you could buy a successful automatic trading system, you could move to Tahiti and spend the rest of your life in leisure, supported by a stream of checks from your broker. So far, the only people who have made money from trading systems are the system sellers. They form a small but colorful cottage industry. If their systems worked, why would they sell them? They could move to Tahiti themselves and cash checks from their brokers! Meanwhile, every system seller has a line. Some say they like programming better than trading. Others claim that they sell their systems only to raise trading capital.

Markets always change and defeat automatic trading systems. Yesterday's rigid rules work poorly today and will probably stop working tomorrow. A competent trader can adjust his methods when he detects trouble. An automatic system is less adaptable and self-destructs.

Airlines pay high salaries to pilots despite having autopilots. They do it because humans can handle unforeseen events. When a roof blows off an airliner over the Pacific or when a plane runs out of gas over the Canadian wilderness, only a human can handle such a crisis. These emergencies have been reported in the press, and in each of them experienced pilots managed to land their airliners by improvising. No autopilot can do that. Betting your money on an automatic system is like betting your life on an autopilot. The first unexpected event will destroy your account.

There are good trading systems out there, but they have to be monitored and adjusted using individual judgment. You have to stay on the ball—you cannot abdicate your responsibility for your success to a trading system.

Traders who have the autopilot fantasy try to repeat what they felt as infants. Their mothers used to fulfill their needs for food, warmth, and comfort. Now they try to re-create the experience of passively lying on their backs and having profits flow to them like an endless stream of free, warm milk.

The market is not your mother. It consists of tough men and women who look for ways to take money away from you instead of pouring milk into your mouth.

The Personality Cult

Most people give lip service to their wish for freedom and independence. When they come under pressure, they change their tune and start looking for "strong leadership." Traders in distress often seek directions from assorted gurus.

When I was growing up in the former Soviet Union, children were taught that Stalin was our great leader. Later we found out what a monster he had been, but while he was alive, most people enjoyed following the leader. He freed them from the need to think for themselves.

"Little Stalins" were installed in every area of society — in economics, biology, architecture, and so on. When I came to the United States and began to trade, I was amazed to see how many traders were looking for a guru — their "little Stalin" in the market. The fantasy that someone else can make you rich deserves its own discussion later in this chapter.

Trade with Your Eyes Open

Every winner needs to master three essential components of trading: a sound individual psychology, a logical trading system, and a good money management plan. These essentials are like three legs of a stool — remove one and the stool will fall, together with the person who sits on it. Losers try to build a stool with only one leg, or two at the most. They usually focus exclusively on trading systems.

Your trades must be based on clearly defined rules. You have to analyze your feelings as you trade, to make sure that your decisions are intellectually sound. You have to structure your money management so that no string of losses can kick you out of the game.

6. MARKET GURUS*

Gurus have been with us ever since the public entered markets. In 1841, the classic book on market manias, *Extraordinary Popular Delusions and the Madness of Crowds,* was published in England. It is still in print today. Its author, Charles Mackay, described the Dutch Tulip Mania, the South Seas Bubble in England, and other mass manias. Human nature changes slowly,

*This section originally appeared as an article, "Market Gurus," in the September 1990 issue of *Futures and Options World.* London, U.K. ©1990 by Alexander Elder.

and today new mass manias, including guru manias, continue to sweep the markets.

Guru manias spring up faster now than they did centuries ago, thanks to modern telecommunications. Even educated and intelligent investors and traders follow market gurus, like the devotees of the false Messiahs in the Middle Ages.

There are three types of gurus in the financial markets: market cycle gurus, magic method gurus, and dead gurus. Some gurus call important market turns. Others promote "unique methods" — new highways to riches. Still others have escaped criticism and invited cult following through the simple mechanism of departing this world.

Market Cycle Gurus

For many decades, the U.S. stock market has generally followed a four-year cycle. Significant bear market lows occurred in 1962, 1966, 1970, 1974, 1978, and 1982. The broad stock market has normally spent 2.5 or 3 years going up and 1 or 1.5 years going down.

A new market cycle guru emerges in almost every major stock market cycle, once every 4 years. A guru's fame tends to last for 2 to 3 years. The reigning period of each guru coincides with a major bull market in the United States.

A market cycle guru forecasts all major rallies and declines. Each correct forecast increases his fame and prompts even more people to buy or sell when he issues his next forecast. As more and more people take notice of the guru, his advice becomes a self-fulfilling prophecy. When you recognize a hot new guru, it pays to follow his advice.

There are thousands of analysts, some of whom are certain to be on a hot streak at any given time. Most analysts become hot at some point in their careers for the same reason a broken clock shows the right time twice a day. Those who have tasted the joy of being on a hot streak sometimes feel crushed when it ends and they wash out of the market. But there are enough old foxes who enjoy their occasional hot streaks, yet continue working as usual after their hot streak ends.

The success of a market cycle guru depends on more than short-term luck. He has a pet theory about the market. That theory — cycles, volume, Elliott Wave, whatever — is usually developed several years prior to reaching stardom. At first, the market refuses to follow an aspiring guru's pet theory. Then the market changes and for several years comes in gear with theory. That is when the star of the market guru rises high and bright above the marketplace.

Compare this to what happens to fashion models as public tastes change. One year, blondes are popular, another year, redheads. Suddenly, last year's blonde star is no longer wanted for the front cover of a major women's magazine. Everybody wants a dark model, or a woman with a birthmark on her face. A model does not change—public tastes do.

Gurus always come from the fringes of market analysis. They are never establishment analysts. Institutional employees play it safe and never achieve spectacular results because each uses similar methods. A market cycle guru is an outsider with a unique theory.

A guru usually earns a living publishing a newsletter and can grow rich selling his advice. Subscriptions can soar from a few hundred annually to tens of thousands. A recent market cycle guru was reported to have hired three people just to open the envelopes with money pouring into his firm.

At investment conferences, a guru is surrounded by a mob of admirers. If you ever find yourself in such a crowd, notice that a guru is seldom asked questions about his theory. His admirers are content to drink in the sound of his voice. They brag to their friends about having met him.

A guru remains famous for as long as the market behaves according to his theory—usually for less than the duration of one 4-year market cycle. At some point the market changes and starts marching to a different tune. A guru continues to use old methods that worked spectacularly well in the past and rapidly loses his following. When the guru's forecasts stop working, public admiration turns to hatred. It is impossible for a discredited market cycle guru to return to stardom.

The reigning guru in the early 1970s was Edson Gould. He based his forecasts on policy changes of the Federal Reserve, as reflected in the discount rate. His famous rule of "three steps and a stumble" stated that if the Federal Reserve raised the discount rate three times, that showed tightening and led to a bear market. Lowering the discount rate in three steps revealed a loosening of the monetary policy and led to a bull market. Gould also developed an original charting technique called speedlines—shallow trendlines whose angles depended on the velocity of a trend and the depth of market reactions.

Gould became very hot during the bear market of 1973–1974. He vaulted to prominence after correctly calling the December 1974 bottom, when the Dow Jones Industrials fell to near 500. The market rocketed higher, Gould presciently identified its important turning points using speedlines, and his fame grew. But soon the United States was flooded with liquidity, inflation intensified, and Gould's methods, developed in a different monetary environment, stopped working. By 1976, he had lost most of his following, and few people today even remember his name.

The new market cycle guru emerged in 1978. Joseph Granville stated that changes in stock market volume preceded changes in prices. He expressed it colorfully: "Volume is the steam that makes the choo-choo go." Granville developed his theory while working for a major Wall Street brokerage firm. He wrote in his autobiography that the idea came to him while sitting on a toilet contemplating the design of floor tiles. Granville took his idea from the bathroom to the chartroom, but the market refused to follow his forecasts. He went broke, got divorced, and slept on the floor of his friend's office. By the late 1970s, the market started to follow Granville's scripts as never before or since, and people began to take notice.

Granville toured the United States speaking to overflow crowds. He arrived on stage in a carriage, issued forecasts, and chided "bagholders" who would not recognize his theory. He played piano, sang, and, on occasion, even dropped his pants to make a point. His forecasts were spectacularly correct; he drew attention to himself and became widely quoted in the mass media. Granville became big enough to move the stock market. When he announced that he was bearish, the Dow dropped over 40 points in a day — a huge decline by the standards of that time. Granville became intoxicated with his success. The market surged higher in 1982, but he remained very bearish and kept advising his dwindling band of followers to continue to sell short. The market rocketed higher into 1983. Granville finally gave up and recommended buying when the Dow doubled in value. He continued to publish a market newsletter, a shadow of his former successful self.

A new guru entered the spotlight in 1984. Robert Prechter has made a name for himself as an Elliott Wave theorist. Elliott was an impecunious accountant who developed his market theory in the 1930s. He believed that the stock market rallied in 5 waves and fell in 3 waves, which in turn could be subdivided into lesser waves.

Like other market cycle gurus before him, Prechter had been writing an advisory letter for many years with modest success. When the bull market penetrated the 1000 level on the Dow, people began to pay attention to the young analyst who kept calling for the Dow to reach 3000. The bull market went from strength to strength, and Prechter's fame grew by leaps and bounds.

In the roaring bull market of the 1980s, Prechter's fame swept outside the narrow world of investment newsletters and conferences. Prechter appeared on national television and was interviewed by popular magazines. In October

1987, he appeared to vacillate, first issuing a sell signal, then telling his followers to get ready to buy. As the Dow crashed 500 points, mass adulation of Prechter gave way to scorn and hatred. Some blamed him for the decline, others were angry that the market never reached his stated target of 3000. Prechter's advisory business shrank, and he largely retired from it.

All market cycle gurus have several traits in common. They become active in the forecasting business several years prior to reaching stardom. Each has a unique theory, a few followers, and some credibility, conferred by sheer survival in the advisory business. The fact that each guru's theory did not work for a number of years is ignored by his followers. When the theory becomes correct, the mass media take notice. When a theory stops working, mass adulation of a guru turns to hatred.

When you recognize that a successful new guru is emerging, it is profitable to jump on his bandwagon. It is even more important to recognize when a guru has reached his peak. All gurus crash—and by definition, they crash from the height of their fame. When a guru becomes accepted by the mass media, it is a sign that he has reached his crest. The mainstream media is wary of outsiders. When several mass magazines devote space to a hot market guru, you know that his end is near.

Another warning sign that a market guru has reached his peak occurs when he is interviewed by *Barron's*—America's largest business weekly. Every January, *Barron's* invites a panel of prominent analysts to dispense wisdom and issue forecasts for the year ahead. The panel is usually made up of "safe" analysts who focus on price/earnings ratios, emerging growth industries, and so on. It is highly atypical of *Barron's* to invite a hot guru with an offbeat theory to its January panel. A guru gets invited only when the public clamors for him, and to exclude him would diminish the prestige of the magazine. Both Granville and Prechter were invited to the January panel when each man was at the crest of his fame. Each guru fell within a few months of appearing on that panel. The next time a market guru is on *Barron's* January panel, do not renew your subscription to his newsletter.

Mass psychology being what it is, new gurus will certainly emerge. An old cycle guru never fully comes back. Once he stumbles, the adulation turns to derision and hatred. An expensive vase, once shattered, can never be fully restored.

Magic Method Gurus

Market cycle gurus are creatures of the stock market, but "method gurus" are more prominent in the derivative markets, especially in the futures markets.

A "method guru" erupts on the financial scene after discovering a new analytic or trading method.

Traders always look for an edge, an advantage over fellow traders. Like knights shopping for swords, they are willing to pay handsomely for their trading tools. No price is too high if it lets them tap into a money pipeline.

A magic method guru sells a new set of keys to market profits. As soon as enough people become familiar with a new method and test it in the markets, it inevitably deteriorates and starts losing popularity. Markets are forever changing, and the methods that worked yesterday are not likely to work today and even less likely to work a year from now.

In the early 1970s, Chicago market letter writer Jake Bernstein became hot by using market cycles to call tops and bottoms. His methods worked well and his fame spread. Bernstein charged high fees for his newsletters, ran conferences, managed funds, and produced an endless flow of books. As usual, the markets changed, becoming less and less cyclical in the 1980s.

Peter Steidlmayer was another method guru whose star rose high above Chicago. He urged his followers to discard old trading methods in favor of his Market Profile. That method promised to reveal the secrets of supply and demand and give true believers an ability to buy at the bottoms and sell at the tops. Steidlmayer teamed up with entrepreneur Kevin Koy, and their frequent seminars attracted upward of 50 people who paid $1600 for a 4-day class. There appeared to be no conspicuous examples of success among Market Profile devotees, and the founders had a nasty falling out. Steidlmayer got a job with a brokerage firm, and both he and Koy continued to give occasional seminars.

Oddly enough, even in this era of fast global links, reputations change slowly. A guru whose image has been destroyed in his own country can make money peddling his theory overseas. That point has been made to me by a guru who compared his continued popularity in Asia to what happens to faded American singers and movie stars. They are unable to attract an audience in the United States, but they can still make a living singing abroad.

Dead Gurus

The third type of a market guru is a dead guru. His books are reissued, his market courses are scrutinized by new generations of eager traders, and the legend of the dear-departed analyst's prowess and personal wealth grows posthumously. The dead guru is no longer among us and cannot capitalize on his fame. Other promoters profit from his reputation and from expired copyrights. One dear-departed guru is R. N. Elliott, but the best example of such a legend is W. D. Gann.

Various opportunists sell "Gann courses" and "Gann software." They claim that Gann was one of the best traders who ever lived, that he left a $50 million estate, and so on. I interviewed W. D. Gann's son, an analyst for a Boston bank. He told me that his famous father could not support his family by trading but earned his living by writing and selling instructional courses. When W. D. Gann died in the 1950s, his estate, including his house, was valued at slightly over $100,000. The legend of W. D. Gann, the giant of trading, is perpetuated by those who sell courses and other paraphernalia to gullible customers.

The Followers of Gurus

The personalities of market gurus differ. Some are dead, but those who are alive range from serious academic types to great showmen. A guru has to produce original research for several years, then get lucky when the market turns his way.

To read about the scandals that surrounded many gurus, try *Winner Takes All* by William Gallacher and *The Dow Jones Guide to Trading Systems* by Bruce Babcock. The purpose of this section is simply analysis of the guru phenomenon.

When we pay a guru, we expect to get back more than we spend. We act like a man who bets a few dollars against a three-card monte dealer on a street corner. He hopes to win more than he put down on an overturned crate. Only the ignorant or greedy take the bait.

Some people turn to gurus in search of a strong leader. They look for a parent-like omniscient provider. As a friend once said, "They walk with their umbilical cords in hand, looking for a place to plug them in." A smart promoter provides such a receptacle, for a fee.

The public wants gurus, and new gurus will come. As an intelligent trader, you must realize that in the long run, no guru is going to make you rich. You have to work on that yourself.

7. SELF-DESTRUCTIVENESS

Trading is a very hard game. A trader who wants to be successful in the long run has to be very serious about what he does. He cannot afford to be naive or to trade because of some hidden psychological agenda.

Unfortunately, trading often appeals to impulsive people, to gamblers, and to those who feel that the world owes them a living. If you trade for the excitement, you are liable to take trades with bad odds and accept unnecessary risks. The markets are unforgiving, and emotional trading always results in losses.

Gambling

Gambling means betting on games of chance or skill. It exists in all societies, and most people have gambled at some point in their lives.

Freud believed that gambling was universally attractive because it was a substitute for masturbation. The repetitive and exciting activity of the hands, the irresistible urge, the resolutions to stop, the intoxicating quality of pleasure, and the feelings of guilt link gambling and masturbation.

Dr. Ralph Greenson, a prominent California psychoanalyst, has divided gamblers into three groups: the normal person who gambles for diversion and who can stop when he wishes; the professional gambler, who selects gambling as his means of earning a livelihood; and the neurotic gambler, who gambles because he is driven by unconscious needs and is unable to stop.

A neurotic gambler either feels lucky or wants to test his luck. Winning gives him a sense of power. He feels pleased, like a baby feeding at a breast. A neurotic gambler always loses because he tries to re-create that omnipotent feeling of bliss instead of concentrating on a realistic long-term game plan.

Dr. Sheila Blume, director of the compulsive gambling program at South Oaks Hospital in New York, calls gambling "an addiction without a drug." Most gamblers are men who gamble for the action. Women tend to gamble as a means of escape. Losers usually hide their losses and try to look and act like winners, but they are plagued by self-doubt.

Trading stocks, futures, and options gives a gambler a high but it does appear more respectable than betting on the ponies. Moreover, gambling in the financial markets has an aura of sophistication and offers a better intellectual diversion than playing numbers with a bookie.

Gamblers feel happy when trades go in their favor. They feel terribly low when they lose. They differ from successful professionals who focus on long-term plans and do not get particularly upset or excited in the process of trading.

Brokers are well aware that many of their clients are gamblers. They often try to avoid leaving messages for traders with their wives, even when they call to confirm a trade. Amateurs are not the only ones involved in gambling — quite a bit of it goes on among professionals. Sonny Kleinfield describes in his book, *The Traders*, the endemic betting on sports events on the floors of financial exchanges.

The key sign of gambling is the inability to resist the urge to bet. If you feel that you are trading too much and the results are poor, stop trading for a month. This will give you a chance to re-evaluate your trading. If the urge to trade is so strong that you cannot stay away from the action for a month, then it is time to visit your local chapter of Gamblers Anonymous or start using the principles of Alcoholics Anonymous, outlined later in this chapter.

Self-Sabotage

After practicing psychiatry for many years, I became convinced that most failures in life are due to self-sabotage. We fail in our professional, personal, and business affairs not because of stupidity or incompetence, but to fulfill an unconscious wish to fail.

A brilliant and witty friend of mine has a lifelong history of demolishing his success. As a young man, he was a successful industrial salesman and was sacked; he entered training as a broker and rose near the top of his firm but was sued; he became a well-known trader but busted out while disentangling himself from previous disasters. He blamed all his failures on envious bosses, incompetent regulators, and an unsupportive wife.

Finally, he hit bottom. He had no job and no money. He borrowed a quote terminal from another busted-out trader and raised capital from a few people who had heard that he had traded well in the past. He knew how to trade and made money for his pool. As the word spread, more people brought in money. My friend was on a roll. At that point, he went on a speaking tour of Asia but continued to trade from the road. He took a side trip into a country famous for its prostitutes, leaving a very large open position with no protective stop. By the time he returned to civilization, the markets had staged a major move and his pool was wiped out. Did he try to figure out his problem? Did he try to change? No — he blamed his broker!

It hurts to look within yourself for the cause of your failure. When traders get in trouble, they tend to blame others, bad luck, or anything else.

A prominent trader came to me for a consultation. His equity was being demolished by a rally in the U.S. dollar, in which he was heavily short. He had grown up fighting a nasty and arrogant father. He had made a name for himself by betting large positions on reversals of established trends. This trader kept adding to his short position because he could not admit that the market, which represented his father, was bigger and stronger than he was.

These are just two examples of how people act out self-destructive tendencies. We sabotage ourselves by acting like impulsive children rather than intelligent adults. We cling to our self-defeating patterns even though they can be treated — failure is a curable disease.

The mental baggage from childhood can prevent you from succeeding in the markets. You have to find your weaknesses in order to change. Keep a trading diary — write down your reasons for entering and exiting every trade. Look for repetitive patterns of success and failure.

The Demolition Derby

Almost every profession and business provides a safety net for its members. Your bosses, colleagues, and clients can warn you when you behave dangerously or self-destructively. There is no such support in trading, which makes it more dangerous than most human endeavors. The markets offer many opportunities to self-destruct without a safety net.

All members of society make small allowances to protect one another from the consequences of our mistakes. When you drive, you try to avoid hitting other cars and they try to avoid hitting you. If someone swings open the door of a parked car, you swerve. If someone cuts in front of you on a highway, you may curse, but you will slow down. You avoid collisions because they are too costly for both parties.

Markets operate without normal human helpfulness. Every trader tries to hit others. Every trader gets hit by others. The trading highway is littered with wrecks. Trading is the most dangerous human endeavor, short of war.

Buying at the high point of the day is like swinging your car door open into the traffic. When your buy order reaches the floor, traders rush to sell to you — to rip your door off along with your arm. Other traders want you to fail because they get the money you lose.

Controlling Self-Destructiveness

Most people go through life making the same mistakes at sixty that they made at twenty. Others structure their lives to succeed in one area while acting out internal conflicts in another. Very few people grow out of their problems.

You need to be aware of your tendency to sabotage yourself. Stop blaming your losses on bad luck or on others and take responsibility for the results. Start keeping a diary—a record of all your trades, with reasons for entering and exiting them. Look for repetitive patterns of success and failure. Those who do not learn from the past are condemned to repeat it.

You need a psychological safety net the way mountain climbers need their survival gear. I found the principles of Alcoholics Anonymous, outlined later in this chapter, to be of great help. Strict money management rules also provide a safety net.

If you seek therapy for your trading problems, choose a competent therapist who knows what trading is about. You are ultimately responsible for your own therapy and must monitor its progress. I usually tell my patients that if a month goes by without clear signs of improvement, then therapy is in trouble. When therapy shows no progress for two months, it is time to seek a consultation with another therapist.

8. TRADING PSYCHOLOGY

Your feelings have an immediate impact on your account equity. You may have a brilliant trading system, but if you feel frightened, arrogant, or upset, your account is sure to suffer. When you recognize that a gambler's high or fear is clouding your mind, stop trading. Your success or failure as a trader depends on controlling your emotions.

When you trade, you compete against the sharpest minds in the world. The field on which you compete has been slanted to ensure your failure. If you allow your emotions to interfere with your trading, the battle is over.

You are responsible for every trade that you make. A trade begins when you decide to enter the market and ends only when you decide to take yourself out. Having a good trading system is not enough. Most traders with good systems wash out of the markets because psychologically they are not prepared to win.

Bending the Rules

Markets offer enormous temptations, like walking through a gold vault or through a harem. Markets evoke powerful greed for more gains and a great fear of losing what we've got. Those feelings cloud our perceptions of opportunities and dangers.

Most amateurs feel like geniuses after a winning streak. It is exciting to believe that you are so good you can bend your own rules and succeed. That's when traders deviate from their rules and go into a self-destruct mode.

Traders gain some knowledge, they win, their emotions kick in, and they self-destruct. Most traders promptly give their "killings" back to the markets. The markets are full of rags to riches to rags stories. The hallmark of a successful trader is his ability to accumulate equity.

You need to make trading as objective as possible. Keep a diary of all your trades with "before and after" charts, keep a spreadsheet listing all your trades, including commissions and slippage, and maintain very strict money management rules. You may have to devote as much energy to analyzing yourself as you do to analyzing the markets.

When I was learning how to trade, I read every book on trading psychology I could find. Many writers offered sensible advice. Some stressed discipline: "You cannot let the markets sway you. Do not make decisions during trading hours. Plan a trade, and trade a plan." Others stressed flexibility: "Do not enter the market with any preconceived notions. Change your plans when markets change." Some experts suggested isolation — no business news, no *Wall Street Journal*, no listening to other traders, just you and the markets. Others advised being open-minded, keeping in touch with other traders and soaking up fresh ideas. Each piece of advice seemed to make sense but contradicted other equally sensible advice.

I kept reading, trading, and focusing on system development. I also continued to practice psychiatry. I never thought the two fields were connected — until I had a sudden insight. The idea that changed how I trade came from psychiatry.

The Insight That Changed My Trading

Like most psychiatrists, I always had some patients with alcohol problems. I also served as a consultant to a major drug rehabilitation program. It did not take me long to realize that alcoholics and addicts were more likely to recover in self-help groups than in classical psychiatric settings.

Psychotherapy, medications, and expensive hospitals and clinics can sober up a drunk but seldom succeed in keeping him sober. Most addicts quickly relapse. They have a much better chance to recover if they become active in Alcoholics Anonymous (AA) or other self-help groups.

Once I realized that AA members were likely to stay sober and rebuild their lives, I became a big fan of Alcoholics Anonymous. I began sending patients with drinking problems to AA and related groups, such as ACOA (Adult Children of Alcoholics). Now, if an alcoholic comes to me for treatment, I insist that he also go to AA. I tell him that to do otherwise would mean wasting our time and his money.

One night, many years ago, I stopped by a friend's office on the way to a party at our department of psychiatry. We had two hours before the party, and my friend, who was a recovering alcoholic, said: "Do you want to take in a movie or go to an AA meeting?" I had sent many patients to AA but had never been to a meeting, since I have never had a drinking problem. I jumped at a chance to attend an AA meeting — it was a new experience.

The meeting was held at a local YMCA. A dozen men and a few women sat on folding chairs in a plain room. The meeting lasted an hour. I was amazed by what I heard — these people seemed to talk about my trading!

They talked about alcohol, but as long as I substituted the word "loss" for "alcohol," most of what they said applied to me! My account equity was still swinging up and down in those days. I left that YMCA room knowing that I had to handle my losses the way AA handles alcoholism.

9. TRADING LESSONS FROM AA

Almost any drunk can stay sober for a few days. Soon, the urge to drink overwhelms him again and he returns to the bottle. He cannot resist his urge because he continues to feel and think like an alcoholic. Sobriety begins and ends inside a person's mind.

Alcoholics Anonymous (AA) has a system for changing the way people think and feel about drinking. AA members use a 12-step program for changing their minds. These 12 steps, described in the book *Twelve Steps and Twelve Traditions*, refer to 12 stages of personal growth. Recovering alcoholics attend meetings where they share their experiences with other recovering alcoholics, supporting each other in their sobriety. Any member can get a sponsor—another AA member whom he can call for support when he feels the urge to drink.

AA was founded in the 1930s by two alcoholics—a doctor and a traveling salesman. They began meeting and helping each other stay sober. They developed a system that worked so well, others began to join them. AA has only one goal—to help its members stay sober. It does no fund-raising, takes no political positions, and runs no promotional campaigns. AA keeps growing thanks only to word of mouth. It owes its success only to its effectiveness.

The 12-step program of AA is so effective that people with other problems now use it. There are 12-step groups for children of alcoholics, smokers, gamblers, and others. I have become convinced that traders can stop losing money in the markets if they apply the key principles of Alcoholics Anonymous to their trading.

Denial

A social drinker enjoys a cocktail or a glass of wine or beer but stops when he feels he's had enough. An alcoholic's chemistry is different. Once an alcoholic takes a drink, he feels an urge to drink more, until he gets drunk.

A drunk often says that he needs to cut down on alcohol, but he cannot admit that his drinking is out of control. Most drunks deny that they are alcoholics. Try telling an alcoholic relative, friend, or employee that his drinking is out of control and damaging his life and you will run into a wall of denial.

An alcoholic often says: "My boss fired me 'cause I was hung over and came in late. My wife took the kids and left 'cause she had no sense to begin with. My landlord is trying to kick me out of the apartment 'cause I'm a little behind on the rent. I'm gonna have to cut down on my drinking, and everything will be all right."

This man has lost his family and his job. He is about to lose the roof over his head. His life is spinning out of control—but he keeps saying that he can cut down on his drinking. This is denial!

Alcoholics deny their problems while their lives are falling apart. Most of them nurse the fantasy of being able to control their drinking. As long as an alcoholic believes that he can "control his drinking," he is headed downhill. Nothing will ever change, even if he gets a new job, a new wife, and a new landlord.

Alcoholics deny that alcohol controls their lives. When they talk of reducing drinking, they talk about managing the unmanageable. They are like a driver whose car spins out of control on a mountain road. When the car careens down a cliff, it is too late to promise to drive carefully. An alcoholic's life careens out of control while he denies he's an alcoholic.

There is a stark parallel between an alcoholic and a trader whose account is being demolished by losses. He keeps changing trading tactics, acting like an alcoholic who tries to solve his problem by switching from hard liquor to beer. A loser denies that he has lost control over his course in the market.

Rock Bottom

A drunk can begin his journey to recovery only after he admits that he is an alcoholic. He must see that alcohol controls his life and not the other way around. Most drunks cannot accept this painful truth. They can face it only after they hit rock bottom.

Some alcoholics hit rock bottom when they develop a life-threatening illness. Others hit rock bottom after being rejected by their family or losing a job. An alcoholic needs to sink to a point so low, so deep down in the gutter, so unbearably painful that it finally penetrates his denial.

The pain of hitting rock bottom feels intolerable. It makes an alcoholic see how deeply he has sunk. This pain penetrates his denial. He sees a stark and simple choice—either turn his life around or die. Only then is an alcoholic ready to begin his journey to recovery.

Profits make traders feel powerful and give them an emotional high. They try to get high again, put on reckless trades, and give back their profits. Most traders cannot stand the pain of a string of severe losses. They die as traders after hitting rock bottom and wash out of the markets. The few survivors realize that the main trouble is not with their methods, the trouble is with their thinking. They can change and become successful traders.

The First Step

An alcoholic who wants to recover has to go through twelve steps—twelve stages of personal growth. He needs to change how he thinks and feels, how he relates to himself and others. The first step of AA is the hardest.

The first step an alcoholic has to take is to admit that he is powerless over

alcohol. He must admit that his life has become unmanageable, that alcohol is stronger than he is. Most alcoholics cannot take that step, drop out, and go on to destroy their lives.

If alcohol is stronger than you, then you can never touch it again, not a sip for as long as you live. You have to give up drinking forever. Most drunks do not want to give up that pleasure. They destroy their lives rather than take the first step of AA. Only the pain of hitting rock bottom can supply the motivation to take that first step.

One Day at a Time

You have probably seen bumper stickers on cars that say "One day at a time" or "Easy does it." Those are AA slogans, and people who drive those cars are probably recovering alcoholics.

Planning for life without alcohol can seem overwhelming. That's why AA encourages its members to live sober one day at a time.

The goal of every AA member is to stay sober today and go to bed sober tonight. Gradually, days become weeks, then months, then years. AA meetings and other activities help each recovering alcoholic stay sober, one day at a time.

Recovering alcoholics receive — and give others — invaluable support and fellowship at these meetings. They are held at all hours, all over the world. Traders have much to learn from those meetings.

An AA Meeting

One of the best things that a trader can do is go to an AA meeting. I especially recommend it to a trader on a losing streak. Call Alcoholics Anonymous and ask about the next "open meeting" or "beginners' meeting" in your area.

A meeting lasts about an hour. You can sit in the back of the room and listen carefully. There is no pressure to speak, and nobody asks for your last name.

Each meeting begins with a long-term member getting up and speaking about his or her personal struggle for recovery from alcoholism. Several other members share their experiences. There is a collection to cover expenses — most people give a dollar. All you have to do is listen carefully,

and every time you hear the word "alcohol," substitute the word "loss" for it. You will feel as if the people in the meeting are talking about your trading!

10. LOSERS ANONYMOUS

A social drinker enjoys an occasional drink, but an alcoholic craves alcohol. He denies that alcohol controls and destroys his life—until he reaches a personal crisis. It may be a life-threatening illness, unemployment, desertion by a family member, or another unbearably painful event. AA calls it "hitting rock bottom."

The pain of hitting rock bottom punctures an alcoholic's denial. He sees a stark choice—to drown or to turn and swim up for air. His first step to recovery is to admit that he is powerless over alcohol. A recovering alcoholic can never drink again.

Loss is to a loser what alcohol is to an alcoholic. A small loss is like a single drink. A big loss is like a bender. A series of losses is like an alcoholic binge. A loser keeps switching between different markets, gurus, and trading systems. His equity shrinks while he is trying to re-create the pleasurable sensation of winning.

Losing traders think and act like alcoholics, except that their speech is not slurred. The two groups are so much alike that you can predict what a loser will do by using alcoholics as a model.

Alcoholism is a curable disease—and so is losing. Losers can change if they start using the principles of Alcoholics Anonymous.

The Urge to Trade

Successful traders treat drawdowns the way social drinkers treat alcohol. They have a little and stop. If they take several losses in a row, they take that as a signal that something is wrong: It is time to stop and rethink their analysis or methods. Losers cannot stop—they keep trading because they are addicted to the excitement of the game and keep hoping for a big win.

One prominent trading advisor wrote that the pleasure of trading was higher than that of sex or flying jet aircraft. Just as an alcoholic proceeds from social drinking to drunkenness, losers take bigger and bigger risks. They cross the line between taking a business risk and gambling. Many losers do not even know that line exists.

Losers feel the urge to trade, just as alcoholics feel the urge to drink. They make impulsive trades, go on trading binges, and try to trade their way out of a hole.

Losers bleed money from their accounts. Most of them bust out, but some turn to managing other people's money after they lose their own; still others sell advisory services, like burned-out drunks who wash glasses in a bar.

Most losers hide their losses from themselves and from everyone else. They keep shuffling money, keep poor records, and throw away brokerage slips. A loser is like an alcoholic who does not want to know how many ounces of liquor he drank.

Into the Hole

A loser never knows why he loses. If he knew, he would have done something about it and become a winner. He keeps trading in a fog. A loser tries to manage his trading the way an alcoholic tries to manage his drinking.

Losers try to trade their way out of a hole. They switch trading systems, buy new software, or take tips from a new guru. They act out a rescue fantasy — a charming belief in Santa Claus. Their desperate belief in magic solutions helps many advisors sell their services to the public.

When losses mount and equity shrinks, a loser acts like an alcoholic threatened with an eviction or a firing. A loser grows desperate and converts outright positions into spreads, doubles up on losing positions, reverses and trades in the opposite direction, and so on. Losers get as much good from these maneuvers as an alcoholic who switches from hard liquor to wine.

A losing trader careens out of control, trying to manage the unmanageable. Alcoholics die prematurely, and most traders bust out of the markets and never come back. New trading methods, hot tips, and improved software cannot help you until you learn to handle yourself. You have to change how you think in order to stop losing and begin your recovery as a trader.

Losers get drunk on losses; they're addicted to losses. Traders prefer profits, but even losses provide plenty of excitement. The pleasure of trading is very high. Few losers are actively trying to lose — but then few alcoholics are consciously trying to end up in the gutter.

A loser keeps getting high from trading while his equity shrinks. Trying to tell him that he is a loser is like trying to take a bottle away from a drunk. A loser has to hit rock bottom before he can begin to recover.

Rock Bottom

Hitting rock bottom feels horrible. It is painful and humiliating. You hit it when you lose money you cannot afford to lose. You hit it when you gamble away your savings. You hit it after you tell your friends how smart you are and later have to ask them for a loan. You hit rock bottom when the market comes roaring at you and yells: "You fool!"

Some people hit rock bottom after only a few weeks of trading. Others keep adding money to their account to postpone the day of reckoning. It hurts to see a loser in the mirror.

We spend our lifetimes building up self-esteem. Most of us have a high opinion of ourselves. It hurts a smart and successful person to hit rock bottom. Your first impulse may be to hide, but remember you are not alone. Almost every trader has been there.

Most people who hit rock bottom die as traders. They slink away from the market and never look back. Brokerage records indicate that 90 out of 100 people trading today will probably be gone from the markets a year from now. They will hit rock bottom, crumble, and leave. They will try to forget trading as they would a bad dream.

Some losers will lick their wounds and wait until the pain fades away. Then they will return to trading, having learned little. They will be fearful, and their fear will further impair their trading.

Very few traders will begin the process of change and growth. For these rare individuals, the pain of hitting rock bottom will interrupt the vicious cycle of getting high from winning and then losing everything and crashing. *When you admit that you have a personal problem that causes you to lose, you can begin building a new trading life. You can start developing the discipline of a winner.*

The First Step

An alcoholic needs to admit that he cannot control his drinking. A trader needs to admit that he cannot control his losses. He needs to admit that he has a psychological problem with the losses and that he is destroying his trading account. The first step of an AA member is to say: "I am an alcoholic, I am powerless over alcohol." As a trader, you have to take your first step and say: "I am a loser, I am powerless over losses."

A trader can recover using the principles of Alcoholics Anonymous. Recovering alcoholics struggle to stay sober, one day at a time. Now you have to struggle to trade without losses, one day at a time.

You may say this is impossible. What if you buy, and the market immediately ticks down? What if you sell short at the bottom tick, and the market rallies? Even the best traders lose money on some trades.

The answer is to draw a line between a businessman's risk and a loss. A trader must take a businessman's risk, but he may never take a loss greater than his predetermined risk.

A storekeeper takes a risk every time he stocks new merchandise. If it does not sell, he will lose money. An intelligent businessman takes only risks that will not put him out of business even if he makes several mistakes in a row. Stocking two crates of merchandise may be a sensible business risk, but stocking a full trailer is probably a gamble.

As a trader, you are in the business of trading. You need to define your businessman's risk — the maximum amount of money you will risk on any single trade. There is no standard dollar amount, just as there is no standard business. An acceptable businessman's risk depends, first of all, on the size of your trading account. It also depends on your trading method and pain tolerance.

The concept of a businessman's risk will change the way you manage your money (see Chapter 10, "Risk Management"). A sensible trader never risks more than 2 percent of account equity on any trade. For example, if you have $30,000 in your account, you may not risk more than $600 per trade, and if you have $10,000, you may not risk more than $200. If your account is small, limit yourself to trading less expensive markets, or mini-contracts. If you see an attractive trade but your stop would have to be placed where more than 2 percent of equity would be at risk — pass that trade. Avoid risking more than 2 percent on a trade the way a recovering alcoholic avoids bars. If you are not sure how much to risk, err on the side of caution.

If you blame excess commissions on a broker and slippage on a floor trader, you give up control of your trading life. Try to reduce both, but take responsibility for them. If you lose even a dollar more than your businessman's risk, including commissions and slippage, you are a loser.

Do you keep good trading records? Poor record-keeping is a sure sign of a gambler and a loser. Good businessmen keep good records. Your trading records must show the date and price of every entry and exit, slippage, commissions, stops, all adjustments of stops, reasons for entering, objectives for exiting, maximum paper profit, maximum paper loss after a stop was hit, and any other necessary data.

If you bail out of a trade within your businessman's risk, it is normal business. There is no bargaining, no waiting for another tick, no hoping for a change. Losing a dollar more than your established businessman's risk is like getting drunk, getting into a brawl, getting sick to your stomach on your way home, and waking up in the gutter with a headache. You would never want that to happen.

A Meeting for One

When you go to an AA meeting, you will see people who have not had a drink in years stand up and say: "Hello, my name is so-and-so, and I am an alcoholic." Why do they call themselves alcoholics after years of sobriety? Because if they think they have beaten alcoholism, they will start drinking again. If a person stops thinking he is an alcoholic, he is free to take a drink, then another, and will probably end up in the gutter again. A person who wants to stay sober must remember that he is an alcoholic for the rest of his life.

Traders would benefit from our own self-help organization — I'd call it Losers Anonymous. Why not Traders Anonymous? Because a harsh name helps to focus attention on our self-destructive tendencies. After all, Alcoholics Anonymous do not call themselves Drinkers Anonymous. As long as you call yourself a loser, you focus on avoiding losses.

Several traders have argued against what they thought was the "negative thinking" of Losers Anonymous. A retired woman from Texas, a highly successful trader, described her approach to me. She is very religious and thinks it would not please the Lord for her to lose money. She cuts her losses very fast because of that. I thought that our methods were similar. The goal is to cut losses due to some objective, external rule.

Trading within a businessman's risk is like living without alcohol. A trader has to admit that he is a loser, just as a drunk has to admit that he is an alcoholic. Then he can begin his journey to recovery.

This is why every morning before trading I sit in front of the quote screen in my office and say: "Good morning, my name is Alex, and I am a loser. I have it in me to do serious financial damage to my account." This is like an AA meeting — it keeps my mind focused on the first principles. Even if I take thousands of dollars out of the market today, tomorrow I will say: "Good morning, my name is Alex and I am a loser."

A friend of mine joked: "When I sit in front of my quote machine in the morning, I say, 'My name is John, and I'm gonna rip your throat out.'" His thinking generates tension. "Losers Anonymous" thinking generates serenity. A trader who feels serene and relaxed can focus on looking for the best and safest trades. A trader who is tense is like a driver who freezes at the wheel. When a sober man and a drunk enter a race, you know who is more likely to win. A drunk may win once in a while thanks to luck, but the sober man is the one to bet on. You want to be the sober man in the race.

11. WINNERS AND LOSERS

We come to the market from different walks of life and bring with us the mental baggage of our upbringing and prior experiences. Most of us find that when we act in the market the way we do in our everyday life, we lose money.

Your success or failure in the market depends on your thoughts and feelings. It depends on your attitudes toward gain and risk, fear and greed, and on how you handle the excitement of trading and risk.

Most of all, your success or failure depends on your ability to use your intellect rather than act out your emotions. A trader who feels overjoyed when he wins and depressed when he loses cannot accumulate equity because he is controlled by his emotions. If you let the market make you feel high or low, you will lose money.

To be a winner in the market you must know yourself and act coolly and responsibly. The pain of losing scares people into looking for magic methods. At the same time, they discard much of what is useful in their professional or business backgrounds.

Like an Ocean

The market is like an ocean—it moves up and down regardless of what you want. You may feel joy when you buy a stock and it explodes in a rally. You may feel drenched with fear when you go short but the market rises and your equity melts with every uptick. These feelings have nothing to do with the market—they exist only inside you.

The market does not know you exist. You can do nothing to influence it. You can only control your behavior.

The ocean does not care about your welfare, but it has no wish to hurt you either. You may feel joy on a sunny day, when a gentle wind pushes your sailboat where you want it to go. You may feel panic on a stormy day when the ocean pushes your boat toward the rocks. Your feelings about the ocean exist only in your mind. They threaten your survival when you let your feelings rather than intellect control your behavior.

A sailor cannot control the ocean, but he can control himself. He studies currents and weather patterns. He learns safe sailing techniques and gains experience. He knows when to sail and when to stay in the harbor. A successful sailor uses his intelligence.

An ocean can be useful — you can fish in it and use its surface to get to other islands. An ocean can be dangerous — you can drown in it. The more rational your approach, the more likely you are to get what you want. When you act out your emotions, you cannot focus on the reality of the ocean.

A trader has to study trends and reversals in the market the way a sailor studies the ocean. He must trade on a small scale while learning to handle himself in the market. You can never control the market but you can learn to control yourself.

A beginner who has a string of profitable trades often feels he can walk on water. He starts taking wild risks and blows up his account. On the other hand, an amateur who takes several losses in a row often feels so demoralized that he cannot place an order even when his system gives him a strong signal to buy or sell. If trading makes you feel elated or frightened, you cannot fully use your intellect. When joy sweeps you off your feet, you will make irrational trades and lose. When fear grips you, you'll miss profitable trades.

A professional trader uses his head and stays calm. Only amateurs become excited or depressed because of their trades. Emotional reactions are a luxury that you cannot afford in the markets.

Emotional Trading

Most people crave excitement and entertainment. Singers, actors, and professional athletes command much higher incomes in our society than do such mundane workmen as physicians, pilots, or college professors. People love to have their nerves tickled — they buy lottery tickets, fly to Las Vegas, and slow down to gawk at road accidents.

Trading is a heady experience and can be very addictive. Losers who drop money in the markets receive a tremendous entertainment value.

The market is among the most entertaining places on the face of the Earth. It is a spectator sport and a participant sport rolled into one. Imagine going to a major-league ball game in which you are not confined to the bleachers. For a few hundred dollars you can run onto the field and join the game. If you hit the ball right, you will get paid like a professional.

You would probably think twice before running onto the field the first few times. This cautious attitude is responsible for the well-known "beginner's luck." Once a beginner hits the ball well a few times and collects his pay, he is likely to get the idea that he is better than the pros and could make a good living at it. Greedy amateurs start running out onto the field too often, even when there are no good playing opportunities. Before they know what hit them, a short string of losses destroys their careers.

Emotional decisions are lethal in the markets. You can see a good model of emotional trading by going to a racetrack, turning around, and watching the humans instead of the horses. Gamblers stomp their feet, jump up and down, and yell at horses and jockeys. Thousands of people act out their emotions. Winners embrace and losers tear up their tickets in disgust. The joy, the pain, and the intensity of wishful thinking are caricatures of what happens in the markets. A cool handicapper who tries to make a living at the track does not get excited, yell, or bet the bulk of his roll on any race.

Casinos love drunk patrons. They pour gamblers free drinks because drunks are more emotional and gamble more. Casinos try to throw out intelligent card-counters. There is less free liquor on Wall Street than in a casino, but at least here they do not throw you out of the game for being a good trader.

In Charge of Your Life

When a monkey hurts its foot on a tree stump, he flies into a rage and kicks the piece of wood. You laugh at a monkey, but do you laugh at yourself when you act like him? If the market drops while you are long, you may double up on your losing trade or else go short, trying to get even. You act emotionally instead of using your intellect. What is the difference between a trader trying to get back at the market and a monkey kicking a tree stump? Acting out of anger, fear, or elation destroys your chance of success. You have to analyze your behavior in the market instead of acting out your feelings.

We get angry at the market, we become afraid of it, we develop silly superstitions. All the while, the market keeps cycling through its rallies and declines like an ocean going through its storms and calm periods. Mark Douglas writes in *The Disciplined Trader* that in the market, "There is no beginning, middle, or end — only what you create in your own mind. Rarely do any of us grow up learning to operate in an arena that allows for complete freedom of creative expression, with no external structure to restrict it in any way."

We try to cajole or manipulate the market, acting like the ancient emperor Xerxes, who ordered his soldiers to horsewhip the sea for sinking his fleet. Most of us are not aware how manipulative we are, how we bargain, how we act out our feelings in the market. Most of us consider ourselves the center of the universe and expect every person or group to be either good or bad to us. This does not work in the market which is completely impersonal.

Leston Havens, a Harvard University psychiatrist, writes: "Cannibalism and slavery are probably the oldest manifestations of human predation and submission. Although both are now discouraged, their continued existence in psychological forms demonstrates that civilization has achieved great success in moving from the concrete and physical to the abstract and psychological, while persisting in the same purposes." Parents threaten their children, bullies hit them, teachers try to bend their will in school. Little wonder that most of us grow up either hiding in a shell or learning how to manipulate others in self-defense. Acting independently does not feel natural to us — but that is the only way to succeed in the market.

Douglas warns, "If the market's behavior seems mysterious to you, it's because your own behavior is mysterious and unmanageable. You can't really determine what the market is likely to do next when you don't even know what you'll do next." Ultimately, "the one thing you can control is yourself. As a trader, you have the power either to give yourself money or to give your money to other traders." He adds, "The traders who can make money consistently . . . approach trading from the perspective of a mental discipline."

Each trader has his own demons to exorcise on the journey to becoming a successful professional. Here are several rules that worked for me as I grew from a wild amateur into an erratic semiprofessional and finally into a professional trader. You may change this list to suit your personality.

1. Decide that you are in the market for the long haul — that is, you want to be a trader even 20 years from now.

2. Learn as much as you can. Read and listen to experts, but keep a degree of healthy skepticism about everything. Ask questions, and do not accept experts at their word.

3. Do not get greedy and rush to trade — take your time to learn. The markets will be there with more good opportunities in the months and years ahead.

4. Develop a method for analyzing the market — that is, "If A happens, then B is likely to happen." Markets have many dimensions — use several analytic methods to confirm trades. Test everything on historical data and then in the markets, using real money. Markets keep changing — you need different tools for trading bull and bear markets and transitional periods as well as a method for telling the difference (see the sections on technical analysis).

5. Develop a money management plan. Your first goal must be long-term survival; your second goal, a steady growth of capital; and your third goal, making high profits. Most traders put the third goal first and are unaware that goals 1 and 2 exist (see Chapter 10, "Risk Management").

6. Be aware that a trader is the weakest link in any trading system. Go to a meeting of Alcoholics Anonymous to learn how to avoid losses or develop your own method for cutting out impulsive trades.

7. Winners think, feel, and act differently than losers. You must look within yourself, strip away your illusions, and change your old ways of being, thinking, and acting. Change is hard, but if you want to be a professional trader, you have to work on changing your personality.

II

Mass Psychology

---

12. WHAT IS PRICE?

Wall Street is named after a wall that kept farm animals from wandering away from the settlement at the tip of Manhattan. The farming legacy lives on in the language of traders. Four animals are mentioned especially often on Wall Street: bulls and bears, hogs and sheep. Traders say: "Bulls make money, bears make money, but hogs get slaughtered."

A bull fights by striking up with his horns. A bull is a buyer — a person who bets on a rally and profits from a rise in prices. A bear fights by striking down with his paws. A bear is a seller — a person who bets on a decline and profits from a fall in prices.

Hogs are greedy. They get slaughtered when they trade to satisfy their greed. Some hogs buy or sell positions that are too large for them and get destroyed by a small adverse move. Other hogs overstay their positions — they keep waiting for profits to get bigger even after the trend reverses. Sheep are passive and fearful followers of trends, tips, and gurus. They sometimes put on a bull's horns or a bearskin and try to swagger. You recognize them by their pitiful bleating when the market becomes volatile.

Whenever the market is open, bulls are buying, bears are selling, hogs and sheep get trampled underfoot, and the undecided traders wait on the sidelines. Quote machines all over the world show a steady stream of quotes — the latest prices for any trading vehicle. Thousands of eyes are focused on each price quote as people make trading decisions.

Arguing About Price

When I ask traders at a seminar, "What is price?" some answer, "Price is a perceived value." Others say, "Price is what a person at one particular point in time is willing to pay another person for a commodity." Someone says, "Price is what the last person paid for it. That's the price right now." Another suggests, "No, it's what the next person will pay."

Traders who cannot give a clear definition of price do not know what they are analyzing. Your success or failure as a trader depends on handling prices — and you had better know what they mean! Some attendees at the seminars I give become agitated as they search for an answer to a seemingly obvious question. Arguments fly back and forth, as in this discussion:

> I'll give you the worst-case example. In the 1929 crash, Singer stock was selling for $100 and all of sudden there's no bid, no bid, no bid, and somebody comes forth — "I gotta sell, what am I bid?" and one of the floor clerks said "one dollar" and he got it. He got the stock.

> Price is what the greater fool is ready to pay.

> Take the '87 market. All of that 500-point decline — stocks weren't worth any less after the decline than before. So it was the difference in the perception and the willingness of the next person to pay for it.

> You might carry that one step further. What you're paying for is absolutely worthless. It is just a piece of paper. The only value that it does have is the intrinsic dividend value, compared to government paper at that time.

> It still has the value of whatever anybody will pay you. If no one wants to pay you for it, it has no value.

> It'll pay you for a yield.

> What if you trade soybeans? You can eat them.

> How about a stock that has no yield?

> But doesn't it have assets?

> The company that issued the stock has value, cash flow.

> I give you one share of IBM; if no one wants to buy it, you can light a cigarette with it.

There is no such thing that no one wants to buy IBM. There is always a bid and an ask.

Take a look at United Airlines. One day the paper says it's $300 and the next day it's $150.

There's no change in the airline, they're still making the same cash flow, they've still got the same book value, and the same assets — what's the difference?

The price of stock has very little to do with the company it represents. The price of IBM stock has very little to do with IBM. As I visualize it, the price of stock is connected by a mile-long rubber band to IBM and it can be wildly higher and wildly lower — IBM just keeps chugging along and it's a very, very remote connection.

Price is the intersection of supply and demand curves.

Each serious trader must know the meaning of price. You need to know what you analyze before you go out and start buying and selling stocks, futures, or options.

Resolving Conflict

There are three groups of traders in the market: buyers, sellers, and undecided traders. "Ask" is what a seller asks for his merchandise. "Bid" is what a buyer offers for that merchandise. Buyers and sellers are always in conflict.

Buyers want to pay as little as possible, and sellers want to charge as much as possible. If members of both groups insist on having their way, no trade can take place. No trade means no price — only wishful quotes of buyers and sellers.

A seller has a choice: to wait until prices rise, or to accept a lower offer for his merchandise. A buyer also has a choice: to wait until prices come down, or to offer to pay more to the sellers.

A trade occurs when there is a momentary meeting of two minds: An eager bull agrees to a seller's terms and pays up, or an eager bear agrees to a buyer's terms and sells a little cheaper. The presence of undecided traders puts pressure on both bulls and bears.

When a buyer and a seller bargain in private, they may haggle at a leisurely pace. The two must move much faster when they bargain at the exchange. They know that they are surrounded by a crowd of other traders who may butt in on their deal at any moment.

The buyer knows that if he thinks for too long, another trader can step in and snap away his bargain. A seller knows that if he tries to hold out for a higher price, another trader may step in and sell at a lower price. The crowd of undecided traders makes buyers and sellers more anxious to accommodate their opponents. A trade occurs when there is a meeting of two minds.

A Consensus of Value

Each tick on your quote screen represents a deal between a buyer and a seller. Buyers are buying because they expect prices to rise. Sellers are selling because they expect prices to fall. Buyers and sellers trade while surrounded by crowds of undecided traders. They may become buyers or sellers as prices change or as time passes.

Buying by bulls pushes markets up, selling by bears pushes markets down, and undecided traders make everything happen faster by creating a sense of urgency in buyers and sellers.

Traders come to the markets from all over the world: in person, via computers, or through their brokers. Everybody has a chance to buy and to sell. Each price is a momentary consensus of value of all market participants, expressed in action. Price is a psychological event — a momentary balance of opinion between bulls and bears. Prices are created by masses of traders — buyers, sellers, and undecided people. The patterns of prices and volume reflect the mass psychology of the markets.

Behavior Patterns

Huge crowds converge on stock, commodity, and option exchanges — either in person or represented by their brokers. Big money and little money, smart money and dumb money, institutional money and private money, all meet on the exchange floor. *Each price represents a momentary consensus of value between buyers, sellers, and undecided traders at the moment of transaction. There is a crowd of traders behind every pattern in the chartbook.*

Crowd consensus changes from moment to moment. Sometimes it gets established in a very low-key environment, and at other times the environment turns wild. Prices move in small increments during quiet times. When a crowd becomes either spooked or elated, prices begin to jump. Imagine bidding for a life preserver aboard a sinking ship—that's how prices leap when masses of traders become emotional about a trend. An astute trader tries to enter the market during quiet times and take profits during wild times.

Technical analysts study swings of mass psychology in the financial markets. Each trading session is a battle between bulls, who make money when prices rise, and bears, who profit when prices fall. The goal of technical analysts is to discover the balance of power between bulls and bears and bet on the winning group. If bulls are much stronger, you should buy and hold. If bears are much stronger, you should sell and sell short. If both camps are about equal in strength, a wise trader stands aside. He lets bullies fight with each other and puts on a trade only when he is reasonably sure who is likely to win.

Prices, volume, and open interest reflect crowd behavior. So do the indicators that are based on them. This makes technical analysis similar to poll-taking. Both combine science and art: They are scientific to the extent that we use statistical methods and computers; they are artistic to the extent that we use personal judgment to interpret our findings.

13. WHAT IS THE MARKET?

What is the reality behind market symbols, prices, numbers, and graphs? When you check prices in your newspaper, watch quotes on your screen, or plot an indicator on your chart, what exactly are you looking at? What *is* the market that you want to analyze and trade?

Amateurs act as if the market is a giant happening, a ball game in which they can join the professionals and make money. Traders from a scientific or engineering background often treat the market as a physical event. They apply to it the principles of signal processing, noise reduction, and similar ideas. By contrast, all professional traders know full well what the market is—it is a huge mass of people.

Every trader tries to take money away from other traders by outguessing them on the probable direction of the market. The members of the market crowd live on different continents. They are united by modern telecommunications in the pursuit of profit at each other's expense. *The market is a huge crowd of people. Each member of the crowd tries to take money away from other members by outsmarting them. The market is a uniquely harsh environment because everyone is against you, and you are against everyone.*

Not only is the market harsh, you have to pay high prices for entering and exiting it. You have to jump over two high barriers — commissions and slippage — before you can collect a dime. The moment you place an order you owe your broker a commission — you are behind the game before you begin. Then floor traders try to hit you with slippage when your order arrives on the floor. They try to take another bite out of your account when you exit your trade. *In trading, you compete against some of the brightest minds in the world while fending off the piranhas of commissions and slippage.*

Worldwide Crowds

In the old days, markets were small and many traders knew one another. The New York Stock Exchange was formed in 1792 as a club of two dozen brokers. On sunny days they used to trade under a cottonwood tree and on rainy days in Fraunces Tavern. The first thing brokers did after they organized the New York Stock Exchange was to stick the public with fixed commissions that lasted for the next 180 years.

Today, only floor traders meet face-to-face. Most of us are linked to the market electronically. Members of the financial crowd watch the same quotes on their terminals, read the same articles in the financial media, and get similar sales pitches from brokers. These links unite us as members of the market crowd even if we are thousands of miles away from the exchange.

Thanks to modern telecommunications, the world is becoming smaller and the markets are growing. The euphoria of London flows to New York, and the gloom of Tokyo infects Hong Kong.

When you analyze the market, you are analyzing crowd behavior. Crowds behave alike in different cultures on all continents. Social psychologists have uncovered several laws that govern crowd behavior. A trader needs to understand how market crowds influence his mind.

Groups, Not Individuals

Most people feel a strong urge to join the crowd and to "act like everybody else." This primitive urge clouds your judgment when you put on a trade. A successful trader must think independently. He needs to be strong enough to analyze the market alone and to carry out his trading decisions.

If eight or ten people place their hands on your head and push you down, your knees will buckle, no matter how strong you are. The crowd may be stupid, but it is stronger than you. Crowds have the power to create trends. Never buck a trend. If a trend is up, you should only buy or stand aside. Never sell short because "the prices are too high" — never argue with the crowd. You do not have to run with the crowd — but you should never run against it.

Respect the strength of the crowd — but do not fear it. Crowds are powerful, but primitive, their behavior simple and repetitive. A trader who thinks for himself can take money from crowd members.

The Source of Money

When you try to make money trading, do you ever stop to wonder where your expected profits will come from? Is there money in the markets because of higher company earnings, or lower interest rates, or a good soybean crop? *The only reason there is money in the markets is that other traders put it there. The money you want to make belongs to other people who have no intention of giving it to you.*

Trading means trying to rob other people while they are trying to rob you. It is a hard business. Winning is especially difficult because brokers and floor traders skim money from losers and winners alike.

Tim Slater compared trading to a medieval battle. A man used to go on a battlefield with his sword and try to kill his opponent, who was trying to kill him at the same time. The winner took the loser's weapons, his chattels, and his wife, and sold his children into slavery. Now we trade on the exchanges instead of doing battle in an open field. When you take money away from a man, it is not that different from drawing his blood. He may lose his house, his chattels, and his wife, and his children may suffer.

An optimistic friend of mine once snickered that there are plenty of poorly prepared people on the battlefield: "Ninety to ninety-five percent of the brokers don't know the first thing about research. They don't know what they're doing. We have the knowledge, and some poor people who do not have it are just giving the money away to charity." This theory sounds good, but it is wrong — there is no easy money in the market.

There are plenty of dumb sheep waiting to be fleeced or slaughtered. The sheep are easy—but if you want a piece of their meat, you've got to fight some very dangerous competitors. There are mean professionals: American gunslingers, English knights, German landsknechts, Japanese samurai, and other warriors, all going after the same hapless sheep. Trading means battling crowds of hostile people while paying for the privilege of entering the battle and leaving it, whether dead, wounded, or alive.

Inside Information

There is at least one group of people who consistently get information before other traders. Records show that corporate insiders consistently make profits in the stock market. Those records reflect legitimate trades that have been reported by insiders to the Securities and Exchange Commission. They represent the tip of the iceberg—but there is a great deal of illegitimate insider trading in the stock market.

People who trade on inside information are stealing money from the rest of us. The insider trials of the 1980s have landed some of the more notorious insiders in jail—Dennis Levine, Ivan Boesky, and others. For a while, hardly a week went by without an arrest, indictment, conviction or a consent decree: The Yuppy Five, Michael Milken, even a psychiatrist in Connecticut who traded after learning about a pending takeover from a patient.

The defendants of the 1980s insider trials were caught because they became greedy and careless—and ran into a federal prosecutor in New York with major political ambitions. The tip of the iceberg has been shaved down, but its bulk continues to float. Do not ask whose ship it will hit—it is your trading account.

Trying to reduce insider trading is like trying to get rid of rats on a farm. Pesticides keep them under control but do not root them out. A retired chief executive of a publicly traded firm explained to me that a smart man does not trade on inside information but gives it to his golfing buddies at a country club. Later they give him inside information on their companies, and both profit without being detected. The insider network is safe as long as its members follow the same code of conduct and do not become too greedy.

Insider trading is legal in the futures markets. Technical analysis helps you detect insider buying and selling. Charts reflect all trades by all market participants—even by the insiders. They leave their tracks on the charts just like everyone else—and it is your job as a technical analyst to follow them to the bank.

14. THE TRADING SCENE

Humans have traded since the dawn of history — it was safer to trade with your neighbors than to raid them. As society developed, money became the medium of exchange. Stock and commodity markets are among the hallmarks of an advanced society. One of the first economic developments in Eastern Europe following the collapse of communism was the establishment of stock and commodity exchanges.

It took Marco Polo, a medieval Italian traveler, 15 years to get from Italy to China. Now when a European trader wants to buy gold in Hong Kong, he can get his order filled in a minute.

Today, stock, futures, and options markets span the globe. In India alone, there are 14 stock exchanges. There are over 65 futures and options exchanges in the world. As Barbara Diamond and Mark Kollar write in their book, *24-Hour Trading*, they make markets in nearly 400 contracts — from gold to greasy wool, from Australian All-Ordinaries Index to dried silk cocoons. All exchanges must meet three criteria, first developed in the agoras of ancient Greece and the medieval fairs of Western Europe: an established location, rules for grading merchandise, and defined contract terms.

Individual Traders

Private traders usually come to the market after a successful career in business or in the professions. An average private futures trader in the United States is a 50-year-old, married, college-educated man. Many futures traders own their own businesses, and many have postgraduate degrees. The two largest occupational groups among futures traders are farmers and engineers.

Most people trade for partly rational, partly irrational reasons. Rational reasons include the desire to earn a large return on capital. Irrational reasons include gambling and a search for excitement. Most traders are not aware of their irrational motives.

Learning to trade takes hard work, time, energy, and money. Few individuals rise to the level of professionals who can support themselves by trading. Professionals are extremely serious about what they do. They satisfy their irrational goals outside the markets, while amateurs act them out in the marketplace.

The major economic role of a trader is to support his broker — to help him pay his mortgage and keep his children in private schools. In addition, the role of a speculator is to help companies raise capital in the stock market and to assume a price risk in the commodities markets, allowing producers to focus on production. These lofty economic goals are far from a speculator's mind when he gives an order to his broker.

Institutional Traders

Institutions are responsible for a huge volume of trading. Their deep pockets give them several advantages. They pay low institutional commissions. They can afford to hire the best researchers, brokers, and traders. Some even strike back at floor traders who steal too much in slippage. The spate of arrests and trials of Chicago floor traders in 1990 and 1991 began when Archer Daniels Midland, a food processing firm, brought in the FBI.

A friend of mine who heads a trading desk at a bank bases some of his decisions on a service provided by a group of former CIA officers. They scan the media to detect early trends in society and send their reports to him. My trader friend culls some of his best ideas from these reports. The substantial annual fee for those experts is small potatoes for his firm compared with the millions of dollars it trades. Most private traders do not have such opportunities. It is easier for institutions to buy the best research.

An acquaintance who used to trade successfully for a Wall Street investment bank found himself in trouble when he quit to trade for himself. He discovered that a real-time quote system in his Park Avenue apartment in Manhattan did not give him news as fast as the squawk box on the trading floor of his old firm. Brokers from around the country used to call him with the latest ideas because they wanted his orders. "When you trade from your house, you are never the first to hear the news," he says.

Some large firms have intelligence networks that enable them to act before the public. One day, when oil futures rallied in response to a fire on a platform in the North Sea, I called a friend at an oil firm. The market was frantic, but he was relaxed—he had bought oil futures half an hour before they exploded. He had gotten a telex from an agent in the area of the fire well before the reports appeared on the newswire. Timely information is priceless, but only a large company can afford an intelligence network.

The firms that deal in both futures and cash markets have two advantages. They have true inside information, and they are exempt from speculative position limits (see Section 40). Recently, I visited an acquaintance at a multinational oil company. After passing through security that was tighter than at Kennedy International Airport, I walked through glass-enclosed corridors. Clusters of men huddled around monitors trading oil products. When I asked my host whether his traders were hedging or speculating, he looked me straight in the eye and said, "Yes." I asked again and received the same answer. Companies crisscross the thin line between hedging and speculating based on inside information.

Employees of trading firms have a psychological advantage — they can be more relaxed because their own money is not at risk. Most individuals do not have the discipline to stop trading when they get on a losing streak, but institutions impose discipline on traders. A trader is given two limits — how much he may risk on a single trade and the maximum amount he may lose in a month. These limits work as stop-loss orders on a trader.

With all these advantages, how can an individual trader compete against institutions and win? First, many institutional trading departments are poorly run. Second, the Achilles heel of most institutions is that they often *have* to trade, while an individual trader is free to trade or stay out of the market. Banks have to be active in the bond market and food processing companies have to be active in the grain market at almost any price. An individual trader is free to wait for the best trading opportunities.

Most private traders fritter away this advantage by overtrading. An individual who wants to succeed against the giants must develop patience and eliminate greed. *Remember, your goal is to trade well, not to trade often.*

Successful institutional traders receive raises and bonuses. Even a high bonus can feel puny to someone who earns many millions of dollars for his firm. Successful institutional traders often talk of quitting and going to trade for themselves.

Only a handful of them manage to make the transition. Most traders who leave institutions get caught up in the emotions of fear, greed, elation, and panic when they start risking their own money. They seldom do well trading for their own account — another sign that psychology is at the root of trading success or failure.

The Swordmakers

Medieval knights shopped for the sharpest swords, and modern traders shop for the best trading tools. The growing access to data, computers, and software creates a more level playing field for traders. Prices of hardware fall almost monthly and software keeps getting better. It is easy for even a computer-illiterate trader to hire a consultant and set up a system (see Section 24).

A computer allows you to speed up your research and follow up on more leads. It is not a substitute for making trading decisions. A computer helps you analyze more markets in greater depth, but the ultimate responsibility for every trade rests with you.

There are three types of trading software: toolboxes, black boxes, and gray boxes. A toolbox allows you to display data, draw charts, plot indicators, and even test your trading system. Toolboxes for options traders include option valuation models. It is as easy to adapt a good toolbox to your needs as it is to adjust your car seat.

What goes inside a black box is secret. You feed it data, and it tells you when to buy and sell. It is like magic — a way to make money without thinking. Black boxes usually come with excellent historical track records. This is only natural because they were created to fit old data! Markets keep changing, and black boxes keep blowing up, but new generations of losers keep buying new black boxes.

Gray boxes straddle the fence between toolboxes and black boxes. These packages are usually put out by prominent market personalities. They disclose the general logic of their system and allow you to adjust some of their parameters.

Advisors

Advisory newsletters are colorful splashes on the trading scene. Freedom of the press allows anyone to put a typewriter on his kitchen table, buy a few stamps, and start sending out a financial advisory letter. Their "track records" are largely an exercise in futility because hardly anybody ever takes every bit of advice in any newsletter.

Some newsletters provide useful ideas and point readers in the direction of trading opportunities. A few offer educational value. Mostly, they sell outsiders an illusion of being an insider, of knowing what happens or is about to happen in the markets.

Newsletters are good entertainment. Your subscription rents you a penpal who sends amusing and interesting letters and never asks you to write back, except for a check at renewal time.

Services that rate newsletters are for-profit affairs run by small businessmen whose well-being depends on the well-being of the advisory industry.

Rating services may occasionally tut-tut an advisor, but they dedicate most of their energy to loud cheerleading.

I used to write an advisory newsletter: worked hard, did not fudge results, and received good ratings. I saw from the inside a tremendous potential for fudging results. This is a well-kept secret of the advisory industry.

When I was getting into letter writing, one of the most prominent advisors told me that I should spend less time on research and more on marketing. The first principle of letter writing is: "If you have to make forecasts, make a lot of them." Whenever a forecast turns out right, double the volume of promotional mail.

Trading Contests

Trading contests are run by small firms or individuals. Contestants pay organizers to monitor their results and publicize the names of winners. Trading contests have two flaws — one mild, and another possibly criminal. This is a scandal waiting to be explored by investigative journalists.

All contests hide information about losers and tell you only about winners. Each dog has its day in the sun, and most losers have at least one good quarter. If you keep entering contests and taking wild chances, eventually you will have a winning quarter, reap the publicity, and attract money management clients.

Many advisors enter trading contests with a small stake, which they chalk off to marketing expense. If they get lucky they receive valuable publicity, while their losses are hidden. Nobody hears about a contestant who destroys his account. I know several traders who are so bad they could not trade candy with a child. They are chronic losers — but all of them appeared on the list of winners of a major contest, with great percentage gains. That publicity allowed them to raise money from the public — which they proceeded to lose. If trading contests disclosed the names and results of all participants, that would promptly kill the enterprise.

A more malignant flaw of trading contests is the financial collusion between some organizers and contestants. Many organizers have a direct financial incentive to rig the results and help their co-conspirators obtain publicity as winners. They use it to raise money from the public.

The proprietor of one of the contests told me that he was raising money for his star winner. How objective can a judge be if he has a business relationship with one of his contestants? It appeared that the amount he could raise depended on how well his "star" performed in his contest. That highly touted star promptly lost money put under his management.

The worst abuses can occur in contests run by brokerage firms. A firm can set up contest rules, attract participants, have them trade through the firm, judge them, publicize their results, and then go for the jugular—raising money from the public for winners to manage, thereby generating fees and commissions. It would be easy for such a firm to create a star. All it would have to do is open several accounts for the designated "winner." At the end of each day it could put the best trades into a contest account and the rest of the trades into other accounts, creating a great "track record." Trading contests can be an attractive tool for fleecing the public.

15. THE MARKET CROWD AND YOU

The market is a loosely organized crowd whose members bet that prices will rise or fall. Since each price represents the consensus of the crowd at the moment of transaction, all traders are in effect betting on the future mood of the crowd. That crowd keeps swinging from indifference to optimism or pessimism and from hope to fear. Most people do not follow their own trading plans because they let the crowd influence their feelings, thoughts, and actions.

Bulls and bears battle in the market, and the value of your investment sinks or soars, depending on the actions of total strangers. You cannot control the markets. You can only decide whether and when to enter or exit trades.

Most traders feel jittery when we enter a trade. Their judgment becomes clouded by emotions after they join the market crowd. These crowd-induced emotions make traders deviate from their trading plans and lose money.

Experts on Crowds

Charles Mackay, a Scottish barrister, wrote his classic book, *Extraordinary Popular Delusions and the Madness of Crowds*, in 1841. He described several mass manias, including the Tulip Mania in Holland in 1634 and the South Seas investment bubble in England in 1720.

The tulip craze began as a bull market in tulip bulbs. The long bull market convinced the prosperous Dutch that tulips would continue to appreciate. Many of them abandoned their businesses to grow tulips, trade them, or become tulip brokers. Banks accepted tulips as collateral and speculators profited. Finally, that mania collapsed in waves of panic selling, leaving many people destitute and the nation shocked. Mackay sighed, "Men go mad in crowds, and they come back to their senses slowly and one by one."

In 1897, Gustave LeBon, a French philosopher and politician, wrote *The Crowd*, one of the best books on mass psychology. A trader who reads it today can see his reflection in a century-old mirror.

LeBon wrote that when people gather in a crowd, "Whoever be the individuals that compose it, however like or unlike be their mode of life, their occupations, their character, or their intelligence, the fact that they have been transformed into a crowd puts them in possession of a sort of collective mind which makes them feel, think, and act in a manner quite different from that in which each individual of them would feel, think, and act were he in a state of isolation."

People change when they join crowds. They become more credulous and impulsive, anxiously search for a leader, and react to emotions instead of using their intellect. An individual who becomes involved in a group becomes less capable of thinking for himself.

The experiments of American social psychologists in the 1950s have proven that people think differently in groups than they do alone. For example, an individual can easily tell which of the two lines on a piece of paper is longer. He loses that ability when he is put into a group whose other members deliberately give wrong answers. Intelligent, college-educated people believe a group of strangers more than they believe their own eyes!

Group members believe others, and particularly group leaders, more than they believe themselves. Theodore Adorno and other sociologists showed in their two-volume study, *The American Soldier*, that the single best predictor of an individual's effectiveness in combat was his relationship with his sergeant. A soldier who trusts his leader will literally follow him to his death. A trader who believes he is following a trend may hold a losing position until his equity is wiped out.

Sigmund Freud explained that groups are held together by the loyalty of members to the leader. Our feelings toward group leaders stem from our childhood feelings toward our fathers — a mixture of trust, awe, fear, the desire for approval, and potential rebellion. When we join groups, our thinking on issues involving that group regresses to the level of a child. A leaderless group cannot hold itself together and falls apart. This explains buying and selling panics. When traders suddenly feel that the trend they have been following has abandoned them, they dump their positions in a panic.

Group members may catch a few trends, but they get killed when trends reverse. When you join a group, you act like a child following a parent. Markets do not care about your well-being. Successful traders are independent thinkers.

Why Join?

People have been joining crowds for safety since the beginning of time. If a group of hunters took on a saber-toothed tiger, most of them were likely to survive. A lone hunter had a slim chance of coming out alive from such an encounter. Loners got killed more often and left fewer offspring. Group members were more likely to survive, and the tendency to join groups appears to have been bred into humans.

Our society glorifies freedom and free will, but we carry many primitive impulses beneath the thin veneer of civilization. We want to join groups for safety and be led by strong leaders. The greater the uncertainty, the stronger our wish to join and to follow.

No saber-toothed tigers roam the canyons of Wall Street, but you probably fear for your financial survival. Your fear swells up because you cannot control changes in prices. The value of your position rises and falls because of buying and selling by total strangers. This uncertainty makes most traders look for a leader who will tell them what to do.

You may have rationally decided to go long or short, but the moment you put on a trade, the crowd starts sucking you in. You need to pay attention to several signs that indicate when you start turning into a sweaty crowd member instead of an intelligent trader.

You start losing your independence when you watch prices like a hawk and feel elated if they go your way or depressed if they go against you. You are in trouble when you start trusting gurus more than yourself and impulsively add to losing positions or reverse them. You lose your independence when you do not follow your own trading plan. When you notice what is happening, try to come back to your senses; if you cannot regain your composure, exit your trade.

Crowd Mentality

People become primitive and action-oriented when they join crowds. Crowds feel simple but strong emotions such as terror, elation, alarm, and joy. Crowds swing from fear to glee, from panic to mirth. A scientist can be cool and rational in his lab but make harebrained trades after being swept up in the mass hysteria of the market. A group can suck you in, whether you trade from a crowded brokerage office or from a remote mountaintop. When you let others influence your trading decisions, you lose your chance of success.

Group loyalty is essential for the survival of a military unit. Joining a union can help you keep a job even if your performance is not very good. But no group can protect you in the market.

The crowd is bigger and stronger than you. No matter how smart you are, you cannot argue with the crowd. You have only one choice — to join the crowd or to act independently.

Many traders are puzzled why markets always seem to reverse immediately after they dump their losing position. This happens because crowd members are gripped by the same fear — and everybody dumps at the same time. Once the fit of selling has ended, the market has nowhere to go but up. Optimism returns to the marketplace, and the crowd feels greedy and goes on a new buying binge.

Crowds are primitive, and your trading strategies should be simple. You do not have to be a rocket scientist to design a winning trading method. If the trade goes against you — cut your losses and run. It never pays to argue with the crowd — simply use your judgment to decide when to join and when to leave.

Your human nature prepares you to give up your independence under stress. When you put on a trade, you feel the desire to imitate others and overlook objective trading signals. This is why you need to develop and follow trading systems and money management rules. They represent your rational individual decisions, made before you enter a trade and become a crowd member.

Who Leads?

You may feel intense joy when prices move in your favor. You may feel angry, depressed, and fearful when prices go against you, and you may anxiously wait to see what the market will do to you next. Traders join crowds when they feel stressed or threatened. Battered by emotions, they lose their independence and begin imitating other group members, especially the group leader.

When children feel frightened, they want to be told what to do and look up to their parents. They transfer that attitude to teachers, doctors, ministers, bosses, and assorted experts. Traders turn to gurus, trading system vendors, newspaper columnists, and other market leaders. But, as Tony Plummer brilliantly pointed out in his book, *Forecasting Financial Markets*, the main leader of the market is price.

Price is the leader of the market crowd. Traders all over the world follow the market's upticks and downticks. Price seems to say to traders, "Follow me, and I will show you the way to riches." Most traders consider themselves independent. Few of us realize how strongly we focus on the behavior of our group leader.

A trend that goes in your favor symbolizes a strong, bountiful parent calling you to share a meal or risk being left out. A trend that goes against you symbolizes an angry, punishing parent. When you are gripped by these feelings, it is easy to overlook objective signals that tell you to exit. You may feel defiant, or bargain, or beg forgiveness — while avoiding the rational act of accepting your loss and getting out of a losing position.

Independence

You need to base your trades on a carefully prepared trading plan and not jump in response to price changes. It pays to write down your plan. You need to know exactly under what conditions you will enter and exit a trade. Do not make decisions on the spur of the moment, when you are vulnerable to being sucked into the crowd.

You can succeed in trading only when you think and act as an individual. The weakest part of any trading system is the trader himself. Traders fail when they trade without a plan or deviate from their plans. Plans are created by reasoning individuals. Impulsive trades are made by sweaty group members.

You have to observe yourself and notice changes in your mental state as you trade. Write down your reasons for entering a trade and the rules for getting out of it, including money management rules. You must not change your plan while you have an open position.

Sirens were sea creatures of Greek myths who sang so beautifully that sailors jumped overboard and drowned. When Odysseus wanted to hear the Sirens' songs, he ordered his men to tie him to the mast and to put wax in their own ears. Odysseus heard the Sirens' song but survived because he could not jump. You ensure your survival as a trader when on a clear day you tie yourself to the mast of a trading plan and money management rules.

16. PSYCHOLOGY OF TRENDS

Each price is the momentary consensus of value of all market participants. It shows their latest vote on the value of a trading vehicle. Any trader can "put in his two cents' worth" by giving an order to buy or to sell, or by refusing to trade at the current level.

Each bar on a chart reflects the battle between bulls and bears. When bulls feel strongly bullish, they buy more eagerly and push markets up. When bears feel strongly bearish, they sell more actively and push markets down.

Each price reflects action or lack of action by all traders in the market. Charts are a window into mass psychology. When you analyze charts, you analyze the behavior of traders. Technical indicators help make this analysis more objective.

Technical analysis is applied social psychology. It aims to recognize trends and changes in crowd behavior in order to make intelligent trading decisions.

Strong Feelings

Ask most traders why prices went up, and you are likely to get a stock answer—more buyers than sellers. This is not true. The number of trading instruments, such as stocks or futures, bought and sold in any market is always equal.

If you want to buy a contract of Swiss Francs, someone has to sell it to you. If you want to sell short a contract of the S&P 500, someone has to buy it from you. The number of stocks bought and sold is equal in the stock market. Furthermore, the number of long and short positions in the futures markets is always equal. Prices move up or down because of changes in the intensity of greed and fear among buyers or sellers.

When the trend is up, bulls feel optimistic and do not mind paying a little extra. They buy high because they expect prices to rise even higher. Bears feel tense in an uptrend, and they agree to sell only at a higher price. When greedy and optimistic bulls meet fearful and defensive bears, the market rallies. The stronger their feelings, the sharper the rally. The rally ends only when many bulls lose their enthusiasm.

When prices slide, bears feel optimistic and do not quibble about selling short at lower prices. Bulls are fearful and agree to buy only at a discount.

As long as bears feel like winners, they continue to sell at lower prices, and
the downtrend continues. It ends when bears start feeling cautious and refuse
to sell at lower prices.

Rallies and Declines

Few traders act as purely rational human beings. There is a great deal of
emotional activity in the markets. Most market participants act on the principle of "monkey see, monkey do." The waves of fear and greed sweep up
bulls and bears.

Markets rise because of greed among buyers and fear among short sellers.
Bulls normally like to buy on the cheap. When they turn very bullish, they
become more concerned with not missing the rally than with getting a cheap
price. A rally continues as long as bulls are greedy enough to meet sellers'
demands.

The sharpness of a rally depends on how traders feel. If buyers feel just a
little stronger than sellers, the market rises slowly. When they feel much
stronger than sellers, the market rises fast. It is the job of a technical analyst
to find when buyers are strong and when they start running out of steam.

Short sellers feel trapped by rising markets, as their profits melt and turn
into losses. When short sellers rush to cover, a rally becomes nearly vertical.
Fear is a stronger emotion than greed, and rallies driven by short covering
are especially sharp.

Markets fall because of greed among bears and fear among bulls.
Normally bears prefer to sell short on rallies, but if they expect to make a lot
of money on a decline, they don't mind shorting on the way down. Fearful
buyers agree to buy only below the market. As long as short sellers are willing to meet those demands and sell at a bid, the decline continues.

As bulls' profits melt and turn into losses, they panic and sell at almost
any price. They are so eager to get out that they hit the bids under the market. Markets can fall very fast when hit by panic selling.

Trend Leaders

Loyalty is the glue that holds groups together. Freud showed that group
members relate to their leader the way children relate to a father. Group

members expect leaders to inspire and reward them when they are good but to punish them when they are bad.

Who leads market trends? When individuals try to control a market, they usually end up badly. For example, the bull market in silver in the 1980s was led by the Hunt brothers of Texas and their Arab associates. The Hunts ended up in a bankruptcy court. They had no money left even for a limousine and had to ride the subway to the courthouse. Market gurus sometimes lead trends, but they never last beyond one market cycle (see Section 6).

Tony Plummer, a British trader, has presented a revolutionary idea in his book, *Forecasting Financial Markets — The Truth Behind Technical Analysis.* He showed that price itself functions as the leader of the market crowd! Most traders focus their attention on price.

Winners feel rewarded when price moves in their favor, and losers feel punished when price moves against them. Crowd members remain blissfully unaware that when they focus on price they create their own leader. Traders who feel mesmerized by price swings create their own idols.

When the trend is up, bulls feel rewarded by a bountiful parent. The longer an uptrend lasts, the more confident they feel. When a child's behavior is rewarded, he continues to do what he did. When bulls make money, they add to long positions and new bulls enter the market. Bears feel they are being punished for selling short. Many of them cover shorts, go long, and join the bulls.

Buying by happy bulls and covering by fearful bears pushes uptrends higher. Buyers feel rewarded while sellers feel punished. Both feel emotionally involved, but few traders realize that they are creating the uptrend, creating their own leader.

Eventually a price shock occurs — a major sale hits the market, and there are not enough buyers to absorb it. The uptrend takes a dive. Bulls feel mistreated, like children whose father hit them with a strap during a meal, but bears feel encouraged.

A price shock plants the seeds of an uptrend's reversal. Even if the market recovers and reaches a new high, bulls feel more skittish and bears become bolder. This lack of cohesion in the dominant group and optimism among its opponents makes the uptrend ready to reverse. Several technical indicators identify tops by tracing a pattern called bearish divergence (see Section 28). It occurs when prices reach a new high but the indicator reaches a lower high than it did on a previous rally. Bearish divergences mark the best shorting opportunities.

When the trend is down, bears feel like good children, praised and rewarded for being smart. They feel increasingly confident, add to their positions, and the downtrend continues. New bears come into the market. Most people admire winners, and the financial media keep interviewing bears in bear markets.

Bulls lose money in downtrends, and that makes them feel bad. Bulls dump their positions, and many switch sides to join bears. Their selling pushes markets lower.

After a while, bears grow confident and bulls feel demoralized. Suddenly, a price shock occurs. A cluster of buy orders soaks up all available sell orders and lifts the market. Now bears feel like children whose father has lashed out at them in the midst of a happy meal.

A price shock plants the seeds of a downtrend's eventual reversal because bears become more fearful and bulls grow bolder. When a child begins to doubt that Santa Claus exists, he seldom believes in Santa again. Even if bears recover and prices fall to a new low, several technical indicators identify their weakness by tracing a pattern called a bullish divergence. It occurs when prices fall to a new low but an indicator traces a more shallow bottom than during the previous decline. Bullish divergences identify the best buying opportunities.

Social Psychology

An individual has a free will and his behavior is hard to predict. Group behavior is more primitive and easier to follow. When you analyze markets, you analyze group behavior. You need to identify the direction in which groups run and their changes.

Groups suck us in and cloud our judgment. The problem for most analysts is that they get caught in the mentality of the groups they analyze.

The longer a rally continues, the more technicians get caught up in bullish sentiment, ignore the danger signs, and miss the reversal. The longer a decline goes on, the more technicians get caught up in bearish gloom and ignore bullish signs. This is why it helps to have a written plan for analyzing the markets. We have to decide in advance what indicators we will watch and how we will interpret them.

Floor traders use several tools for tracking the quality and intensity of a crowd's feelings. They watch the crowd's ability to break through recent support and resistance levels. They keep an eye on the flow of "paper" — customer orders that come to the floor in response to price changes. Floor traders listen to the changes in pitch and volume of the roar on the exchange floor.

If you trade away from the floor, you need other tools for analyzing crowd behavior. Your charts and indicators reflect mass psychology in action. *A technical analyst is an applied social psychologist, often armed with a computer.*

17. MANAGING VERSUS FORECASTING

I once ran into a very fat surgeon at a seminar. He told me that he had lost a quarter of a million dollars in three years trading stocks and options. When I asked him how he made his trading decisions, he sheepishly pointed to his ample gut. He gambled on hunches and used his professional income to support his habit. There are two alternatives to "gut feel": One is fundamental analysis; the other is technical analysis.

Major bull and bear markets result from fundamental changes in supply and demand. Fundamental analysts follow crop reports, study the actions of the Federal Reserve, track industry utilization rates, and so on. Even if you know those factors, you can lose money trading if you are out of touch with intermediate- and short-term trends. They depend on the crowd's emotions.

Technical analysts believe that prices reflect everything known about the market, including all fundamental factors. Each price represents the consensus of value of all market participants — large commercial interests and small speculators, fundamental researchers, technicians, and gamblers.

Technical analysis is a study of mass psychology. It is partly a science and partly an art. Technicians use many scientific methods, including mathematical concepts of game theory, probabilities, and so on. Many technicians use computers to track sophisticated indicators.

Technical analysis is also an art. The bars on a chart coalesce into patterns and formations. When prices and indicators move, they produce a sense of flow and rhythm, a feeling of tension and beauty that helps you sense what is happening and how to trade.

Individual behavior is complex, diverse, and difficult to predict. Group behavior is primitive. Technicians study the behavior patterns of market crowds. They trade when they recognize a pattern that preceded past market moves.

Poll-Taking

Political poll-taking is a good model of technical analysis. Technicians and polltakers try to read the mass mind. Polltakers do it for political gain, technicians for financial gain. Politicians want to know their chances of being elected or re-elected. They make promises to constituents and then ask polltakers about their odds of winning.

Polltakers use scientific methods: statistics, sampling procedures, and so on. They also need a flair for interviewing and phrasing questions; they have to be plugged into the emotional undercurrents of their party. Poll-taking is a combination of science and art. If a polltaker says he is a scientist, ask him why every major political polltaker in the United States is affiliated with either the Democratic or Republican party. True science knows no party.

A market technician must rise above party affiliation. Be neither a bull nor a bear, but only seek the truth. A biased bull looks at a chart and says, "Where can I buy?" A biased bear looks at the same chart and tries to find where he can go short. A top-flight analyst is free of bullish or bearish bias.

There is a trick to help you detect your bias. If you want to buy, turn your chart upside down and see whether it looks like a sell. If it still looks like a buy after you flip it, then you have to work on getting a bullish bias out of your system. If both charts look like a sell, then you have to work on purging a bearish bias.

A Crystal Ball

Most traders take price swings personally. They feel very proud when they make money and love to talk about their profits. When a trade goes against them they feel like punished children and try to keep their losses secret. You can read traders' emotions on their faces.

Many traders believe that the aim of a market analyst is to forecast future prices. The amateurs in most fields ask for forecasts, while professionals simply manage information and make decisions based on probabilities. Take medicine, for example. A patient is brought to an emergency room with a knife sticking out of his chest — and the anxious family members have only two questions: "Will he survive?" and "when can he go home?" They ask the doctor for a forecast.

But the doctor is not forecasting—he is taking care of problems as they emerge. His first job is to prevent the patient from dying from shock, and so he gives him pain-killers and starts an intravenous drip to replace lost blood. Then he removes the knife and sutures damaged organs. After that, he has to watch against infection. He monitors the trend of a patient's health and takes measures to prevent complications. He is managing—not forecasting. When a family begs for a forecast, he may give it to them, but its practical value is low.

To make money trading, you do not need to forecast the future. You have to extract information from the market and find out whether bulls or bears are in control. You need to measure the strength of the dominant market group and decide how likely the current trend is to continue. You need to practice conservative money management aimed at long-term survival and profit accumulation. You must observe how your mind works and avoid slipping into greed or fear. A trader who does all of this will succeed more than any forecaster.

Read the Market, Manage Yourself

A tremendous volume of information pours out of the markets during trading hours. Changes in prices tell us about the battles of bulls and bears. Your job is to analyze this information and bet on the dominant market group.

Dramatic forecasts are a marketing gimmick. People who sell advisory services or raise money know that good calls attract paying customers, while bad calls are quickly forgotten. My phone rang while I was writing this chapter. One of the famous gurus, currently down on his luck, told me that he identified a "once-in-a-lifetime buying opportunity" in a certain agricultural market. He asked me to raise money for him and promised to multiply it a hundredfold in six months! I do not know how many fools he hooked, but dramatic forecasts have always been good for fleecing the public.

Use your common sense when you analyze markets. When some new development puzzles you, compare it to life outside the markets. For example, indicators may give you buy signals in two markets. Should you buy the market that declined a lot before the buy signal or the one that declined a little? Compare this to what happens to a man after a fall. If he falls down a flight of stairs, he may dust himself off and run up again. But if he falls out of a third story window, he's not going to run anytime soon; he needs time to recover. Prices seldom rally very hard immediately after a bad decline.

Successful trading stands on three pillars. You need to analyze the balance of power between bulls and bears. You need to practice good money management. You need personal discipline to follow your trading plan and avoid getting high in the markets.

III

Classical Chart Analysis

18. CHARTING

Chartists study market action, trying to identify recurrent price patterns. Their goal is to profit from trading when patterns recur. Most chartists work with bar graphs showing high, low, and closing prices and volume. Some also watch opening prices and open interest. Point-and-figure chartists track only price changes and ignore time, volume, and open interest.

Classical charting requires only a pencil and paper. It appeals to visually oriented people. Those who plot data by hand often develop a physical feel for prices. Computers speed charting at a cost of losing some of that feel.

The biggest problem in charting is wishful thinking. Traders often convince themselves that a pattern is bullish or bearish depending on whether they want to buy or to sell.

Early in this century Herman Rorschach, a Swiss psychiatrist, designed a test for exploring a person's mind. He dropped ink on 10 sheets of paper and folded each in half, creating a symmetrical inkblot. Most people who peer at these sheets describe what they see: parts of the anatomy, animals, buildings, and so on. In reality, there are only inkblots! Each person sees what's on his mind. Most traders use charts as a giant Rorschach test. They project their hopes, fears, and fantasies onto the charts.

Brief History

The first chartists in the United States appeared at the turn of the century. They included Charles Dow, the author of a famous stock market theory, and

William Hamilton, who succeeded Dow as the editor of the *Wall Street Journal.* Dow's famous maxim was "The averages discount everything." He meant that changes in the Dow Jones Industrial and Rail Averages reflected all knowledge and hopes about the economy and the stock market.

Dow never wrote a book, only the *Wall Street Journal* editorials. Hamilton took over the job after Dow died and struck a blow for charting when he wrote "The Turn of the Tide," an editorial following the 1929 crash.

Hamilton laid out the principles of Dow theory in his book, *The Stock Market Barometer.* Robert Rhea, a newsletter publisher, brought the theory to its pinnacle in his 1932 book, *The Dow Theory.*

The decade of the 1930s was the Golden Age of charting. Many innovators found themselves with time on their hands after the crash of 1929. Schabaker, Rhea, Elliott, Wyckoff, Gann, and others published their research during that decade. Their work went in two distinct directions. Some, such as Wyckoff and Schabaker, saw charts as a graphic record of supply and demand in the markets. Others, such as Elliott and Gann, searched for a perfect order in the markets — a fascinating but futile undertaking (see Section 6).

In 1948, Edwards (who was a son-in-law of Schabaker) and Magee published *Technical Analysis of Stock Trends.* They popularized such concepts as triangles, rectangles, head-and-shoulders, and other chart formations, as well as support and resistance and trendlines. Other chartists have applied these concepts to commodities.

Markets have changed a great deal since the days of Edwards and Magee. In the 1940s, daily volume of an active stock on the New York Stock Exchange was only several hundred shares, while in the 1990s it often exceeds a million. The balance of power in the stock market has shifted in favor of bulls. Early chartists wrote that stock market tops were sharp and fast, while bottoms took a long time to develop. That was true in their deflationary era, but the opposite has been true since the 1950s. Now bottoms tend to form quickly while tops tend to take longer.

The Meaning of a Bar Chart

Chart patterns reflect the tides of greed and fear among traders. This book focuses on daily charts, but you can apply many of its principles to other data. The rules for reading weekly, daily, hourly, or intraday charts are very similar.

Each price is a momentary consensus of value of all market participants

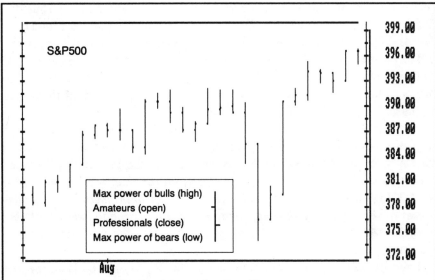

Figure 18–1. The Meaning of a Bar Chart

Opening prices are set by amateurs, whose orders accumulate overnight and hit the market in the morning. Closing prices are largely set by market professionals, who trade throughout the day. Note how often opening and closing prices are at opposite ends of a bar.

The high of each bar marks the maximum power of bulls during that bar. The low of each bar marks the maximum power of bears during that bar. Slippage tends to be less when you enter or exit positions during short bars.

expressed in action. Each price bar provides several pieces of information about the balance of power between bulls and bears (Figure 18-1).

The **opening price** of a daily or a weekly bar usually reflects the amateurs' opinion of value. They read morning papers, find out what happened the day before, and call their brokers with orders before going to work. Amateurs are especially active early in the day and early in the week.

Traders who researched the relationship between opening and closing prices for several decades found that opening prices most often occur near the high or the low of the daily bars. Buying or selling by amateurs early in the day creates an emotional extreme from which prices recoil later in the day.

In bull markets, prices often make their low for the week on Monday or

Tuesday on profit taking by amateurs, then rally to a new high on Thursday or Friday. In bear markets, the high for the week is often set on Monday or Tuesday, with a new low toward the end of the week, on Thursday or Friday.

The **closing prices** of daily and weekly bars tend to reflect the actions of professional traders. They watch the markets throughout the day, respond to changes, and become especially active near the close. Many of them take profits at that time to avoid carrying trades overnight.

Professionals as a group usually trade against the amateurs. They tend to buy lower openings, sell short higher openings, and unwind their positions as the day goes on. Traders need to pay attention to the relationship between opening and closing prices. *If prices closed higher than they opened, then market professionals were probably more bullish than amateurs. If prices closed lower than they opened, then market professionals were probably more bearish than amateurs.* It pays to trade with the professionals and against the amateurs.

The **high of each bar** represents the maximum power of bulls during that bar. Bulls make money when prices go up. Their buying pushes prices higher, and every uptick adds to their profits. Finally, bulls reach a point where they cannot lift prices — not even by one more tick. The high of a daily bar represents the maximum power of bulls during the day, and the high of a weekly bar marks the maximum power of bulls during the week; the high of a 5-minute bar reflects the maximum power of bulls during that 5-minute period. *The highest point of a bar represents the maximum power of bulls during that bar.*

The **low of each bar** represents the maximum power of bears during that bar. Bears make money when prices go down. They keep selling short, their selling pushes prices lower, and every downtick adds to their profits. At some point they run out of either capital or enthusiasm, and prices stop falling. *The low of each bar shows the maximum power of bears during that bar.* The low of a daily bar marks the maximum power of bears during that day, and the low of a weekly bar identifies the maximum power of bears during that week.

The **closing tick of each bar** reveals the outcome of a battle between bulls and bears during that bar. If prices close near the high of the daily bar, it shows that bulls won the day's battle. If prices close near the low of the day, it shows that bears won the day. Closing prices on daily charts of the futures markets are especially important. The amount of money in your account depends on them because your account equity is "marked to market" each night.

The **distance between the high and the low** of any bar reveals the intensity of conflict between bulls and bears. An average bar marks a relatively cool market. A bar that is only half as long as average reveals a sleepy, disinterested market. A bar that is two times taller than average shows a boiling market where bulls and bears battle all over the field.

Slippage (see Section 3) is usually lower in quiet markets. It pays to enter your trades during short or normal bars. Tall bars are good for taking profits. Trying to put on a position when the market is running is like jumping on a moving train. It is better to wait for the next one.

Japanese Candlesticks

Japanese rice traders began using candlestick charts some two centuries before the first chartists appeared in America. Instead of bars, these charts have rows of candles with wicks at both ends. The body of each candle represents the distance between the opening and closing prices. If the closing price is higher than the opening, the body is white. If the closing price is lower, the body is black.

The tip of the upper wick represents the high of the day, and the bottom of the lower wick represents the low of the day. The Japanese consider highs and lows relatively unimportant, according to Steve Nison, author of *Japanese Candlestick Charting Techniques*. They focus on the relationship between opening and closing prices and on patterns that include several candles.

The main advantage of a candlestick chart is its focus on the struggle between amateurs who control openings and professionals who control closings. Unfortunately, most candlestick chartists fail to use many tools of Western analysts. They ignore volume and have no trendlines or technical indicators. These gaps are being filled by modern American analysts such as Greg Morris, whose *Candlepower* software combines Western technical indicators with classical candlestick patterns.

Market Profile

This charting technique for tracking accumulation and distribution during each trading session was developed by J. Peter Steidlmayer. **Market Profile** requires access to real-time data—a constant flow of quotes throughout the day. It assigns one letter of the alphabet to each half-hour of trading. Each price level reached during that half-hour is marked with its own letter.

As prices change, more and more letters fill the screen, creating a bell-shaped curve. When prices erupt in a trend, Market Profile reflects that by becoming elongated. Market Profile is sometimes combined with Liquidity Data Bank. It tracks intraday volume of trading by several groups—floor traders, hedgers, and off-the-floor traders.

Efficient Markets, Random Walk, and Nature's Law

Efficient Market theory is an academic notion that nobody can outperform the market because any price at any given moment incorporates all available information. Warren Buffet, one of the most successful investors of our century, commented: "I think it's fascinating how the ruling orthodoxy can cause a lot of people to think the earth is flat. Investing in a market where people believe in efficiency is like playing bridge with someone who's been told it doesn't do any good to look at the cards."

The logical flaw of Efficient Market theory is that it equates knowledge with action. People may have knowledge, but the emotional pull of the crowd often leads them to trade irrationally. A good analyst can detect repetitive patterns of crowd behavior on his charts and exploit them.

Random Walk theorists claim that market prices change at random. Of course, there is a fair amount of randomness or "noise" in the markets, just as there is randomness in any other crowd milling around. An intelligent observer can identify repetitive behavior patterns of a crowd and make sensible bets on their continuation or reversal.

People have memories, they remember past prices, and their memories influence their buying and selling decisions. Memories help create support under the market and resistance above it. Random Walkers deny that memories of the past influence our behavior in the present.

As Milton Friedman has pointed out, prices carry information about the availability of supply and the intensity of demand. Market participants use that information to make their buying and selling decisions. For example, consumers buy more merchandise when it is on sale and less when prices are high. Financial traders are just as capable of logical behavior as homemakers in a supermarket. When prices are low, bargain hunters step in. A shortage can lead to a buying panic, but high prices choke off demand.

Nature's Law is the rallying cry of a clutch of mystics who oppose Random Walkers in the financial markets. Mystics claim that there is a perfect order in the markets, which they say move like clockwork in response to immutable natural laws. R. N. Elliott even titled his last book *Nature's Law*.

The "perfect order" crowd gravitates to astrology and looks for links between prices and the movements of the planets. Most mystics try to hide their astrological bent, but it is easy to draw them out of a shell. Next time someone talks to you about natural order in the markets, ask him about astrology. He will probably jump at the chance to come out of the closet and talk about the stars.

Those who believe in perfect order in the markets accept that tops and bottoms can be predicted far into the future. Amateurs love forecasts, and mysticism provides a great marketing gimmick. It helps sell courses, trading systems, and newsletters.

Mystics, Random Walk academics, and Efficient Market theorists have one trait in common. They are equally divorced from the reality of the markets. Extremists argue with one another but they think alike.

19. SUPPORT AND RESISTANCE

A ball hits the floor and bounces. It drops after it hits the ceiling. Support and resistance are like a floor and a ceiling, with prices sandwiched between them. Understanding support and resistance is essential for understanding price trends and chart patterns. Rating their strength helps you decide whether the trend is likely to continue or to reverse.

Support is a price level where buying is strong enough to interrupt or reverse a downtrend. When a downtrend hits support, it bounces like a diver who hits the bottom and pushes away from it. Support is represented on a chart by a horizontal or near-horizontal line connecting several bottoms (Figure 19-1).

Resistance is a price level where selling is strong enough to interrupt or reverse an uptrend. When an uptrend hits resistance, it stops or tumbles down like a man who hits his head on a branch while climbing a tree. Resistance is represented on a chart by a horizontal or near-horizontal line connecting several tops.

It is better to draw support and resistance lines across the edges of congestion areas instead of extreme prices. The edges show where masses of traders have changed their minds, while the extreme points reflect only panic among the weakest traders.

Minor support or resistance causes trends to pause, while major support or resistance causes them to reverse. Traders buy at support and sell at resistance, making their effectiveness a self-fulfilling prophecy.

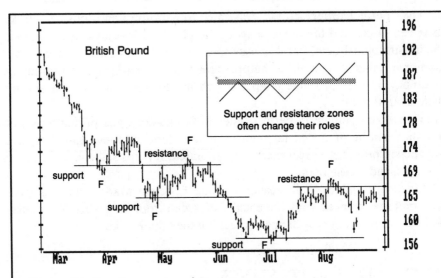

Figure 19–1.   Support and Resistance

Draw horizontal lines through the upper and lower edges of congestion areas. The bottom line marks the support–the level at which buyers over-power sellers. The upper line identifies resistance, where sellers over-power buyers. Areas of support and resistance often switch their roles. Note how the level of support in March became the line of resistance in May. The strength of these barriers increases each time prices touch them and bounce away.

Beware of false breakouts from support and resistance. The letter F marks false breakouts on this chart. Amateurs tend to follow breakouts, while professionals tend to fade (trade against) them. At the right edge of the chart, prices are hitting strong resistance. This is the time to look for a shorting opportunity, with a protective stop slightly above the line of resistance.

Memories, Pain, and Regret

Support and resistance exist because people have memories. Our memories prompt us to buy and sell at certain levels. Buying and selling by crowds of traders creates support and resistance.

If traders remember that prices have recently stopped falling and turned up from a certain level, they are likely to buy when prices approach that level again. If traders remember that an uptrend has recently reversed after rising to a certain peak, they tend to sell and go short when prices approach that level again.

For example, all major rallies in the stock market from 1966 until 1982 ended whenever the Dow Jones Industrial Average rallied to 950 or 1050. The resistance was so strong that traders named it "A Graveyard in the Sky." Once the bulls rammed the market through that level, it became a major support area.

Support and resistance exist because masses of traders feel pain and regret. Traders who hold losing positions feel intense pain. Losers are determined to get out as soon as the market gives them another chance. Traders who missed an opportunity feel regret and also wait for the market to give them a second chance. Feelings of pain and regret are mild in trading ranges where swings are small and losers do not get hurt too badly. Breakouts from trading ranges create intense pain and regret.

When the market stays flat for a while, traders get used to buying at the lower edge of the range and shorting at the upper edge. In uptrends, bears who sold short feel pain and bulls feel regret that they did not buy more. Both feel determined to buy if the market gives them a second chance. The pain of bears and regret of bulls make them ready to buy, creating **support** during reactions in an uptrend.

Resistance is an area where bulls feel pain, bears feel regret, and both are ready to sell. When prices break down from a trading range, bulls who bought feel pain, feel trapped, and wait for a rally to let them get out even. Bears regret that they have not shorted more and wait for a rally to give them a second chance to sell short. Bulls' pain and bears' regret create resistance—a ceiling above the market in downtrends. The strength of support and resistance depends on the strength of feelings among masses of traders.

Strength of Support and Resistance

A congestion area that has been hit by several trends is like a cratered battlefield. Its defenders have plenty of cover, and an attacking force is likely to slow down. The longer prices stay in a congestion zone, the stronger the emotional commitment of bulls and bears to that area. When prices approach that zone from above, it serves as support. When prices rally into it from below, it acts as resistance. A congestion area can reverse its role and serve as either support or resistance.

The strength of every support or resistance zone depends on three factors: its length, its height, and the volume of trading that has taken place in it. You can visualize these factors as the length, the width, and the depth of a congestion zone.

The longer a support or resistance area — its length of time or the number of hits it took — the stronger it is. Support and resistance, like good wine, become better with age. A 2-week trading range provides only minimal support or resistance, a 2-month range gives people time to become used to it and creates intermediate support or resistance, while a 2-year range becomes accepted as a standard of value and offers major support or resistance.

As support and resistance levels grow old, they gradually become weaker. Losers keep washing out of the markets, replaced by newcomers who do not have the same emotional commitment to old price levels. People who lost money only recently remember full well what happened to them. They are probably still in the market, feeling pain and regret, trying to get even. People who made bad decisions several years ago are probably out of the markets and their memories matter less.

The strength of support and resistance increases each time that area is hit. When traders see that prices have reversed at a certain level, they tend to bet on a reversal the next time prices reach that level.

The taller the support and resistance zone, the stronger it is. A tall congestion zone is like a tall fence around a property. A congestion zone whose height equals 1 percent of current market value (four points in the case of the S&P 500 at 400) provides only minor support or resistance. A congestion zone that is 3 percent tall provides intermediate support or resistance, and a congestion zone that is 7 percent tall or higher can grind down a major trend.

The greater the volume of trading in a support and resistance zone, the stronger it is. High volume in a congestion area shows active involvement by traders — a sign of strong emotional commitment. Low volume shows that traders have little interest in transacting at that level — a sign of weak support or resistance.

Trading Rules

1. Whenever the trend you are riding approaches support or resistance, tighten your protective stop. A protective stop is an order to sell below the market when you are long or to cover shorts above the market when you are short. This stop protects you from getting badly hurt by

an adverse market move. A trend reveals its health by how it acts when it hits support or resistance. If it is strong enough to penetrate that zone, it accelerates, and your tight stop is not touched. If a trend bounces away from support or resistance, it reveals its weakness. In that case, your tight stop salvages a good chunk of profits.

2. Support and resistance are more important on long-term charts than on short-term charts. Weekly charts are more important than dailies. A good trader keeps an eye on several timeframes and defers to the longer one. If the weekly trend is sailing through a clear zone, the fact that the daily trend is hitting resistance is less important. When a weekly trend approaches support or resistance, you should be more inclined to act.

3. Support and resistance levels are useful for placing stop-loss and pro-tect-profit orders. The bottom of a congestion area is the bottom line of support. If you buy and place your stop below that level, you give the uptrend plenty of room. More cautious traders buy after an upside breakout and place a stop in the middle of a congestion area. A true upside breakout should not be followed by a pullback into the range, just as a rocket is not supposed to sink back to its launching pad. Reverse this procedure in downtrends.

Many traders avoid placing stops at round numbers. This superstition began with off-the-cuff advice by Edwards and Magee to avoid placing stops at round numbers because "everybody" was placing them there. Now, if traders buy copper at 92, they place a stop at 89.75 rather than 90. When they sell a stock short at 76, they place a protective stop at 80.25 rather than 80. These days there are fewer stops at round numbers than at fractional numbers. It is better to place your stops at logical levels, round or not.

True and False Breakouts

Markets spend more time in trading ranges than they do in trends. Most breakouts from trading ranges are false breakouts. They suck in trend-fol-lowers just before prices return into the trading range. A false breakout is the bane of amateurs, but professional traders love them.

Professionals expect prices to fluctuate without going very far most of the time. They wait until an upside breakout stops reaching new highs or a downside breakout stops making new lows. Then they pounce—they fade the breakout (trade against it) and place a protective stop at the latest extreme point. It is a very tight stop, and their risk is low, while there is a big profit potential from a pullback into the congestion zone. The risk/reward ratio is so good that professionals can afford to be wrong half the time and still come out ahead of the game.

The best time to buy an upside breakout on a daily chart is when your analysis of the **weekly** chart suggests that a new uptrend is developing. True breakouts are confirmed by heavy **volume**, while false breakouts tend to have light volume. True breakouts are confirmed when technical **indicators** reach new extreme highs or lows in the direction of the trend, while false breakouts are often marked by divergences between prices and indicators.

20. TREND AND TRADING RANGE

Traders try to profit from changes in prices: Buy low and sell high, or sell short high and cover low. Even a quick look at a chart reveals that markets spend most of their time in trading ranges. They spend less time in trends.

A **trend** exists when prices keep rising or falling over time. In an **uptrend**, each rally reaches a higher high than the preceding rally and each decline stops at a higher level than the preceding decline. In a **downtrend**, each decline falls to a lower low than the preceding decline and each rally stops at a lower level than the preceding rally. In a **trading range,** most rallies stop at about the same high and declines peter out at about the same low.

A trader needs to identify trends and trading ranges. It is easier to trade during trends (Figure 20-1). It is harder to make money when prices are flat unless you write options, which requires a special skill.

Trading in trends and in trading ranges calls for different tactics. When you go long in an uptrend or sell short in a downtrend, you have to give that trend the benefit of the doubt and not be shaken out easily. It pays to buckle your seat belt and hang on for as long as the trend continues. When you trade in a trading range, you have to be nimble and close out your position at the slightest sign of a reversal.

Another difference in trading tactics between trends and trading ranges is the handling of strength and weakness. You have to follow strength during trends—buy in uptrends and sell short in downtrends. When prices are in a trading range, you have to do the opposite—buy weakness and sell strength.

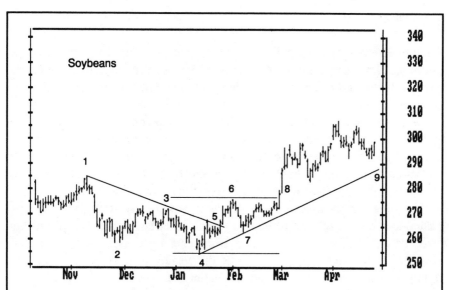

Figure 20–1.   Trend and Trading Range

A pattern of lower bottoms and lower tops defines downtrends. Soybeans declined from November until the middle of January. Bottom 4 was lower than bottom 2, and peak 3 lower than peak 1. The break of the downtrendline at point 5 signaled the end of the downtrend. A broken downtrend can lead to either a trading range or an uptrend.

The November–January downtrend has dissolved into a trading range, defined by horizontal lines drawn through the low 4 and highs 3 and 6. When the decline from high 6 stopped at a higher low 7 without reaching the bottom of the range, you could draw a preliminary uptrendline. A breakout from the range at point 8 confirmed the beginning of a new uptrend.

At the right edge of the chart, prices are hovering just above their uptrendline. It is a buying opportunity because the trend is up. The downside risk of a trade can be limited by placing a stop either below the latest low or below the trendline. Notice that daily trading ranges (the distances from highs to lows) are relatively narrow. This is typical of a healthy trend. Trends often end after several wide-range days–a sign of blowoff action.

Mass Psychology

An uptrend emerges when bulls are stronger than bears and their buying forces prices up. If bears manage to push prices down, bulls return in force, break the decline, and force prices to a new high. Downtrends occur when bears are stronger and their selling pushes markets down. When a flurry of buying lifts prices, bears sell short into that rally, stop it, and send prices to new lows.

When bulls and bears are equally strong or weak, prices stay in a trading range. When bulls manage to push prices up, bears sell short into that rally and prices fall. Bargain hunters step in and break the decline; bears cover shorts, their buying fuels a minor rally, and the cycle repeats.

A trading range is like a fight between two equally strong gangs. They push one another back and forth on a street corner but neither can control the turf. A trend is like a fight where a stronger gang chases the weaker gang down the street. Every once in a while the weaker gang stops and puts up a fight but then is forced to turn and run again.

Prices in trading ranges go nowhere, just as crowds spend most of their time in aimless milling. Markets spend more time in trading ranges than in trends because aimlessness is more common among people than purposeful action. When a crowd becomes agitated, it surges and creates a trend. Crowds do not stay excited for long — they go back to meandering. Professionals tend to give the benefit of the doubt to trading ranges.

The Hard Right Edge

Identifying trends and trading ranges is one of the hardest tasks in technical analysis. It is easy to find them in the middle of a chart, but the closer you get to the right edge, the harder it gets.

Trends and trading ranges clearly stand out on old charts. Experts show those charts at seminars and make it seem easy to catch trends. Trouble is, your broker does not allow you to trade in the middle of the chart. He says you must make your trading decisions at the hard right edge of the chart!

The past is fixed and easy to analyze. The future is fluid and uncertain. By the time you identify a trend, a good chunk of it is gone. Nobody rings a bell when a trend dissolves into a trading range. By the time you recognize that change, you will lose some money trying to trade as if the market was still trending.

Many chart patterns and indicator signals contradict one another at the right edge of the chart. You have to base your decisions on probabilities in an atmosphere of uncertainty.

Most people cannot accept uncertainty. They have a strong emotional need to be right. They hang onto losing positions, waiting for the market to turn and make them whole. Trying to be right in the market is very expensive. Professional traders get out of losing trades fast. When the market deviates from your analysis, you have to cut losses without fuss or emotions.

Methods and Techniques

There is no single magic method for identifying trends and trading ranges. There are several methods, and it pays to combine them. When they confirm one another, their message is reinforced. When they contradict one another, it is better to pass up a trade.

1. Analyze the pattern of highs and lows. When rallies keep reaching higher levels and declines keep stopping at higher levels, they identify an uptrend. The pattern of lower lows and lower highs identifies a downtrend, and the pattern of irregular highs and lows points to a trading range (Figure 20-1).

2. Draw an uptrendline connecting significant recent lows and a downtrendline connecting significant recent highs (see Section 21). The slope of the latest trendline identifies the current trend (Figures 20-1, 20-2, 21-1).

A significant high or low on a daily chart is the highest high or the lowest low for at least a week. As you study charts, you become better at identifying those points. Technical analysis is partly a science and partly an art.

3. Plot a 13-day or longer exponential moving average (see Section 25). The direction of its slope identifies the trend. If a moving average has not reached a new high or low in a month, then the market is in a trading range.

4. Several market indicators, such as MACD (see Section 26) and the Directional system (Section 27), help identify trends. The Directional system is especially good at catching early stages of new trends.

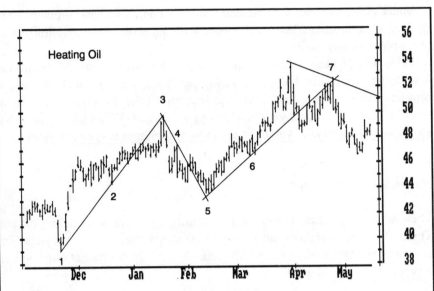

Figure 20–2.   Trendlines Identify Trends

The most important message of a trendline is the direction of its slope. When the slope is up, trade that market from the long side. When the slope is down, trade that market from the short side.

The uptrendline connecting bottoms 1 and 2 identifies an uptrend. It tells you to trade heating oil only from the long side. Notice that sometimes prices break their uptrendline but later pull back to it from below (3). This is a superb shorting opportunity. This happens again at point 7, where prices rise to their old uptrendline after breaking it.

When you trade in the direction of the trendline, you are usually trading in the direction of the market tide. At the right edge of the chart, you need to look for a shorting opportunity because the trend is down. Do not sell short immediately, because prices are too far below their downtrendline and your stop would have to be too wide. It is essential to wait for trades with a good risk/reward ratio. Patience is a virtue for a trader.

Trade or Wait

When you identify an uptrend and decide to buy, you have to decide whether to buy immediately or wait for a dip. If you buy fast, you get in gear with the trend, but your stops are likely to be farther away and you risk more.

If you wait for a dip, you will risk less but will have four groups of competitors: longs who want to add to their positions, shorts who want to get out even, traders who never bought, and traders who sold too early but are eager to buy. The waiting area for a pullback is very crowded! Markets are not known for their charity, and a deep pullback may well signal the beginning of a reversal. This reasoning also applies to downtrends. Waiting for pullbacks while a trend is gathering steam is an amateur's game.

If the market is in a trading range and you are waiting for a breakout, you have to decide whether to buy in anticipation of a breakout, during a breakout, or on a pullback after a valid breakout. If you trade multiple positions, you can buy a third in anticipation, a third on a breakout, and a third on a pullback.

Whatever method you use, there is one money management rule that will keep you out of the riskiest trades. The distance from the entry point to the level of a protective stop should never be more than 2 percent of your account equity (see Chapter 10). No matter how attractive a trade is, pass it up if it requires a wider stop.

Money management tactics are different in trends and trading ranges. It pays to put on a smaller position in a trend but use a wider stop. Then you will be less likely to get shaken out by reactions while you keep risk under control. You may put on a bigger position in a trading range but use a tighter stop.

Finding good entry points is extremely important in trading ranges. You have to be very precise because the profit potential is so limited. A trend is more forgiving of a sloppy entry, as long as you trade in the direction of the trend. Old traders chuckle: "Do not confuse brains with a bull market." When you cannot tell whether the market is in a trend or in a trading range, remember that professionals give the benefit of the doubt to trading ranges. If you are not sure, stand aside.

Professionals love trading ranges because they can slide in and out of positions with little risk of being impaled on a trend. Since they pay low or no commissions and suffer little slippage, it is profitable for them to trade in gently fluctuating markets. Those of us who trade away from the floor are better off trying to catch trends. You can trade less frequently during trends, and your account suffers less from commissions and slippage.

Conflicting Timeframes

Most traders ignore the fact that markets usually are both in a trend and in a trading range at the same time! They pick one timeframe such as daily or

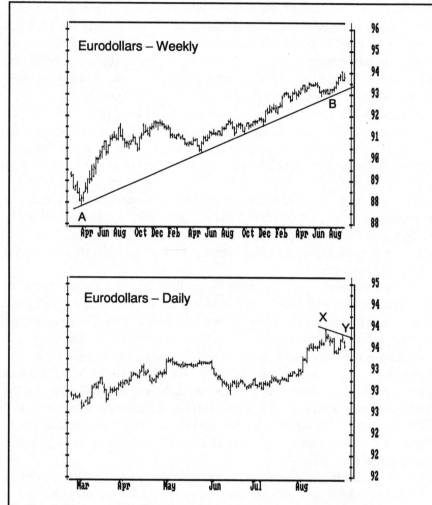

Figure 20–3. Conflicting Trends in Different Timeframes

The weekly chart of Eurodollars shows a perfect uptrend A–B. At the same time, the daily chart shows that a downtrend X–Y is beginning. Which of them will you follow? Contradictory signals in different timeframes in the same market are among the most common and thorny dilemmas in trading. You need to watch markets in more than one timeframe and know how to handle their conflicting signals. The Triple Screen trading system helps you solve this problem (see Section 43).

hourly and look for trades on daily charts. With their attention fixed on daily or hourly charts, trends from other timeframes, such as weekly or 10-minute trends, keep sneaking up on them and wreaking havoc with their plans.

Markets exist in several timeframes simultaneously (see Section 36). They exist on a 10-minute chart, an hourly chart, a daily chart, a weekly chart, and any other chart. The market may look like a buy on a daily chart but a sell on a weekly chart, and vice versa (Figure 20-3). The signals in different timeframes of the same market often contradict one another. Which of them will you follow?

When you are in doubt about a trend, step back and examine the charts in a timeframe that is larger than the one you are trying to trade. This search for a greater perspective is one of the key principles of the Triple Screen trading system (see Section 43).

A losing trader often thinks he would be better off if he had a real-time quote machine on his desk. One of the universal fantasies of losers is that they would be winners if they could get their data faster and focused on a shorter timeframe. But they lose money even faster with a quote system! When that happens, some losers say they would be better off trading right on the exchange floor, without any delay for data transmission. But more than half of floor traders wash out in their first year; being in the middle of the action does not do losers any good.

The conflicting signals in different timeframes of the same market are one of the great puzzles in market analysis. What looks like a trend on a daily chart may show up as a blip on a flat weekly chart. What looks like a flat trading range on a daily chart shows rich uptrends and downtrends on an hourly chart, and so on. When professionals are in doubt, they look at the big picture, but amateurs focus on the short-term charts.

21. TRENDLINES

Charts reveal the actions of bulls and bears. Bottoms of declines show where bears stopped and bulls regained control of the market. Peaks of rallies show where bulls ran out of steam and bears gained control. A line connecting two nearby bottoms shows the lowest common denominator of bullish power. A line that connects two nearby tops shows the lowest common denominator of the power of bears. Those lines are called **trendlines**. Traders use them to identify trends.

When prices rally, draw an uptrendline across the bottoms. When prices decline, draw a downtrendline across the tops. Projecting those lines into the future helps anticipate buying and selling points.

The most important feature of a trendline is its angle—it identifies the dominant market force. When a trendline points up, it shows that bulls are in control. Then it pays to buy with a protective stop below the trendline. When a trendline points down, it shows that bears are in control. Then it pays to sell short and protect your position with a stop above the trendline.

Trendlines are among the oldest tools of traders. Modern computerized tools for identifying trends include moving averages, the Directional system, and MACD (Chapter 4).

How to Draw a Trendline

Most chartists draw a trendline through extreme high and low points, but it is better to draw it through the edges of congestion areas (Figure 21-1). Those edges show where the majority of traders have reversed direction. Technical analysis is poll-taking—and polltakers want to track opinions of masses, not of a few extremists. Drawing trendlines through the edges of congestion areas is somewhat subjective. You have to watch out for the temptation to slant your ruler.

Panic dumping by bulls at the bottoms and panic covering by bears at the tops create extremes, which appear as long "tails" on the charts. You want to base your trendlines on the edges of congestion areas and not on tails because tails show little about the crowd other than its tendency to panic.

The extreme points are very important—but not for drawing trendlines. Markets usually recoil from those tails, offering opportunities to short-term traders (Figure 21-1). As Steidlmayer pointed out, a bar that looks like a finger sticking out of a tight chart pattern provides a valuable reference point for short-term traders.

Markets constantly fluctuate, seeking an area that generates the highest volume of trading. A tail shows that a certain price has been rejected by the market. It usually leads to a swing in the opposite direction. As soon as you recognize a tail, trade against it. Place your protective stop halfway through the tail. If the market starts "chewing its tail," it is time to get out.

Victor Sperandeo described another method for drawing trendlines in his book, *Trader Vic*. His technique helps identify reversals of well-established trends (Figure 21-2).

Sperandeo draws an uptrendline from the lowest low of the move to the

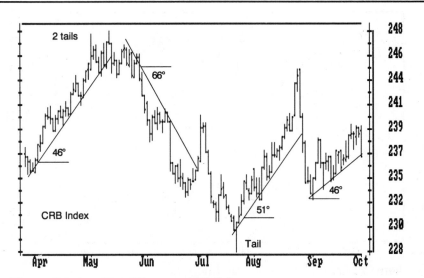

Figure 21–1.   Trendlines and "Tails"

Draw trendlines through the edges of congestion areas and leave out the extreme prices. Tails are long bars at the ends of trends–they spring outside of congestion areas. Markets recoil from tails, offering good trading opportunities in the opposite direction.

   Notice how the angles of uptrends tend to recur, month after month. Knowing this can help you draw preliminary trendlines. At the right edge of the chart, prices are touching their uptrendline–buy as soon as you see a bar that fails to reach a new low.

highest minor low prior to the highest high. That line may not pass through prices between those two points. When that trendline is broken, it gives the first signal of a trend change. The second signal is given when prices retest the recent high and back away from it. The third signal occurs when prices break through the previous minor low. It confirms that the uptrend has reversed. A mirror image of this method applies to downtrends.

Rating Trendlines

The single most important feature of a trendline is its slope. When a trend-line slants up, bulls are in control and it pays to look for buying opportuni-

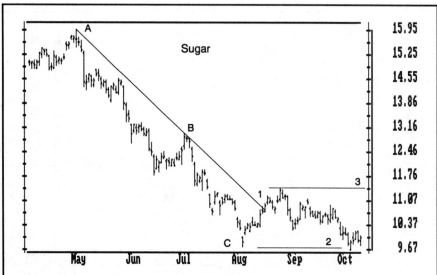

Figure 21–2.   1–2–3 Reversal Method

Draw a trendline from the highest high (A) to the highest minor high (B) preceding the lowest low (C) so that it does not pass through prices between A and B. The break of this trendline (1) is the first signal of a trend change. A test of the recent low (2) gives the second signal of a trend change. This is a good time to start buying. When prices break through their minor high (3), they will confirm that the trend has reversed. This method, described by Victor Sperandeo, helps catch major reversals rather than shorter-term swings.

ties. When a trendline slants down, bears are in control and it pays to look for shorting opportunities. You can rate the importance of any trendline by examining five factors: the timeframe of the trendline, its length, the number of times prices touch it, its angle, and volume.

The longer the timeframe, the more important the trendline. A trendline on a weekly chart identifies a more important trend than a daily trendline. A trendline on a daily chart identifies a more important trend than an hourly trendline, and so on.

The longer the trendline, the more valid it is. A short trendline reflects mass behavior over a short period. A longer trendline reflects mass behavior over a longer time. The longer a trend continues, the greater its inertia. A major bull market may follow its trendline for several years.

The more contacts between prices and trendline, the more valid that line.

When the trend is up, a return to the trendline shows a rebellion among bears. When the trend is down, a rally to the trendline shows a rebellion by the bulls. When prices pull back to a trendline and then bounce away from it, you know that the dominant market group has beaten the rebels.

A preliminary trendline is drawn across only two points. Three points of contact make that line more valid. Four or five points of contact show that the dominant market crowd is firmly in control.

The angle between a trendline and the horizontal axis reflects the emotional intensity of the dominant market crowd. A steep trendline shows that the dominant crowd is moving rapidly. A relatively flat trendline shows that the dominant crowd is moving slowly. A shallow trendline is likely to last longer, like a turtle racing against a hare.

It pays to measure the angle of every trendline and write it down on your chart (Figure 21-1). This can be done using a computer, a protractor, or a Chinese Charting Tool. Comparing angles of trendlines shows whether the dominant market crowd is becoming more bullish or bearish. It is uncanny how often trendlines trace the same angle time and again in a given market. It may be because the key players seldom change.

Sometimes prices accelerate away from their trendline. Then you can draw a new, steeper trendline. It shows that a trend is speeding up, becoming unsustainable (Figure 21-3). When you draw a new, steeper trendline, tighten your stop, place it immediately below the latest trendline, and adjust that stop at every new bar. The breaking of a steep trendline is usually followed by a sharp reversal.

When the trend is up, volume normally expands when prices rally and shrinks when they decline. This shows that rallies attract traders while declines leave them cold. The opposite occurs in downtrends — volume expands on declines and shrinks on rallies. A pullback on heavy volume threatens a trendline because it shows that the rebellious crowd is growing.

If volume expands when prices move in the direction of a trendline, it confirms that trendline; if volume shrinks when prices pull back to a trendline, it also confirms the trendline. If volume expands when prices return to a trendline, it warns of a potential break; if volume shrinks when prices pull away from a trendline, it warns that the trendline is in danger.

Trendline Breaks

The breaking of a well-established trendline shows that the dominant market crowd has lost its power. You have to be careful not to anticipate trading signals — most traders lose money when they jump the gun.

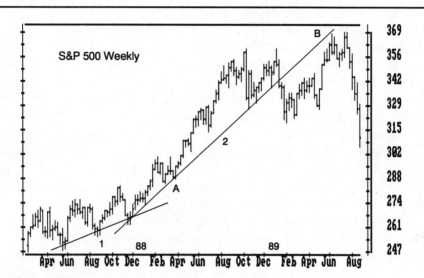

Figure 21–3.   When Trendlines Accelerate

The stock market rose slowly but steadily from its 1987 bottom. You could buy each time prices touched their shallow uptrendline (1). The uptrend accelerated in 1988, and at point A, a new uptrendline (2) had to be drawn. When the new, steeper trendline was broken, it indicated that the bull move was over. The market offered, as it sometimes does, an excellent shorting opportunity at point B, when it pulled back to its old uptrendline before crashing.

A trendline is not a glass floor under the market — one crack and it is gone. It is more like a fence that bulls or bears can lean on. They can even violate it a bit without toppling it, the way animals shake a fence. A trendline break is valid only if prices close on the other side of a trendline. Some traders insist that a trendline has to be penetrated by two or three percentage points of price ($8–$12 in the case of $400/oz. gold).

After a very steep uptrend is broken, prices often rally again, retest their old high, and touch their old uptrendline from below (Figures 20-2, 21-3). When that happens, you have a near-perfect shorting opportunity: a combination of a double top, a pullback to an old trendline, and perhaps a bearish divergence from technical indicators. The reverse also applies to downtrends.

Trading Rules

1. Trade in the direction of the slope of a trendline. If it points up, look for buying opportunities and avoid shorting. When the slope is down, trade from the short side and avoid buying.

2. A trendline provides support or resistance. When prices rise, place buy orders at the uptrendline and protective orders below. Reverse the procedure in downtrends.

3. Steep trendlines precede sharp breaks. If a trendline is steeper than 45°, place your stop right at the trendline and adjust it daily.

4. Prices often retest their latest extreme after breaking a steep trendline. A pullback rally to an old high on falling volume and with indicator divergences provides an excellent shorting opportunity. A decline to an old low after a downtrendline is broken provides a low-risk buying opportunity.

5. Draw a channel line parallel to a trendline and use it as a target for profit taking.

Trendline Channels

A **channel** consists of two parallel lines that contain prices (Figure 21-4). If you draw an uptrendline across the bottoms of reactions, you can draw a channel line parallel to it across the tops of rallies. When you draw a downtrendline across the tops of rallies, you can also draw a channel line parallel to it across the bottoms of declines.

Channel lines, like trendlines, should be drawn across the edges of congestion areas, leaving out the extreme highs and lows. The presence of a channel line reinforces the validity of the trendline itself. The validity of channel lines depends on how many times they were touched by prices.

A channel line marks the area of bulls' maximum power in an uptrend and bears' maximum power in a downtrend. The wider the channel, the stronger the trend. It pays to trade in the direction of the channel's slope, going long in the lower quarter or half of a rising channel and selling short in the upper quarter or half of a falling channel. Profits should be taken at the opposite channel wall (see also Section 45).

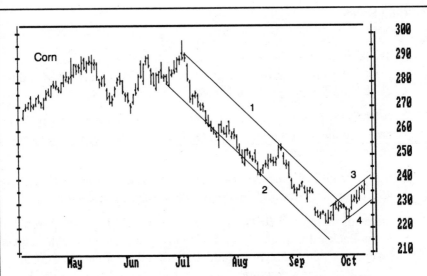

Figure 21–4.   Trendline Channels and Preliminary Trendlines

The downtrendline 1, drawn across rally peaks, identifies a bear market in corn. A channel line 2 is drawn across the lows, parallel to the trendline. The channel line helps track the maximum power of bears in a downtrend. The best shorting opportunities are in the upper half of a falling channel, while the best buying opportunities are in the lower half of a rising channel.

When prices break out above their downtrendline, channels can help you draw a preliminary uptrendline. First, draw a new channel line 3 to connect the last two rally tops. Then draw line 4 parallel to it, touching the latest bottom. This is the new preliminary uptrendline.

At the right edge of the chart, corn is trending higher. It is expensive–near its upper channel line. If you want to go long, place an order to buy in the vicinity of the new uptrendline 4.

A Preliminary Trendline

Normally, a trendline touches at least two points on a chart. There is a little-known technique for drawing a preliminary trendline through only one point (Figure 21-4).

When prices break their downtrend and rally above it, you can assume that the downtrend has ended and a new uptrend may begin. Connect the two latest peaks — this is the channel line of the new uptrend. Draw a line parallel to it through the latest low. This preliminary uptrendline, drawn parallel to a channel line, tells you where to expect the next bottom. It often points to excellent buying opportunities. This procedure tends to work better at bottoms than at the tops.

More on Trendlines

When prices break their uptrend, measure the **vertical distance** from the trendline to the latest top and project it down from the breaking point. If the crowd can become optimistic enough to swing prices so many dollars above the trendline, then it is likely to become equally pessimistic and swing prices the same distance down from the trendline. Reverse this procedure in downtrends. This method gives you the minimum target for a new move, which is often exceeded.

Trendlines can also be applied to **volume** and to **indicators**. The slope of a trendline of volume shows whether more or fewer people are becoming involved in the market. A rising trendline of volume confirms the current price trend. A falling trendline of volume shows that the market crowd is refusing to follow the current price trend. Among technical indicators, the Relative Strength Index (see Section 31) is especially well suited for trendline analysis. It often breaks its trendlines in advance of prices, providing an early warning of a trend change.

22. GAPS

A **gap** is a chart pattern that consists of two adjacent bars, where the low of one bar is higher than the high of the other bar (Figure 22-1). It shows that no trades took place at a certain price, only at higher and lower levels. *Webster's Dictionary* defines: "Gap: 1. a hole or opening, as in a wall or fence, made by breaking or parting; breach. 2. an interruption of continuity in space or time; hiatus; lacuna."

Gaps occur when prices jump in response to a sudden imbalance of buy or sell orders. A scary piece of news often triggers gaps. Gaps on daily charts show reactions to events that took place while the market was closed. Had the news come out during trading hours, a gap might have occurred only on intraday charts and perhaps have led to a wider daily range.

For example, a strike at a major copper mine is bullish for copper. If the news comes out in the evening, the shorts become frightened and want to

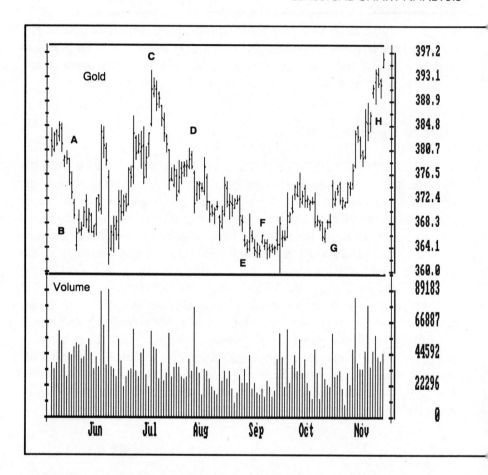

cover. They flood the pit with buy orders before the opening bell. Floor traders respond by opening copper above the previous day's high. The smart money, incidentally, has probably bought copper before the strike was announced. Smart money tends to put on trades when markets are quiet, but amateurs tend to jump on the news.

Gaps show that the trading crowd is spooked, that losers are getting hurt and dumping their positions. When you know that bulls or bears are hurting, you can figure out what they are likely to do next and trade accordingly.

Some gaps are valid; others are phony. Valid gaps occur when the market skips a price level. Phony gaps occur when a financial instrument trades in another market while the market you analyze is closed. For example, daily charts of Chicago currency futures are full of phony gaps. Currencies trade in Tokyo, London, and elsewhere while the Chicago Mercantile Exchange is

---

Figure 22–1. Gaps

Cover this chart with a sheet of paper and slide it slowly from left to right.

A. A breakaway gap. Sell short and place a stop a few ticks above the gap's upper rim.

B. An exhaustion gap–prices pull back into it the next day. The downtrend is over. Cover shorts immediately.

C. Another exhaustion gap, marked by a lack of new highs after the gap. Several days of churning offer good shorting opportunities with a stop above the high.

D. A continuation gap in a downtrend. Go short, with a stop a few ticks above the gap's upper rim. Prices hit that stop a few days later–no method is fail-safe.

E. An exhaustion gap, closed two days after it opened. Cover shorts immediately.

F. A common gap in the midst of a congestion area, closed the next day. No action recommended.

G. A breakaway gap. Go long and place a protective stop a few ticks below the gap's lower rim.

H. A continuation gap. Add to longs and place a protective stop a few ticks below the gap's lower rim. The gap at the right edge of this chart could be either a continuation or an exhaustion gap. Relatively quiet volume suggests continuation. If you buy, place a protective stop a few ticks below the lower rim of this gap.

---

closed. When the exchange reopens, its prices gap simply to reflect price changes overseas.

All gaps can be divided into four major groups: common, breakaway, continuation, and exhaustion. You need to identify them because each tells a different story and calls for different trading tactics.

Common Gaps

Common gaps are rapidly closed—prices return into the gap within a few days. Common gaps usually occur in quiet trendless markets. They are seen in futures contracts for late delivery, in thinly traded stocks, and at sold-out, low-volume market bottoms.

Common gaps show no follow-through—no new highs after an upside gap or new lows after a downside gap. Volume may slightly increase on the day of a common gap, but the following days show a return to average volume. The lack of new highs or lows and indifferent volume show that neither bulls nor bears have strong feelings about the market. Common gaps are the least useful of all gaps for trading.

Common gaps occur more often than other gaps. It takes very little to create them in a dull market. A Comex floor trader at one of our seminars spoke of how he could push gold up or down $2 an ounce on a quiet day. He was known as a big trader and if he suddenly began bidding for 20 contracts at a time, other floor traders stepped back, figuring he knew something. Gold would gap up, and the trick for him was to sell before that gap was closed.

An **ex-dividend gap** is a common gap that occurs in the stock market on the day a dividend becomes payable. For example, if the dividend is 50 cents, then each share is worth 50 cents less after that dividend is paid. This is similar to a drop in the price of a cow after it delivers a calf. Once the calf is born, the price of the cow falls by the amount of the calf's price because it is no longer included with the cow. Ex-dividend gaps were common in the old days. Today, the average daily range of a dividend-paying stock is greater than the amount of its dividend, and the ex-dividend drop seldom results in a gap.

Breakaway Gaps

A breakaway gap occurs when prices leap out of a congestion zone on heavy volume and begin a new trend. A breakaway gap can remain open for weeks or months, and sometimes years. The longer the range that preceded the gap, the longer the subsequent trend.

An upside breakaway gap is usually followed by new highs for several days in a row, and a downside breakaway gap is followed by a series of new lows. There is a sharp increase in volume on the day of the breakaway gap and for several days after that. Volume on the day of the gap may be twice as high as the average volume for the previous few days.

A breakaway gap marks a major change in mass mentality—it reveals a great pressure behind the new trend. The sooner you jump aboard the new trend, the better.

Most gaps are common gaps that are quickly closed. Professional traders like to fade them—trade against gaps. You have to be careful because if you do it mechanically, sooner or later a breakaway gap will clobber you. It takes deep pockets to hold a losing position for months, waiting for a gap to close.

Continuation Gaps

A continuation gap occurs in the midst of a powerful trend, which continues to reach new highs or new lows without filling the gap. It is similar to a breakaway gap but occurs in the middle of a trend rather than in the beginning. Continuation gaps show a new surge of power among the dominant market crowd. The inflationary bull markets in commodities in the 1970s had many of them.

A continuation gap can help you estimate how far a trend is likely to carry. Measure the vertical distance from the beginning of a trend to the gap, and then project it from the gap in the direction of the trend. When the market approaches that target, it is time to begin taking profits.

Volume confirms continuation gaps when it jumps at least 50 percent above the average for the previous few days. If prices do not reach new highs or new lows for several days after a gap, you are probably dealing with a treacherous exhaustion gap.

Exhaustion Gaps

An exhaustion gap is not followed by new highs during uptrends or new lows during downtrends — prices churn and then return into the gap and close it. Exhaustion gaps appear at the ends of trends. Prices rise or fall for several weeks or months, and then gap in the direction of the trend. At first, an exhaustion gap looks like a continuation gap — a leap in the direction of the trend on heavy volume. If prices fail to reach new highs or new lows for several days after the gap, it is probably an exhaustion gap.

An exhaustion gap is confirmed only when prices reverse and close it. This gap is like the last spurt of a tired athlete. He springs away from the pack but cannot sustain the pace; as soon as others close in on him, you know that he will lose the race.

Trading Rules

1. Common gaps do not offer good trading opportunities, but if you must trade, fade them. If prices gap up, sell short as soon as the market stops reaching new highs and place a protective stop above the high of the past few days; cover shorts and take profits at the lower rim of the

gap. If prices gap down, go long as soon as the market stops reaching new lows and place a protective stop below the low of the past few days; place an order to sell and take profits at the upper rim of the gap.

2. If a market gaps out of a long trading range on a burst of volume and continues to make new highs or lows, you are probably dealing with a breakaway gap. If prices have gapped to the upside, buy and place a protective stop at the lower rim of the gap. A valid breakaway gap almost never gets closed. Reverse the procedure in downtrends. Waiting for a pullback when a new trend has just begun may leave you on the sidelines.

3. Trading a continuation gap is similar to trading a breakaway gap — buy early and place a protective stop at the lower rim of the gap. Reverse the procedure in downtrends. Tighten your stops when a trend approaches its target as projected by the continuation gap.

4. A valid breakaway or continuation gap must be confirmed by a series of several new highs or lows. Otherwise, you may be dealing with an exhaustion gap. If the market refuses to reach new highs or lows in the direction of the gap, exit your trade and re-evaluate the market from the sidelines.

5. Exhaustion gaps offer attractive trading opportunities because they are often followed by violent reversals. When you identify an upside exhaustion gap, sell short and place a protective stop above the latest high. Once prices begin to slide, weak bulls will start bailing out. Stay short as long as prices continue to reach new lows and cover the day after prices fail to make a new low. Reverse the procedure in downtrends. Because of high volatility, exhaustion gaps are easier to trade using options, especially buying puts at the tops.

More on Gaps

An **island reversal** is a combination of a continuation gap and a breakaway gap in the opposite direction. An island reversal looks like an island, separated from the rest of price action by a gulf in which no trading took place. It begins as a continuation gap, followed by a compact trading range with high trading volume. Then prices gap in the opposite direction and leave behind an island of prices. This pattern occurs very seldom, but it marks major reversal areas. Trade against the trend that preceded an island.

It pays to watch for gaps in **related markets**. If gold shows a breakaway gap but silver and platinum do not, then you may get a chance to position for a "catch-up move" in a market that has not yet become frenzied.

Gaps can serve as **support and resistance levels**. If greater volume occurred after an upside gap, it indicates very strong support. If greater volume occurred before the gap, then support is less strong.

Technical indicators help identify types of gaps. The Force Index (see Section 42) is based on price and volume. If Force Index shows only a minor change on the day of a gap, it is probably a common gap. When Force Index reaches a record high or a low level for several weeks, it confirms breakaway and continuation gaps.

Intraday charts show many **opening gaps**, when prices open outside the previous day's range. When there is an imbalance of public buy and sell orders before the opening, floor traders open markets higher or lower. If outsiders want to buy, floor traders sell to them at such a high price that the slightest dip will make them money. If customers want to sell, floor traders will take merchandise off their hands — at a price that is low enough to profit from the slightest bounce. Professionals play it cool — they know that crowds seldom stay excited for long and prices tend to pull back into yesterday's range. They sell above that range or buy below, waiting to unwind their positions and take profits when the opening gap is closed.

If you trade the S&P 500 futures, remember that their opening gaps are almost always closed. If the S&P 500 futures open higher, they almost always sink during the day and touch their previous day's high. If they open lower, they almost always rally during the day and touch their previous day's low. Savvy day-traders tend to sell short higher openings and buy lower openings. This is not a mechanical method — you have to buy or sell only after indicators tell you that the force behind the opening gap has been spent and the market is ready to close the gap.

23. CHART PATTERNS

The patterns you see on your chart or computer screen are the trails left by bulls and bears. A chartist is a hunter who follows subtle signs, visible only to those who know what to look for. Chart patterns can help you decide when a trend is likely to continue or to reverse.

There are two main groups of patterns: continuation and reversal. **Continuation** patterns include flags and pennants. They suggest trading in the direction of the current trend. **Reversal** patterns include head and shoulders, inverse head and shoulders, and double tops and bottoms. They indicate it is time to take profits on existing positions. Some patterns can serve as either continuation or reversal formations. Triangles and rectangles are notorious for doing that double duty.

When several chart patterns point in the same direction, their signals are reinforced. For example, if an uptrendline gets broken when a head-and-shoulders top is being completed, they both confirm that the uptrend is ending. When different patterns give conflicting messages, their signals cancel one another, and it is better not to trade.

Head-and-Shoulders Tops

A healthy uptrend moves up in steps. Most rallies reach higher peaks than the preceding rally and declines stop at a higher level than the previous decline. When an uptrend fails to reach a higher high or a decline falls below the previous low, it shows that bulls are losing their grip.

Head-and-shoulders tops mark the ends of uptrends (Figure 23-1). The "head" is a price peak surrounded by two lower peaks, or "shoulders." A neckline connects the lows of declines from the left shoulder and the head. The neckline does not have to be horizontal—it may be flat, rising, or falling. A downsloping neckline is especially bearish—it shows that bears are becoming stronger.

When prices fail to rally above the head, they confirm that a head-and-shoulders top is developing. The right shoulder may be higher or lower than the left and may be shorter or longer. The decline from the right shoulder breaks the neckline. When that happens, the uptrend is dead.

After breaking the neckline, prices sometimes pull back to it on low volume. This feeble rally offers an excellent shorting opportunity, with a logical stop just above the neckline.

Head-and-shoulders tops often have typical volume patterns. Volume is often lower on the head than on the left shoulder. It is even lower on the right shoulder. Volume tends to increase when prices break the neckline. When prices pull back to it, volume is very thin.

A head-and-shoulders pattern provides an approximate target for the new downtrend. You can obtain it by measuring the distance from the top of the head to the neckline and projecting this down from the neckline.

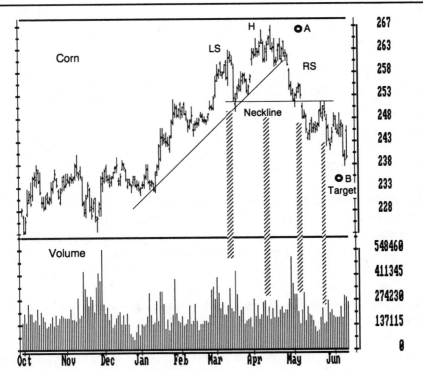

Figure 23–1. Head and Shoulders

An uptrend remains healthy as long as each new rally reaches a new high. Rising volume confirms rallies. Volume falls when prices reach the head (H) and flashes a warning to tighten stops on long positions. The decline from the head breaks the uptrendline and signals that the uptrend is over.

The head, in this case, is an "island reversal" (see "Gaps," Section 22)–a very bearish pattern. Volume shoots up ominously during the decline from the head. The right shoulder (RS) is much smaller than the left–another sign of weakness. Low volume on the right shoulder also points to a good shorting opportunity.

The decline from the right shoulder breaks the neckline. This completes the head-and-shoulders pattern. There is an excellent shorting opportunity when prices pull back to the neckline from below on low volume. The distance from the top of the head to the neckline (A) provides a target for the decline (B). At the right edge of the chart, hold shorts because prices continue to fall on rising volume and have not reached their target; place a protective stop at the top of the past 5 days' range.

Trading Rules

Once you identify a head-and-shoulders top, you need to make two trading decisions: what to do about your long position and how to go about shorting. You have three choices for managing your longs: sell them outright, tighten your stops, or sell some and hold the rest.

Many traders take the fourth choice—they simply freeze and do nothing. Trading is a complex, nontrivial game that demands making decisions in an atmosphere of uncertainty.

Your decision depends on how certain you feel about the pattern. It also depends on the size of your account. A large account allows you to buy and sell gradually. Having to trade a single contract in a small account demands precise timing—it is a good school for a beginning trader.

You must analyze your charts in more than one timeframe (see Section 36). If weekly charts are toppy, a head-and-shoulders pattern on the dailies should prompt you to run for the exit. If weeklies are strong, then it is often better to simply tighten the stops. Technical indicators can also help you decide how urgent it is to sell.

Markets often are more volatile at tops, with wide swings between short-term highs and lows. Selling short and placing a stop above the latest high may expose you to more risk than the maximum amount allowed per contract in your account (see Chapter 10). You may have to pass up the trade or buy puts to keep your monetary risk within allowed limits.

1. Sell when you recognize the head or the right shoulder of a head-and-shoulders pattern, based on low volume, a break of an uptrend, and a divergence between indicators and prices.

2. The decline from the head establishes a neckline. If you still hold a long position, place a stop below the neckline.

3. The rally to the right shoulder is usually marked by low volume and glaring weakness in technical indicators; it offers the last good opportunity to cash out of the uptrend. Technical indicators often reach higher levels on the right shoulder than on the head but they never exceed the levels reached during the left shoulder. When you sell short into the right shoulder, place your stop at the top of the head. Make that order "stop-and-reverse"—if stopped out of the short position, reverse and go long (see "The Hound of the Baskervilles" signal).

4. Once the neckline is broken, a pullback on low volume offers an excellent shorting opportunity, with a protective stop slightly above the neckline.

The Hound of the Baskervilles

This signal occurs when a reliable chart or indicator pattern does not lead to the action you expect and prices move in the opposite direction. A head-and-shoulders pattern indicates that the uptrend is over. If prices continue to rise, they give the Hound of the Baskervilles signal.

This signal is named after the story by Sir Arthur Conan Doyle in which Sherlock Holmes was called to solve a murder at a country estate. He found the essential clue when he realized that the family dog did not bark while the murder was being committed. That meant the dog knew the criminal and the murder was an inside job. The *signal was given by the lack of expected action* — by the lack of barking!

When the market refuses to bark in response to a perfectly good signal, it gives you the Hound of the Baskervilles signal. This shows that something is fundamentally changing below the surface. Then it is time to get in gear with the new powerful trend.

A head-and-shoulders pattern gives a strong sell signal. If the market refuses to collapse but rallies from the right shoulder, it gives you its Hound of the Baskervilles signal. When prices rise above the head, it is time to cover shorts, reverse, and go long. An aborted head-and-shoulders top often leads to a very strong rally. Buy the upside breakout, and place a protective stop slightly below the top of the head.

Inverse Head and Shoulders

Some traders call this pattern a head-and-shoulders bottom — a mirror image of a head-and-shoulders top. It looks like a silhouette of a person upside down: the head at the lowest point, surrounded by two shoulders. This pattern develops when a downtrend loses its force and gets ready to reverse (Figure 23-2).

In a valid downtrend, each new low falls lower than the previous low, and each rally stops at a lower level. A strong rally from the head allows you to

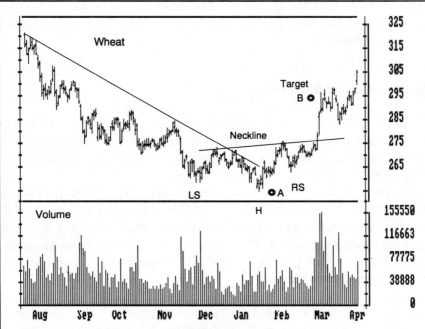

Figure 23–2.   Inverse Head and Shoulders

While the downtrend is in effect, high volume confirms all declines until the left shoulder (LS). The decline into the head (H) comes on low volume–a warning to the bears. The rally out of the head breaks above the downtrendline and signals that the downtrend is over.

Low volume during the right shoulder (RS) and the upward-sloping neckline indicate that a powerful rally is coming. The burst of volume during the neckline break confirms the new uptrend. No pullback ever reached this neckline.

The preliminary target (B) is as high above the neckline as the head of the pattern (A) is below it. It is common for rallies out of head-and-shoulders bottoms to exceed their targets. The best buying opportunity was at the right shoulder, with a protective stop a few ticks below the head. At the right edge of the chart, a gap confirms a strong uptrend. Place a protective stop on long positions a few ticks below the gap's lower rim.

draw a neckline. When a decline from the neckline fails to reach the level of the head, it creates the right shoulder. When prices rally from the right shoulder above the neckline on increased volume, they complete the head-and-shoulders bottom and a new uptrend begins.

Sometimes a head-and-shoulders bottom is followed by a pullback to the neckline on low volume, offering an excellent buying opportunity. Measure the distance from the bottom of the head to the neckline and project it upward from the point where the neckline was broken. This gives you a minimum measurement for a rally, which is frequently exceeded.

The tactics for trading inverse head and shoulders is similar to head-and-shoulders tops. You risk less money trading at bottoms because prices are less volatile, and you can use closer stops.

Rectangles

A **rectangle** is a chart pattern that contains price movements between two parallel lines. They are usually horizontal but can sometimes slant up or down (see "Lines and Flags," later in this section). Rectangles and triangles can serve as continuation or reversal patterns.

You need four points to draw a rectangle: The upper line connects two rally tops, and the lower line connects two bottoms (Figure 23-3). These lines should be drawn through the edges of congestion areas rather than across the extreme highs and lows (see Section 19).

The upper line of a rectangle identifies resistance, while the lower line identifies support. The upper line shows where bulls run out of steam; the lower line shows where bears become exhausted. A rectangle shows that bulls and bears are evenly matched. The key question is whether bulls or bears will eventually win the battle within this pattern.

If volume swells when prices approach the upper border of a rectangle, an upside breakout is more likely. If volume increases when prices approach the lower border, a downside breakout is more likely. A valid breakout from a rectangle is usually confirmed by an increase in volume — one-third to one-half higher than the average of the previous five days. If volume is thin, it is likely to be a false breakout.

Rectangles tend to be wider in uptrends and narrower in downtrends. The longer a rectangle, the more significant a breakout. Breakouts from rectangles on weekly charts are especially important because they mark important victories for bulls or bears.

There are several techniques for projecting how far a breakout is likely to go. Measure the height of a rectangle and project it from the broken wall in

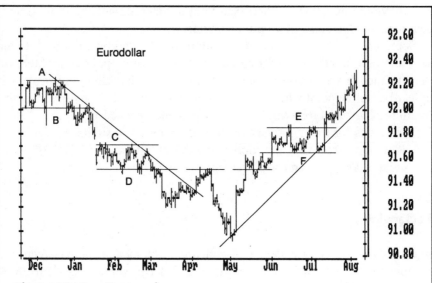

Figure 23–3. Rectangles

The upper border of each rectangle is drawn across two or more highs. The lower border is drawn across two or more lows. A rectangle may serve either as a continuation or a reversal pattern. As long as a major trendline is intact, a rectangle is more likely to serve as a continuation pattern.

After prices break out of a rectangle, they often return and touch its wall from the outside (B, D, and E). These pullbacks offer excellent entries into low-risk trades in the direction of the breakout, with a protective stop inside the rectangle.

The same price levels tend to serve as both support and resistance. Notice how line D turned from support into resistance and back into support. At the right edge of the chart, prices are well above their uptrendline, and it is better to wait for a pullback before buying.

the direction of the breakout. This is the minimum target. The maximum target is obtained by taking the length of the rectangle and projecting it vertically from the broken wall in the direction of a breakout. Tony Plummer writes that a rectangle is a part of a spiral-like development of a trend. He recommends measuring the height of a rectangle, multiplying it by three

Fibonacci ratios (1.618, 2.618, and 4.236), and projecting those measurements in the direction of the breakout to obtain a price target.

Trading Rules

Floor traders can profit from trading short-term swings between a rectangle's walls, but the big money is made by trading in the direction of a breakout.

1. When trading within a rectangle, buy at the lower boundary and sell short at the upper boundary. Oscillators can help you decide when prices are ready to reverse within a rectangle. Stochastic, the Relative Strength Index, and Williams %R (see Chapter 4) mark price reversals within rectangles when they hit their reference lines and change direction.

   If you buy at the lower border of a rectangle, place your protective stop slightly below that rectangle. If you sell short near the upper wall of a rectangle, place a protective stop slightly above that border. You have to be very nimble and take profits at the first sign of a reversal. It is dangerous to hold on for a few extra ticks within a rectangle.

2. To find out whether an upside or a downside breakout is more likely, analyze the market in a longer timeframe than the one you are trading. If you want to catch a breakout on a daily chart, identify the weekly trend because a breakout is more likely to go in its direction (see Section 43).

3. Once you buy an upside breakout or sell short a downside breakout, place your protective stop slightly inside the rectangle. There may be a pullback to the rectangle wall on light volume, but prices should not return into a rectangle after a valid breakout.

Lines and Flags

A **line** is a kind of a rectangle — a lengthy congestion area. In Dow theory, a line is a correction against the primary trend. It is a congestion zone whose height is approximately 3 percent of current stock market value. When the stock market "draws a line" instead of reacting more deeply against its major trend, it shows a particularly strong primary trend.

A **flag** is a rectangle whose boundaries are parallel but slant up or down.

Breakouts tend to go against the slope of the flag. If a flag slants upward, a downside breakout is more likely. If the flag slants down, an upside breakout is more likely.

If you see a downsloping flag in an uptrend, place a buy order above the latest peak of the flag to catch an upside breakout. A rising flag in an uptrend marks distribution, and a downside breakout is more likely. Place an order to sell short below the latest low of that flag. Reverse the procedure in downtrends.

Triangles

A **triangle** is a congestion area whose upper and lower boundaries converge on the right (Figure 23-4). It can serve either as a reversal or, more often, as a continuation pattern. Some technicians call triangles **coils**. The market winds up and the energy of traders becomes compressed, ready to spring from a triangle.

A small triangle whose height is 10 to 15 percent of the preceding trend is more likely to serve as a **continuation** pattern. Many uptrends and downtrends are punctuated by these triangles, as sentences are punctuated by commas. Large triangles whose height equals a third or more of the preceding trend are more likely to serve as **reversal** patterns. Finally, some triangles simply fizzle out into listless trading ranges.

Triangles can be divided into three major groups, depending on their angles. The upper and lower lines of **symmetrical** triangles converge at the same angles. If the upper line is inclined 30 degrees to the horizontal, then the lower line is also inclined 30 degrees. Symmetrical triangles reflect a fair balance of power between bulls and bears and are more likely to serve as continuation patterns.

An **ascending** triangle has a relatively flat upper boundary and a rising lower boundary. Its flat upper boundary shows that bulls are maintaining their strength and can lift prices to the same level, while bears are losing their ability to drive prices lower. An ascending triangle is more likely to result in an upside breakout.

A **descending** triangle has a relatively flat lower boundary, while its upper boundary slants down. Its flat lower boundary shows that bears are maintaining their strength and continue to drive prices down, while bulls are losing their capacity to lift prices. A descending triangle is more likely to lead to a downside breakout.

Figure 23–4.   Triangles

Each triangle is defined by two converging lines. The upper line connects two or more peaks, and the lower line connects two or more bottoms.

A triangle whose lower boundary is rising is called an ascending triangle (marked Asc T on the chart). It tells you to expect an upside breakout. A descending triangle (Desc T) has a declining upper boundary. It shows that prices are more likely to break down. A symmetrical triangle (Symm T) shows that the forces of bulls and bears are evenly matched and the trend is likely to continue.

Valid breakouts tend to occur during the first two thirds of a triangle's length. Sometimes prices pull back to a triangle after a breakout. Those pullbacks offer excellent entry points into trades in the direction of the breakout.

Volume tends to shrink as triangles get older. If volume jumps on a rally toward the upper boundary, an upside breakout is more likely. If volume becomes heavier when prices fall toward the lower boundary, a downside breakout is more likely. Valid breakouts are accompanied by a burst of volume — at least 50 percent above the average for the past 5 days.

Valid breakouts occur during the first two thirds of a triangle. It is better not to trade breakouts from the last third of a triangle. If prices stagnate all the way into the apex, they are likely to remain flat. A triangle is like a fight between two tired boxers who keep leaning on each other. An early breakout shows that one of the fighters is stronger. If prices stay within a triangle all the way into the apex, that shows that both boxers are exhausted and no trend is likely to emerge.

Charts of related markets often show triangles at the same time. If gold, silver, and platinum all trace triangles and gold breaks out to the upside, then platinum and silver are likely to follow. This approach works well with currencies, especially with closely related ones, such as the German Mark and Swiss Franc. It also works with stocks in the same group — compare General Motors to Ford but not to IBM.

Triangles provide a minimum target for a move following a breakout. Measure the height of a triangle at its base and project vertically from the point where the triangle was broken. If you are dealing with a small triangle in the midst of a dynamic trend, that minimum measurement is likely to be exceeded. You can also use the Fibonacci projections mentioned earlier.

Trading Rules

It's better not to trade minor swings within a triangle unless that triangle is very large. As a triangle grows older, the swings become narrower. Profit potential shrinks, while slippage and commissions continue to take just as bad a bite from your account as before.

1. If you trade inside a triangle, use oscillators such as Stochastic (see Section 30) and Elder-ray (see Section 41). They can help you catch minor swings.

2. In trying to decide whether a triangle on a daily chart is likely to lead to an upside or a downside breakout, look at the weekly chart (see Section 43). If the weekly trend is up, then a triangle on the daily charts is more likely to break out to the upside, and vice versa.

3. When you want to buy an upside breakout, place a buy order slightly above the upper boundary of a triangle. Keep lowering your order as the triangle becomes narrower. If you want to short a downside break-

out, place a sell order slightly below the lower boundary. Keep raising it as the triangle becomes narrower. Once you are in a trade, place a protective stop slightly inside the triangle. Prices may pull back to the wall, but they should not return deep inside a triangle following a valid breakout.

4. When a breakout from a triangle is followed by a pullback, pay attention to volume. A pullback on heavy volume threatens to abort the breakout, but a pullback on light volume offers a good opportunity to add to your position.

5. When prices approach the last third of a triangle, cancel your buy or sell orders. Breakouts from the last third of a triangle are very unreliable.

Atypical Triangles

A **pennant** is a small triangle whose lines are slanted in the same direction. Pennants that slant against the trend serve as continuation patterns. There is an old saying "The pennant flies at half-mast" — a rally is likely to travel as far after the pennant as it did before. A pennant that slants in the direction of the trend indicates exhaustion — a trend is nearing a reversal.

A **widening triangle** occurs when prices set a series of higher highs and lower lows. This pattern shows that the market is becoming hysterically volatile, with bulls and bears pouring in. The fight between bulls and bears becomes too hot for the uptrend to continue — a widening triangle kills an uptrend.

A **diamond** starts out as a widening triangle and ends as a symmetrical triangle. You have to squint very hard to recognize it. Diamonds are prime examples of Rorschach-type patterns for chartists. If you look long enough, you will find them, but their trading usefulness is minimal. I used to look for diamonds . . . and most of them were fake zirconium.

Double Tops and Bottoms

Double tops occur when prices rally to the area of the previous high. Double bottoms occur when prices fall near the previous low. The second top or bottom can be slightly above or below the first. This often confuses beginning analysts.

Savvy traders use technical indicators to identify double tops and bottoms. They are often marked by bullish and bearish divergences. Buying at double bottoms and selling short at double tops offer some of the best trading opportunities.

IV

Computerized Technical Analysis

---

24. COMPUTERS IN TRADING

To be a successful trader, you must understand markets better than your competitors do. You can analyze them more thoroughly using a computer. Many traders who compete with you in the markets already have these machines.

Manual charting can help you develop an intuitive, physical feel for prices. You can buy some graph paper and plot several stocks or commodities each day. Once you post your charts, write down at what level you will be a buyer or a seller and where you will place your stops.

After you do that for a while, you will probably want to analyze more markets using technical indicators. Then it is time to look for a computer and technical analysis software.

Driving or Walking

A trader without a computer is like a man traveling on a bicycle. His legs grow strong and he sees a lot of scenery, but his progress is slow. When you travel on business and want to get to the point fast, you get a car.

A computer can help you track and analyze more markets in depth. It can take over routine tasks and free up your mind for thinking. A computer allows you to use more indicators and spot more opportunities in the markets. Trading is an information game. A computer helps you process more information.

Computerized technical analysis is more objective than classical charting. You can argue about whether a head-and-shoulders pattern is present—but there is never an argument about an indicator's direction. When an indicator points up, it is clearly up, and when it is down, it is clearly down.

Switching from manual charting to computerized analysis is like giving up an abacus for a calculator. It may slow you down for a while, as you learn to push the keys, but the eventual increase in speed is worth the effort.

Three Steps to Computerized Analysis

There are three steps to becoming a computerized trader. First you must choose software, then a computer, and finally data for analysis. Different programs require different computers, which is why it pays to choose software first. Software tells a computer how to process data and how to display the results. Each program has a unique list of features and its own look and feel.

Draw a list of tasks you want your computer to perform for you and show it to computerized traders. Contact a traders' group such as Club 3000 to see what its members like. Many traders call Financial Trading Seminars, Inc. for our opinion on the best packages. Magazines for traders, such as *Futures* and *Technical Analysis of Stocks and Commodities* carry many ads for technical analysis software. Read those ads and software reviews, and send away for demo diskettes.

Once you narrow down your choices to two or three programs, call the companies whose software you like and ask for names of users in your area. Insist on names of real users—your best source of practical and unbiased advice. Many traders feel isolated and enjoy contact with other traders. They like to show their equipment and tell you about the quality of technical support.

Most programs for technical analysis fall into one of three groups: toolboxes, black boxes, and gray boxes. Toolboxes are for serious traders, black boxes are for people who believe in Santa Claus, and gray boxes are in between. When considering a new package, ask yourself which group it belongs to.

Toolboxes

If you want to work with wood or metal, you can go to a hardware store and buy a toolbox with a set of tools. You must learn how to use those tools to work smarter and more efficiently. A technical analysis toolbox provides a set of electronic tools for processing market data.

A toolbox draws daily and weekly charts, splits the screen into several windows, and plots prices and indicators. A good toolbox includes many popular indicators, such as moving averages, channels, MACD, MACD-Histogram, Stochastic, the Relative Strength Index, and a dozen others. It allows you to fine-tune all indicators. For example, it lets you switch from a 5-day to a 9-day Stochastic at the push of a button.

A quality package allows you to write your own indicators into the system. You may have a favorite formula that you want to follow, along with ready-made indicators. Avoid programs that limit you to canned indicators.

A good toolbox allows you to compare any two markets and analyze their spreads. If you trade options, your toolbox must include an options valuation model. Advanced packages allow you to test the profitability of trading systems.

There are good toolboxes at all price levels. At the high end, CompuTrac's™ list of indicators runs to two pages, it allows you to test profitability, and it is highly automated. Most of the charts in this book were drawn using CompuTrac. Financial Trading Seminars, Inc. maintains a list of recommended resources for computerized traders — software packages at all price levels, data services, computer configurations, and so on. This list is updated every few months and offered to traders as a public service. You can receive this timely information by contacting our company at the address that appears in the back of this book.

Black Boxes

Black box software tells you what to buy and sell and when to buy or sell it without telling you why. You put data into a black box, lights blink, gears click, and out comes a piece of paper telling you what to do. Thousands of traders pay good money for this.

Most black boxes are sold by hustlers to gullible or insecure traders. Black boxes always come with impressive track records showing profitable past performance. Every black box self-destructs because markets keep changing. Even systems with built-in optimization do not work because we do not know what kind of optimization will be needed in the future. There is no substitute for mature judgment in trading. The only way to make money from a black box is to sell one.

Each black box is guaranteed to fail, even if sold by an honest developer. Complex human activities such as trading cannot be automated. Machines can help but not replace humans.

Trading with a black box means using a slice of someone else's intelligence, as it existed at some point in the past. Markets change, and experts change their minds, but a black box keeps churning out its buy and sell signals. Trading with a black box is like having sex using a penile implant — you may deceive your partner for a while, but you will never deceive yourself.

Gray Boxes

Like a black box, a gray box generates trading signals based on a proprietary formula. Unlike a black box, it gives you a general understanding of its formula and allows you to fine-tune its operations to some degree. The closer a gray box is to a toolbox, the better it is.

Well-known gray boxes include such programs as MESA. It is considered the best program for identifying market cycles.

Computers

Different software programs run on different machines. This is why it is better to choose your software before you buy a computer. Get the most modern machine, so that it will remain useful for years. Traders keep demanding more memory and speed — I never heard anyone complain about having too much of either. Buy a fast modem for collecting data from a database. Get a laser printer if you need to print high-quality charts.

Most programs allow you to automate studies and print them out. You push a button and leave the computer alone. When you return, there is a ream of charts with indicators piled in front of the printer. The tedious work is done, and you can go to work making trading decisions.

It pays to hire a person who already uses the package to set up your system. I often do that when I start using a new piece of software — it saves a lot of time and energy. Once you know which buttons to push, you can run most programs without knowing much about computers.

Market Data

Each trader needs to start with a historical database and update it daily. In the old days, both had to be created manually. Now historical data for any given market costs less than a dollar per month, and updates are cheap. It takes less than a minute to update a dozen markets by modem, using your regular phone line. There are many reliable databases offering a variety of stock, currency, futures, and options data.

Some traders collect their data around the clock. They use satellite dishes, FM receivers, and dedicated phone lines. Real-time data is necessary for day-trading, but not for position trading.

Position traders enter and exit positions within days or weeks. Day-traders enter and exit trades within a few hours if not minutes. You need to become a competent position trader before you can day-trade. You can compare position trading and day-trading to playing a video game at level one or level nine. You run the same mazes and dodge the same monsters, but the pace of the game is so fast that at level nine your reactions must be almost automatic. If you stop to think, you are dead. Learn to analyze the markets and trade at level one — learn to be a position trader before attempting to day-trade.

When you buy historical data, it pays to cover two bull markets and two bear markets. Starting to analyze a new market, I usually review a monthly chartbook covering 20 years of trading to see whether the market is historically high or low. I buy three to five years' worth of weekly data and one year of daily data.

When you begin using a computer, focus on six or fewer markets and add more later. For example, you may follow Treasury Bonds, Standard & Poor's 500, gold, and Japanese Yen or the German Mark. Change this list if you want to follow agricultural or industrial markets. Choose a few technical indicators, and run them daily on each market. After you learn them well, add new ones. I use a battery of 10 or 12 indicators at any given time, plus one new indicator. I watch it for several months and compare its signals to others. If it proves useful, I add it to the standard package.

Three Major Groups of Indicators

Indicators can help you identify trends and their turning points. They can provide a deeper insight into the balance of power between bulls and bears. Indicators are more objective than chart patterns.

The trouble with indicators is that they often contradict one another. Some of them work best in trending markets, others in flat markets. Some are good at catching turning points, while others are better at following trends.

Most beginners look for a single indicator — a silver bullet to kill the confusion in the markets. Others lump together many indicators and try to average their signals. Either way, a careless beginner with a computer is like a teenager with a sports car — an accident waiting to happen. A serious trader needs to know which indicators work best under different conditions. Before you use any indicator, you must understand what it measures and how it works. Only then can you have confidence in its signals.

Professionals divide indicators into three groups: trend-following indicators, oscillators, and miscellaneous. Trend-following indicators work best when markets are moving but give bad and dangerous signals when the markets are flat. Oscillators catch turning points in flat markets but give premature and dangerous signals when the markets begin to trend. Miscellaneous indicators provide special insights into mass psychology. The secret of successful trading is to combine several indicators from different groups so that their negative features cancel each other out while their positive features remain undisturbed. This is the aim of the Triple Screen trading system (see Section 43).

Trend-following indicators include moving averages, MACD (moving average convergence-divergence), MACD-Histogram, the Directional System, On-Balance Volume, Accumulation/Distribution, and others. Trend-following indicators are coincident or lagging indicators — they turn after trends reverse.

Oscillators help identify turning points. They include Stochastic, Rate of Change, Smoothed Rate of Change, Momentum, the Relative Strength Index, Elder-ray, the Force Index, Williams %R, the Commodity Channel Index, and others. Oscillators are leading or coincident indicators and often turn ahead of prices.

Miscellaneous indicators provide insights into the intensity of bullish or bearish market opinion. They include the New High–New Low Index, the Put-Call Ratio, Bullish Consensus, Commitments of Traders, the Advance/Decline Index, the Traders' Index, and so on. They can be leading or coincident indicators.

25. MOVING AVERAGES

Wall Street old-timers claim that moving averages were brought to the financial markets by antiaircraft gunners. They used moving averages to site guns on enemy planes during World War ll and applied this method to prices. The two early experts on moving averages were Richard Donchian and J. M. Hurst — neither apparently a gunner. Donchian was a Merrill Lynch employee who developed trading methods based on moving average crossovers. Hurst was an engineer who applied moving averages to stocks in his now-classic book, *The Profit Magic of Stock Transaction Timing.*

A moving average (MA) shows the average value of data in its time window. A 5-day MA shows the average price for the past 5 days, a 20-day MA shows the average price for the past 20 days, and so on. When you connect each day's MA values, you create a moving average line.

$$\text{Simple MA} = \frac{P_1 + P_2 + \ldots + P_N}{N}$$

where P is the price being averaged

           N is the number of days in the moving average (selected by trader)

The value of MA depends on two factors: values that are being averaged and the width of the MA time window. Suppose you want to calculate a 3-day simple moving average of a stock. If it closes at 19, 21, and 20 on three consecutive days, then a 3-day simple MA of closing prices is 20 (19 + 21 + 20, divided by 3). Suppose that on the fourth day the stock closes at 22. It makes its 3-day MA rise to 21 — the average of the last three days (21 + 20 + 22), divided by 3.

There are three main types of moving averages: simple, exponential, and weighted. Most traders use simple MAs because they are easy to calculate, and Donchian and Hurst used them in precomputer days. Simple MAs, however, have a fatal flaw — they change twice in response to each price.

Twice as Much Bark

A simple MA changes twice in response to each piece of data. First, it changes when a new piece of data is added to the moving average. That is good — we want our MA to reflect changes in prices. The bad thing is that MA changes again when an old price is dropped off at the end of the moving average window. When a high price is dropped, a simple MA ticks down. When a low price is dropped, a simple MA rises. Those changes have nothing to do with the current reality of the market.

Imagine that a stock hovers between 80 and 90, and its 10-day simple MA stands at 85 but includes one day when the stock reached 105. When that high number is dropped at the end of the 10-day window, the MA dives, as if in a downtrend. That meaningless dive has nothing to do with the current reality of the market.

When an old piece of data gets dropped off, a simple moving average jumps. A simple MA is like a guard dog that barks twice—once when someone approaches the house, and once again when someone walks away from it. You do not know when to believe that dog. Traders use simple MAs out of inertia. A modern computerized trader is better off using exponential moving averages.

Market Psychology

Each price is a snapshot of the current mass consensus of value (see Section 12). A single price does not tell you whether the crowd is bullish or bearish—just as a single photo does not tell you whether a person is an optimist or a pessimist. If, on the other hand, someone brings ten photos of a person to a lab and gets a composite picture, it will reveal that person's typical features. If you update a composite photo each day, you can monitor trends in that person's mood.

A moving average is a composite photograph of the market—it combines prices for several days. The market consists of huge crowds, and a moving average identifies the direction of mass movement.

The most important message of a moving average is the direction of its slope. When it rises, it shows that the crowd is becoming more optimistic—bullish. When it falls, it shows that the crowd is becoming more pessimistic—bearish. When the crowd is more bullish than before, prices rise above a moving average. When the crowd is more bearish than before, prices fall below a moving average.

Exponential Moving Averages

An exponential moving average (EMA) is a better trend-following tool than a simple MA. It gives greater weight to the latest data and responds to changes faster than a simple MA. At the same time, an EMA does not jump in response to old data. This guard dog has better ears, and it barks only when someone approaches the house.

$$\text{EMA} = P_{\text{tod}} \cdot K + \text{EMA}_{\text{yest}} \cdot (1 - K)$$

where $K = \dfrac{2}{N + 1}$

N = the number of days in the EMA (chosen by the trader).

P_{tod} = today's price.

EMA_{yest} = the EMA of yesterday.

Technical analysis software allows you to select the EMA length and calculate it at a push of a key. To do it by hand, follow these steps:

1. Choose the EMA length (see below). Let us say, we want a 10-day EMA.

2. Calculate the coefficient K for that length (see above). For example, if you want a 10-day EMA, K equals 2 divided by 10 + 1, or 0.18.

3. Calculate a simple MA for the first 10 days — add closing prices and divide the sum by 10.

4. On the 11th day, multiply the closing price by K, multiply the previous day's MA by $(1 - K)$, and add the two. The result is the 10-day EMA.

5. Keep repeating step 4 on each subsequent day to obtain the latest EMA (see worksheet, Figure 25-1).

An EMA has two major advantages over a simple MA. First, it assigns greater weight to the last trading day. The latest mood of the crowd is more important. In a 10-day EMA, the last closing price is responsible for 18 percent of EMA value, while in a simple MA all days are equal. Second, EMA does not drop old data the way a simple MA does. Old data slowly fades away, like a mood of the past lingering in a composite photo.

Choosing the Length of a Moving Average

A relatively short EMA is more sensitive to price changes — it allows you to catch new trends sooner. It also changes its direction more often and produces more whipsaws. A whipsaw is a rapid reversal of a trading signal. A relatively long EMA leads to fewer whipsaws but misses turning points by a wider margin.

Gold

Day	Close	10-EMA
1	447.3	
2	456.8	
3	451.0	
4	452.5	
5	453.4	
6	455.5	
7	456.0	
8	454.7	
9	453.5	
1 0	456.5	453.7
1 1	459.5	454.8
1 2	465.2	456.6
1 3	460.8	457.4
1 4	460.8	458.0

Figure 25–1. Ten-Day EMA Worksheet

Begin by calculating a simple moving average. The first value in column 3 is a simple MA. Then calculate an exponential moving average on each subsequent day, according to the formula provided in the chapter.

When computers first became available, traders crunched numbers to find the "best" moving averages for different markets. They found which MAs worked in the past—but it did not help them trade because markets kept changing. Our brokers do not let us trade the past.

It pays to tie EMA length to a cycle if you can find it. A moving average should be half the length of the dominant market cycle (see Section 36). If you find a 22-day cycle, use an 11-day moving average. If the cycle is 34 days long, then use a 17-day moving average. Trouble is, cycles keep changing their length and disappearing. Some traders use software such as MESA to look for valid cycles, but MESA shows that noise is greater than cycle amplitude most of the time.

Finally, traders can fall back on a simple rule of thumb: The longer the trend you are trying to catch, the longer the moving average you need. You need a bigger fishing rod to catch a bigger fish. A 200-day moving average works for long-term stock investors who want to ride major trends. Most traders can use an EMA between 10 and 20 days. A moving average should not be shorter than 8 days to avoid defeating its purpose as a trend-following tool. I have been using a 13-day exponential moving average for most of my trading in the past several years.

Trading Rules

A successful trader does not forecast the future — he monitors the market and manages his trading position (see Section 17). Moving averages help us to trade in the direction of the trend. The single most important message of a moving average is the direction of its slope. It shows the direction of the market's inertia. When an EMA rises, it is best to trade the market from the long side, and when it falls, it pays to trade from the short side (Figure 25-2).

1. When an EMA rises, trade that market from the long side. Buy when prices dip near or slightly below the moving average. Once you are long, place a protective stop below the latest minor low and move the stop to the break-even point as soon as prices close above their EMA.

2. When the EMA falls, trade that market from the short side. Sell short when prices rally toward or slightly above the EMA, and place a protective stop above the latest minor high. Lower that stop to the break-even point as soon as prices close below their EMA.

3. When the EMA goes flat and only wiggles a little, it identifies an aimless, trendless market. Do not trade using a trend-following method.

Mechanical Systems

The old mechanical trading methods using moving averages usually had four steps: (1) Buy when the MA rises and prices close above it; (2) sell when prices close below the MA; (3) sell short when the MA declines and prices close below it; (4) cover shorts when prices close above the MA. This mechanical method works in trending markets but leads to whipsaws when markets go flat.

Trying to filter out whipsaws with mechanical rules is self-defeating — fil-

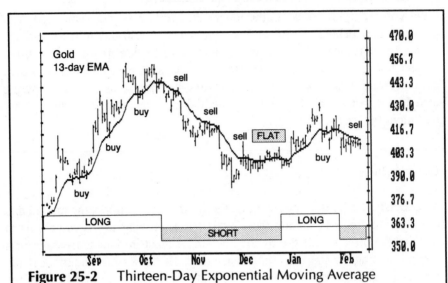

Figure 25-2   Thirteen-Day Exponential Moving Average

When the EMA rises, it shows that the trend is up and the market should be traded from the long side. The best time to buy is when prices return to their EMA–not when they are high above it. Those trades offer a better risk/reward ratio.

When the EMA declines, it shows that the trend is down and the market should be traded from the short side. It is best to sell when prices rally back to their EMA. When the EMA goes flat, as it did in December, it tells you that the market has stopped trending. Stop using a trend-following method but continue to track this indicator, waiting for it to enter a trend.

ters reduce profits as much as losses. An example of a filter is a rule that requires that prices close on the other side of MA not once, but twice, or that they penetrate MA by a certain margin. Mechanical filters reduce losses, but they also diminish the best feature of a moving average—its ability to lock onto a trend early.

The favorite approach of Donchian, one of the originators of trading with moving averages, was to use crossovers of 4-, 9-, and 18-day MAs. Trading signals were given when all three MAs turned in the same direction. His method, like other mechanical trading methods, only worked in strongly trending markets.

A trader must accept that an EMA, like any other trading tool, has good and bad sides. Moving averages help you identify and follow trends, but they lead to whipsaws in trading ranges. We will look for an answer to this dilemma in Chapter 9 on the Triple Screen trading system.

More on Moving Averages

Moving averages serve as **support and resistance** zones. A rising MA tends to serve as a floor below prices, and a falling MA serves as a ceiling above them. That's why it pays to buy near a rising MA, and sell short near a falling MA.

Moving averages can be applied to **indicators** as well as prices. Some traders use a 5-day **moving average of volume**. When volume falls below its 5-day MA, it shows reduced public interest in the minor trend, which is likely to reverse. When volume overshoots its MA, it shows strong public interest and confirms the price trend.

The proper way to plot a simple moving average is to **lag** it behind prices by half its length. For example, a 10-day simple MA properly belongs in the middle of a 10-day period, and it should be plotted underneath the 5th or 6th day. An exponential moving average is more heavily weighted toward the latest data, and a 10-day EMA should be plotted underneath the 7th or 8th day. Most software packages allow you to lag a moving average.

Moving averages can be based not only on closing prices but also on the **mean between the high and the low**. MAs of closing prices are used for daily analysis, but day-traders prefer to apply MAs to median prices.

An exponential moving average assigns greater weight to the latest day of trading, but a **weighted moving average** (WMA) allows you to assign any weight to any day, depending on what you deem important. WMAs are so complicated that traders are better off using EMAs.

26. MOVING AVERAGE CONVERGENCE-DIVERGENCE (MACD) AND MACD-HISTOGRAM

Moving averages identify trends by filtering out daily price ripples. A more advanced indicator was constructed by Gerald Appel, an analyst and money manager in New York. Moving Average Convergence-Divergence, or MACD for short, consists not of one, but three exponential moving averages. It appears on the charts as two lines whose crossovers give trading signals.

How to Create MACD

The original MACD indicator consists of two lines: a solid line (called the MACD line) and a dashed line (called the Signal line). The MACD line is made up of two exponential moving averages (EMAs). It responds to changes in prices relatively quickly. The Signal line is made up of the MACD line smoothed with another EMA. It responds to changes in prices more slowly.

Buy and sell signals are given when the fast MACD line crosses above or below the slow Signal line. The MACD indicator is included in most programs for technical analysis. Few traders calculate it by hand—a computer does the job faster and more accurately.

To create MACD:

1. Calculate a 12-day EMA of closing prices.

2. Calculate a 26-day EMA of closing prices.

3. Subtract the 26-day EMA from the 12-day EMA, and plot their difference as a solid line. This is the fast MACD line.

4. Calculate a 9-day EMA of the fast line, and plot the result as a dashed line. This is the slow Signal line (see the worksheet, Figure 26-1).

Market Psychology

Each price reflects the consensus of value among the mass of market participants at the moment of the trade. A moving average represents an average consensus of value in a selected period—a composite photo of mass consensus. A long moving average tracks long-term consensus, and a short moving average tracks short-term consensus.

Crossovers of the MACD and Signal lines identify shifts in the balance of power of bulls and bears. The fast MACD line reflects mass consensus over a shorter period. The slow Signal line reflects mass consensus over a longer period. When the fast MACD line rises above the slow Signal line, it shows

Crude Oil

DAY	CLOSE	12–EMA	26–EMA	MACD	SIGNAL	MACD-HIST
1	20.70	20.39	20.46	-0.07	-0.16	0.09
2	20.55	20.41	20.47	-0.06	-0.14	0.08
3	20.72	20.46	20.49	-0.03	-0.12	0.09
4	21.03	20.55	20.53	0.02	-0.09	0.11
5	21.10	20.63	20.57	0.06	-0.06	0.12
6	21.29	20.73	20.62	0.11	-0.02	0.13
7	21.09	20.79	20.66	0.13	0.01	0.12
8	21.48	20.90	20.72	0.18	0.04	0.14
9	21.23	20.95	20.76	0.19	0.07	0.12

Figure 26–1. MACD and MACD-Histogram Worksheet

To obtain MACD lines and an MACD-Histogram take these steps:

1. Calculate the 12-day and 26-day exponential moving averages of closing prices.
2. Subtract the 26-day EMA from the 12-day EMA to obtain the fast MACD line.
3. Calculate a 9-day EMA of the fast MACD line to obtain the slow Signal line. Plot both lines to obtain the classic MACD indicator.
4. Subtract the Signal line from the MACD line to obtain an MACD-Histogram.

that bulls dominate the market, and it is better to trade from the long side. When the fast line falls below the slow line, it shows that bears dominate the market and it pays to trade from the short side.

Trading Rules

Crossovers between the MACD and Signal lines identify changing market tides. Trading in the direction of a crossover means going with the flow of the market. This system generates fewer trades and whipsaws than a mechanical system based on a single moving average.

1. When the fast MACD line crosses above the slow Signal line, it gives a buy signal. Go long, and place a protective stop below the latest minor low.

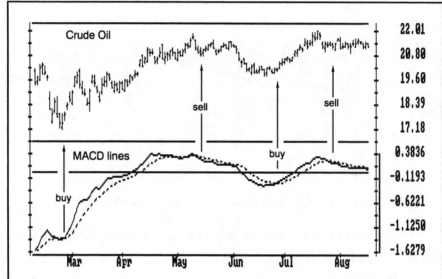

Figure 26–2. MACD Lines

When the fast MACD line crosses above the slow Signal line, it gives a buy signal. Sell signals are given when the fast line crosses below the slow line. These rules help catch all the major trends and generate fewer whipsaws than crossovers of prices and a single moving average.

2. When the fast line crosses below the slow line, it gives a sell signal. Go short, and place a protective stop above the latest minor high (Figure 26-2).

More on MACD

Many traders try to **optimize** MACD by using other moving averages than the standard 12-, 26-, and 9-bar EMAs; 5–34–7 is another popular choice. Some traders try to link MACD to market **cycles**. The trouble is cycles are not present in the markets most of the time (see Section 36). If you use cycles, the first EMA should be one quarter the length of the dominant cycle and the second EMA half the cycle length. The third EMA is a smoothing device whose length does not have to be tied to a cycle. Beware of optimizing MACD too often. If you fiddle with MACD long enough, you can make it give you any signal you want using the same data.

A **"quick-and-dirty"** way to plot MACD is used by traders whose software does not include this indicator. Some packages allow you to draw only two EMAs. In that case, you can use crossovers between two EMAs, such as 11-day and 26-day EMAs as a proxy for MACD and Signal lines.

MACD-Histogram

MACD-Histogram offers a deeper insight into the balance of power between bulls and bears than the original MACD. It shows not only whether bulls or bears are in control but also whether they are growing stronger or weaker. It is one of the best tools available to a market technician.

MACD-Histogram = MACD line – Signal line

MACD-Histogram measures the difference between the MACD line and the Signal line (see worksheet, Figure 26-1). It plots that difference as a histogram — a series of vertical bars. That distance may appear puny, but a computer rescales it to fill the screen.

If the fast line is above the slow line, MACD-Histogram is positive and plotted above the zero line. If the fast line is below the slow line, MACD-Histogram is negative and plotted below the zero line. When the two lines touch, MACD-Histogram equals zero.

When the spread between the MACD and Signal lines increases, MACD-Histogram becomes taller or deeper, depending on its direction. When the two lines draw closer, MACD-Histogram becomes shorter.

The slope of MACD-Histogram is defined by the relationship between any two neighboring bars. If the last bar is higher (like the height of letters m–M), the slope of MACD-Histogram is up. If the last bar is lower (like the depth of letters P–p), then the slope of MACD-Histogram is down.

Market Psychology

MACD-Histogram shows the difference between long-term and short-term consensus of value. The fast MACD line reflects market consensus over a shorter period. The slow Signal line reflects market consensus over a longer period. MACD-Histogram tracks the difference between these two lines.

The slope of MACD-Histogram identifies the dominant market group. A rising MACD-Histogram shows that bulls are becoming stronger. A falling MACD-Histogram shows that bears are becoming stronger.

When the fast MACD line rallies faster than the slow Signal line, MACD-Histogram rises. It shows that bulls are becoming stronger than they have been—it is a good time to trade from the long side. When the fast MACD line drops faster than the slow line, MACD-Histogram falls. It shows that bears are becoming stronger—it is a good time to trade from the short side.

When the slope of MACD-Histogram moves in the same direction as prices, the trend is safe. When the slope of MACD-Histogram moves in a direction opposite to that of prices, the health of the trend is questioned. It is best to trade in the direction of the slope of MACD-Histogram because it shows whether bulls or bears dominate the market.

The slope of MACD-Histogram is more important than its position above or below the centerline. The best sell signals are given when MACD-Histogram is above its centerline but its slope turns down, showing that bulls have become exhausted. The best buy signals occur when MACD-Histogram is below its centerline but its slope turns up, showing that bears have become exhausted.

Trading Rules

MACD-Histogram gives two types of trading signals. One is common and occurs at every price bar. The other is rare and occurs only a few times a year in any market—but it is extremely strong.

The common signal is given by the slope of MACD-Histogram (Figure 26-3). When the current bar is higher than the preceding bar, the slope is up. It shows that bulls are in control and it is time to buy. When the current bar is lower than the preceding bar, the slope is down. It shows that bears are in control and it is time to be short. When prices go one way but MACD-Histogram moves the other way, it shows that the dominant crowd is losing its enthusiasm and the trend is weaker than it appears.

1. Buy when MACD-Histogram stops falling and ticks up. Place a protective stop below the latest minor low.

2. Sell short when MACD-Histogram stops rising and ticks down. Place a protective stop above the latest minor high.

MACD-Histogram ticks up and down on the daily charts so often that is

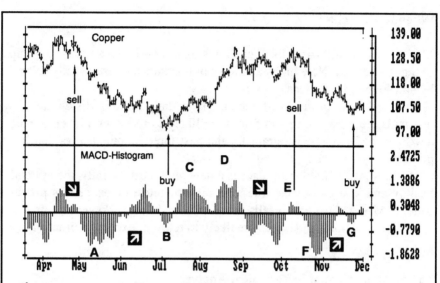

Figure 26–3. MACD-Histogram Divergences

MACD-Histogram confirms trends when it reaches new highs or lows together with prices. The new lows in MACD-Histogram at points A and F confirm downtrends. New lows in the indicator tell traders that the downtrend is likely to retest or exceed bottoms A and F. New highs C and D in MACD-Histogram confirm uptrends. They show that the uptrend is likely to retest or exceed peaks C and D.

Divergences between MACD-Histogram and prices identify major turning points. These signals rarely occur, but when they do, they often let you catch major reversals and the beginnings of new trends. The bullish divergence A–B flags a major buying opportunity. Prices are at a new low, but the indicator is tracing a higher bottom. It shows that bears are exhausted and bulls are ready to gain the upper hand.

The bearish divergence D–E identifies a major selling opportunity. At the right edge of the chart, there is a bullish divergence, F–G. The best time to buy is when MACD-Histogram ticks up from its second bottom, G. Once you go long, place a protective stop below the price bottom G. Move the stop up as the trend progresses.

not practical to buy and sell every time it turns. The changes of slope of MACD-Histograms are much more meaningful on the weekly charts, which is why it is included in the Triple Screen trading system (see Section 43).

When to Expect a New Peak or Valley

MACD-Histogram works like headlights on a car — it gives traders a glimpse of the road ahead. New highs and lows in this indicator are usually followed by new high or low prices.

A record peak for the past three months in daily MACD-Histogram shows that bulls are very strong and prices are likely to rise even higher. A record new low for MACD-Histogram for the past three months shows that lower prices are likely ahead.

When MACD-Histogram reaches a new high during a rally, the uptrend is healthy and you can expect the next rally to retest or exceed its previous peak. If MACD-Histogram falls to a new low during a downtrend, it shows that bears are strong and prices are likely to retest or exceed their latest low.

The Strongest Signal in Technical Analysis

Divergences between MACD-Histogram and prices occur only a few times a year in any given market, but they give some of the most powerful messages in technical analysis. These divergences identify major turning points and give "extra-strength" buy or sell signals. They do not occur at every important top and bottom, but when you see one, you know that a major reversal is probably at hand.

When prices rally to a new high, but MACD-Histogram traces a lower top, it creates a bearish divergence (Figure 26-3). A lower top in MACD-Histogram shows that bulls are internally weak even though prices are higher. When bulls are running out of steam, bears are ready to grab control. Bearish divergences between MACD-Histogram and prices identify weakness at market tops. They give sell signals when most traders feel excited about a breakout to a new high!

3. Sell short when MACD-Histogram ticks down from its second, lower top, while prices are at a new high. Place a protective stop above the latest high.

As long as prices keep falling to new lows and MACD-Histogram keeps going lower, it confirms the downtrend. If prices fall to a new low but MACD-Histogram traces a more shallow low, it creates a bullish divergence. It shows that prices are falling out of inertia, bears are weaker than they seem, and bulls are ready to gain control. Bullish divergences between

MACD-Histogram and prices identify strength at market bottoms. They give buy signals when most traders feel fearful about a breakdown to a new low!

4. Buy when MACD-Histogram ticks up from its second, more shallow bottom while prices are at a new low. Place a protective stop below the latest low.

If a bullish divergence between MACD-Histogram and price is aborted and prices fall to a new low, you will be stopped out. Continue to watch MACD-Histogram. If it traces a more shallow third bottom while prices decline to a new low, you are dealing with a "triple bullish divergence" — an especially strong buy signal. Buy again as soon as MACD-Histogram ticks up from its shallow third bottom. The reverse applies to shorting triple bearish divergences.

More on MACD-Histogram

MACD-Histogram works in any timeframe: weekly, daily, and intraday. The signals of weekly MACD-Histogram lead to greater price moves than the daily or intraday indicators. This principle applies to all indicators — signals in longer timeframes lead to greater price moves.

When you use MACD and MACD-Histogram on the weekly charts, you do not have to wait until Friday to get your signals. A major trend can change in the middle of the week — the market does not watch the calendar. Because of this, weekly studies have to be performed each day.

27. THE DIRECTIONAL SYSTEM

The Directional system is a trend-following method. It was developed by J. Welles Wilder, Jr., in the mid-1970s and modified by several analysts. The Directional system identifies trends and shows when a trend is moving fast enough to make it worth following. It helps traders take chunks of profit out of the middle of important trends.

How to Construct the Directional System

Directional Movement is defined as the portion of today's range that is outside of the previous day's range. The Directional system checks whether

Japanese Yen

Date	High	Low	Close	+DI$_{13}$	−DI$_{13}$	DX	ADX
7/1	72.24	71.87	71.92	30	20	20	20
7/2	71.83	71.63	71.69	29	23	12	19
7/3	71.65	71.33	71.36	27	27	0	18
7/5	72.10	71.83	72.06	31	23	15	18
7/8	71.94	71.78	71.90	30	23	13	18
7/9	72.02	71.77	71.79	30	22	15	18
7/10	71.95	71.87	71.90	29	21	16	18
7/11	72.13	71.82	71.85	30	20	20	18
7/12	73.20	71.94	73.11	41	16	44	20
7/15	72.94	72.65	72.80	38	15	43	22
7/16	72.75	72.55	72.58	36	16	38	23
7/17	72.91	72.62	72.71	37	15	42	24
7/18	73.07	72.29	72.42	32	18	28	24
7/19	73.06	72.69	73.06	29	16	29	24
7/22	72.70	72.22	72.36	26	21	11	23
7/23	72.76	72.62	72.69	25	20	11	22
7/24	72.96	72.38	72.48	23	22	2	20
7/25	72.42	71.64	71.76	20	30	20	20
7/26	72.50	71.96	72.37	19	27	17	20
7/29	72.34	72.08	72.25	18	26	18	20
7/30	72.47	72.18	72.26	19	25	14	20
7/31	72.59	72.31	72.51	20	23	7	19
8/1	72.59	72.30	72.41	19	22	7	18
8/2	72.92	72.28	72.58	23	20	7	17
8/5	72.95	72.56	72.80	22	19	7	16
8/6	73.57	72.94	73.50	28	17	24	17
8/7	73.29	73.07	73.21	27	16	26	18
8/8	73.15	72.84	73.06	25	18	16	18
8/9	73.18	72.67	72.81	23	20	7	17
8/12	72.92	72.72	72.88	22	19	7	16

Figure 27-1. Directional System Worksheet

+DI$_{13}$ and −DI$_{13}$ are based on positive and negative directional movements and the true ranges of the past 13 days. DX is derived from +DI$_{13}$ and −DI$_{13}$, and ADX is made by smoothing DX. See formulas in the chapter.

today's range extends above or below the previous day's range and averages that data over a period of time. These complex calculations (see worksheet, Figure 27-1) are best performed on a computer. The Directional system is included in most software programs for technical analysis.

1. **Identify "Directional Movement" (DM)** by comparing today's high-to-low range with yesterday's high-to-low range. Directional Movement is the largest part of today's range outside of yesterday's range. There are four types of DM (Figure 27-2). DM is always a positive number (+DM and −DM refer simply to movement above or below yesterday's range).

2. **Identify the "True Range" (TR)** of the market you analyze. It is always a positive number, the largest of three:
    A. The distance from today's high to today's low
    B. The distance from today's high to yesterday's close
    C. The distance from today's low to yesterday's close

3. **Calculate daily Directional Indicators (+DI and −DI).** They allow you to compare different markets by expressing their directional movement as a percentage of each market's true range. Each DI is a positive number: +DI equals zero on a day that has no directional movement up; −DI equals zero on a day that has no directional movement down.

    $$+DI = \frac{+DM}{TR} \qquad -DI = \frac{-DM}{TR}$$

4. **Calculate smoothed Directional Lines (+DI$_{13}$ and −DI$_{13}$).** Smooth +DI and −DI are created with moving averages. Most software packages allow you to pick any period for smoothing, such as a 13-day moving average. You get two indicator lines: smoothed Positive and Negative Directional lines, +DI$_{13}$ and −DI$_{13}$. Both numbers are positive. They are usually plotted in different colors, or as a solid and a dashed line.
    The relationship between Positive and Negative lines identifies trends. When +DI$_{13}$ is on top, it shows that the trend is up, and when −DI$_{13}$ is on top, it shows that the trend is down. The crossovers of +DI$_{13}$ and −DI$_{13}$ give buy and sell signals.

5. **Calculate the Average Directional Indicator (ADX).** This unique component of Directional system shows when a trend is worth following. ADX measures the spread between Directional Lines +DI$_{13}$ and −DI$_{13}$. It is calculated in two steps:

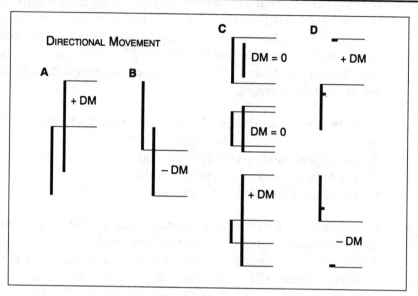

Figure 27–2.   Directional Movement

Directional Movement is the largest part of today's range that is outside of yesterday's range.

A. If today's range extends above yesterday's range, Directional Movement is positive (+DM).

B. If today's range extends below yesterday's range, Directional Movement is negative (–DM).

C. If today's range is inside of yesterday's range or extends above and below it by equal amounts, there is no Directional Movement (DM = 0). If today's range extends both above and below yesterday's range, DM is positive or negative, depending on which part of the "outside range" is larger.

D. On a limit up day, +DM equals the distance from today's close to yesterday's high. On a limit down day, –DM equals the distance from today's close to yesterday's low.

A. Calculate the daily Directional Indicator DX:

$$DX = \frac{+DI_{13} - -DI_{13}}{+DI_{13} + -DI_{13}} \cdot 100$$

For example, $+DI_{13} = 34$; $-DI_{13} = 18$. Then,

$$DX = \frac{34 - 18}{34 + 18} \cdot 100 = \frac{16}{52} \cdot 100 = 30.77, \text{ rounded off} = 31$$

> B. Calculate the Average Directional Indicator ADX by smoothing DX with a moving average, such as a 13-day EMA.

When a trend proceeds in a healthy manner, the spread between two smoothed Directional lines increases and ADX rises. ADX declines when a trend reverses or when a market enters a trading range. It pays to use a trend-following method when ADX rises and not when ADX declines.

Crowd Behavior

The Directional system tracks changes in mass bullishness and bearishness by measuring the capacity of bulls and bears to move prices outside of the previous day's range. If today's high is above yesterday's high, it shows that the market crowd is becoming more bullish. If today's low is below yesterday's low, it shows that the market crowd is becoming more bearish.

The relative position of Directional lines identifies trends. When the Positive Directional line is above the Negative Directional line, it shows that bullish traders dominate the market. When the Negative Directional line rises above the Positive Directional line, it shows that bearish traders are stronger. It pays to trade in the direction of the upper Directional line.

The Average Directional Indicator ADX rises when the spread between Directional lines increases. This shows that market leaders are becoming stronger, losers are getting weaker, and the trend is likely to continue. When the ADX rises, it pays to trade in the direction of the upper Directional line, using a trend-following method.

ADX declines when the spread between $+DI_{13}$ and $-DI_{13}$ narrows down. This shows that the dominant market group is losing its strength, while the underdogs are gaining. Then the market is in turmoil, and it is better not to use trend-following methods.

Trading Rules

1. Trade only from the long side when $+DI_{13}$ is above $-DI_{13}$. Trade only from the short side when $-DI_{13}$ is above $+DI_{13}$. The best time to be long is when both $+DI_{13}$ and ADX are above $-DI_{13}$ and ADX rises. This shows that the uptrend is getting stronger. Go long and place a

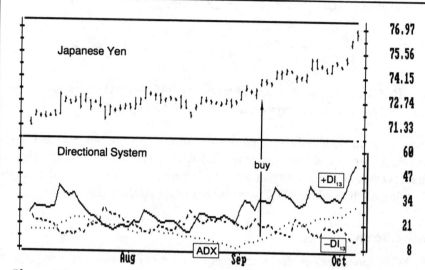

Figure 27–3.   Signals of the Directional System

Directional lines identify trends. When +DI is on top, the trend is up, and it pays to trade the market from the long side. When –DI is on top, it shows that the trend is down and it pays to trade the market from the short side. The best time to use a trend-following method is when ADX is rising and is above the lower Directional line. Those are two signs of dynamic trends.

The Directional system gives its best signals after ADX spends several weeks below both Directional lines. That happens in quiet, dull markets. Once ADX "wakes up" and rises by four steps (for example, from 10 to 14), it gives a strong signal to trade in the direction of the upper Directional line. It often flashes this signal at the beginning of major market moves. On this chart, ADX rallied from 9 to 13 in September, just prior to a dynamic rally in the Japanese Yen. Since the +DI was on top when the signal occurred, it signalled to go long.

protective stop below the latest minor low. The best time to be short is when $-DI_{13}$ and ADX are above $+DI_{13}$ and ADX rises. This shows that bears are becoming stronger. Go short and place a protective stop above the latest minor high.

2. When ADX declines, it shows that the market is becoming less direc-

tional. There are usually many whipsaws, just as there are turbulences in the water during the change of tide. When ADX points down, it is better not to use a trend-following method.

3. When ADX falls below both Directional lines, it identifies a flat, sleepy market. Do not use a trend-following system but start getting ready, because major trends emerge from such lulls.

4. The single best signal of the Directional system comes after ADX falls below both Directional lines. The longer it stays there, the stronger the base for the next move. When ADX rallies from below both Directional lines, it shows that the market is waking up from a lull. When ADX rises by four steps (i.e., from 9 to 13) from its lowest point below both Directional lines, it "rings a bell" on a new trend. It shows that a new bull market or bear market is being born (Figure 27-3). Buy if $+DI_{13}$ is on top and place a stop below the latest minor low. Sell short if $-DI_{13}$ is on top and place a stop above the latest minor high.

   For example, if ADX rises from 8 to 12 while both lines are above 12 and $+DI_{13}$ is on top, it indicates that a new uptrend is beginning. If ADX rises from 9 to 13 while both lines are above 13 and $-DI_{13}$ is on top, it shows that a new downtrend is starting.

The Directional System is unique in telling you when a major new trend is likely to begin. It rings a bell once or twice a year in any given market. It signals when a new baby bull or baby bear is being born. Monetary risk is usually low at that time, due to low volatility while the trend is still young.

5. When ADX rallies above both Directional lines, it identifies an overheated market. When ADX turns down from above both Directional lines, it shows that the major trend has stumbled. It is a good time to take profits. If you trade multiple contracts, you definitely want to take partial profits.

Market indicators give hard signals and soft signals. For example, a violation of a price low or a change in direction of a moving average are hard signals. A downturn of ADX is a soft signal. Once you see ADX turn down, you ought to be very, very careful about adding to positions. You should start taking profits, reducing positions, and looking to get out of your position rather than adding to it.

28. MOMENTUM, RATE OF CHANGE, AND SMOOTHED RATE OF CHANGE

When greed or fear grips a mass of traders, the crowd surges. Oscillators measure the speed of that surge and track its momentum.

Technical indicators are divided into three main groups. Trend-following indicators help identify trends. Oscillators help find turning points. Miscellaneous indicators, such as the New High–New Low Index, track general changes in mass psychology.

Oscillators identify the emotional extremes of market crowds. They allow you to find unsustainable levels of optimism and pessimism. Professionals tend to fade those extremes. They bet against them, for a return to normalcy. When the market rises and the crowd gets up on its hind legs and roars from greed, professionals sell short. They buy when the market falls and the crowd howls in fear. Oscillators help them to time those trades.

Overbought and Oversold

Martin Pring compares trend-following indicators and oscillators to the footprints of a man walking his dog on a leash. The man leaves a fairly straight trail — like a trend-following indicator. The dog's trail swings right and left as far as the leash allows — like an oscillator. When the dog reaches the end of its leash, it is likely to turn and run the other way.

You can follow the trail of a man to find the trend of the pair. When the dog deviates from that trail by the length of its leash, it usually turns around. Usually, but not always. If a dog sees a cat or a rabbit, it may become excited enough to pull its owner off his trail. Traders need to use judgment when using oscillator signals.

An oscillator becomes overbought when it reaches a high level associated with tops in the past. Overbought means too high, ready to turn down. An oscillator becomes oversold when it reaches a low level associated with bottoms in the past. Oversold means too low, ready to turn up.

Overbought and oversold levels are marked by horizontal reference lines on the charts. The proper way to draw those lines is to place them so that an oscillator spends only about 5 percent of its time beyond each line. Place overbought and oversold lines so that they cut across only the highest peaks and the lowest valleys of an oscillator for the past six months. Readjust these lines once every three months.

When an oscillator rises or falls beyond its reference line, it helps a trader to pick a top or a bottom. Oscillators work spectacularly well in trading ranges, but they give premature and dangerous trading signals when a new trend erupts from a range. When a strong trend begins, oscillators start acting like a dog that pulls its owner off his path.

An oscillator can stay overbought for weeks at a time when a new, strong uptrend begins, giving premature sell signals. It can stay oversold for weeks in a steep downtrend, giving premature buy signals. Knowing when to use oscillators and when to rely on trend-following indicators is a hallmark of a mature analyst (see Section 43).

Types of Divergences

Oscillators, as well as other indicators, give their best trading signals when they diverge from prices. Bullish divergences occur when prices fall to a new low while an oscillator refuses to decline to a new low. They show that bears are losing power, prices are falling out of inertia, and bulls are ready to seize control. Bullish divergences often mark the ends of downtrends.

Bearish divergences occur in uptrends—they identify market tops. They emerge when prices rally to a new high while an oscillator refuses to rise to a new peak. A bearish divergence shows that bulls are running out of steam, prices are rising out of inertia, and bears are ready to take control.

There are three classes of bullish and bearish divergences (Figure 28-1). Class A divergences identify important turning points—the best trading opportunities. Class B divergences are less strong, and class C divergences are least important. Valid divergences are clearly visible—they seem to jump from the charts. If you need a ruler to tell whether there is a divergence, assume there is none.

Class A bearish divergences occur when prices reach a new high but an oscillator reaches a lower high than it did on a previous rally. Class A bearish divergences usually lead to sharp breaks. Class A bullish divergences occur when prices reach a new low but an oscillator traces a higher bottom than during its previous decline. They often precede sharp rallies.

Class B bearish divergences occur when prices make a double top but an oscillator traces a lower second top. Class B bullish divergences occur when prices make a double bottom but an oscillator traces a higher second bottom.

Class C bearish divergences occur when prices rise to a new high but an indicator stops at the same level it reached during the previous rally. It shows

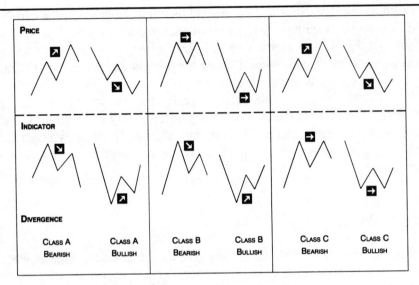

Figure 28–1. Types of Divergences

Divergences between prices and indicators give some of the most powerful signals in technical analysis. Divergences are defined by the differences in height or depth of prices and indicators.

Class A bearish divergence–prices reach a new peak while an indicator reaches a lower peak. This is the strongest sell signal.

Class A bullish divergence–prices fall to a new low while an indicator stops at a more shallow low than before. This is the strongest buy signal.

Class B bearish divergence–prices trace a double top while an indicator reaches a lower peak. This is the second strongest sell signal.

Class B bullish divergence–prices trace a double bottom while an indicator traces a higher second bottom. This is the second strongest buy signal.

Class C bearish divergence–prices reach a new peak while an indicator traces a double top. This is the weakest bearish divergence.

Class C bullish divergence–prices fall to a new low while an indicator makes a double bottom. This is the weakest bullish divergence.

that bulls are becoming neither stronger nor weaker. Class C bullish divergences occur when prices fall to a new low but the indicator traces a double bottom.

Class A divergences almost always identify good trades. Class B and C divergences more often lead to whipsaws. It is best to ignore them, unless they are strongly confirmed by other indicators.

Triple Bullish or Bearish Divergences consist of three price bottoms and three oscillator bottoms or three price tops and three oscillator tops. They are even stronger than regular divergences. In order for a triple divergence to occur, a regular bullish or bearish divergence first has to abort. That's another good reason to practice tight money management! If you lose only a little on a whipsaw, you will not suffer — and you will have both the money and psychological strength to re-enter a trade.

Momentum and Rate of Change

Momentum and Rate of Change measure trend acceleration — its gain or loss of speed. These leading indicators show when a trend speeds up, slows down, or maintains its rate of progress. They usually reach a peak before the trend reaches its high and reach a bottom before prices hit their low.

As long as oscillators keep reaching new highs, it is safe to hold long positions. As long as they keep reaching new lows, it is safe to hold short positions. When an oscillator reaches a new high, it shows that an uptrend is gaining speed and is likely to continue. When an oscillator traces a lower peak, it shows that an uptrend has stopped accelerating, like a rocket that has run out of fuel. When it flies only because of inertia, you have to get ready for a reversal. The same reasoning applies to oscillator lows in downtrends.

Momentum and Rate of Change compare today's closing price to a price a selected period of time ago. Momentum subtracts a past price from today's price; Rate of Change divides today's price by a past price.

$$M = P_{\text{tod}} - P_{\text{tod} - n} \qquad \text{RoC} = \frac{P_{\text{tod}}}{P_{\text{tod} - n}}$$

where M = Momentum.
$\quad\quad\quad$ RoC   = Rate of Change.
$\quad\quad\quad$ P_{tod} = Today's closing price.
$\quad\quad\quad$ $P_{\text{tod} - n}$ = Closing price n days ago (chosen by trader).

For example, a 7-day **Momentum** of closing prices equals today's closing price minus the closing price 7 days ago. Momentum is positive if today's price is higher, negative if today's price is lower, and at zero if today's price equals the price of 7 days ago. The slope of the line connecting momentum values for each day shows whether momentum is rising or falling.

A 7-day **Rate of Change** (RoC) divides the latest price by the closing price 7 days ago. If they are equal, RoC equals 1. If today's price is higher, then RoC is greater than 1, and if today's price is lower, then RoC is less than 1. The slope of the line that connects values for each day shows whether Rate of Change is rising or falling (see worksheet, Figure 28-2).

A trader must choose the width of the time window for Momentum or RoC. As a rule of thumb, it pays to keep oscillator windows fairly narrow. Use wide windows for trend-following indicators whose goal it is to catch trends. Use narrow windows for oscillators to detect short-term changes in the markets.

Momentum and RoC share a flaw with simple moving averages — they jump twice in response to each piece of data. They react to each new price, and they jump again when that piece of data leaves the oscillator's window. Smoothed Rate of Change takes care of this problem.

Crowd Psychology

Each price reflects the consensus of value of all market participants at the moment of transaction. Momentum and RoC compare today's price (today's consensus of value) to a previous price (an earlier consensus of value). They measure changes in mass optimism or pessimism.

To find out whether a child is growing fast enough, you can measure his height each month and compare it with his height six months ago. Then you find out whether your child is growing normally, growing so slowly that you should take him to a doctor, or growing fast enough to think about applying for a basketball scholarship. Momentum and RoC tell you whether a trend is accelerating, slowing down, or moving at the same speed.

When Momentum or RoC rises to a new peak, it shows that the optimism of the market crowd is growing, and prices are likely to rally higher. When Momentum or RoC falls to a new low, it shows that the pessimism of the market crowd is increasing, and lower prices are likely ahead.

When prices rise but Momentum or RoC falls, it warns you that a top is near — it is time to think of taking profits on long positions or tightening stops. If prices reach a new high but Momentum or RoC reaches a lower top,

Crude Oil

Date	Close	Mtm:7	RoC:7	13-EMA	S-RoC 13/21
6/6	20.51	-0.84	96.07	21.04	100.51
6/7	20.45	-0.71	96.64	20.95	99.68
6/10	20.09	-1.36	93.66	20.83	98.61
6/11	20.20	-1.06	95.01	20.74	98.14
6/12	20.31	-0.94	95.58	20.68	97.96
6/13	20.01	-1.11	94.74	20.58	97.65
6/14	20.00	-0.64	96.90	20.50	97.25
6/17	20.13	-0.38	98.15	20.45	96.94
6/18	20.10	-0.35	98.29	20.40	96.56
6/19	19.91	-0.18	99.10	20.33	96.07
6/20	20.17	-0.03	99.85	20.30	95.94
6/21	20.21	-0.10	99.51	20.29	96.04
6/24	20.00	-0.01	99.95	20.25	95.90
6/25	20.10	0.10	100.50	20.23	95.72
6/26	20.09	-0.04	99.80	20.21	95.49
6/27	20.46	0.36	101.79	20.24	95.66
6/28	20.53	0.62	103.11	20.29	95.67
7/01	20.65	0.48	102.38	20.34	95.88
7/02	20.70	0.49	102.42	20.39	96.10
7/03	20.55	0.55	102.75	20.41	96.27
7/05	20.72	0.62	103.08	20.46	96.84
7/08	21.03	0.94	104.68	20.54	97.64
7/09	21.10	0.64	103.13	20.62	98.41
7/10	21.29	0.76	103.70	20.71	99.45
7/11	21.09	0.44	102.13	20.77	100.14
7/12	21.48	0.78	103.77	20.87	100.93
7/15	21.23	0.68	103.31	20.92	101.65
7/16	21.37	0.65	103.14	20.99	102.37
7/17	21.81	0.78	103.71	21.10	103.21
7/18	21.66	0.56	102.65	21.18	103.85

Figure 28–2. Momentum, Rate of Change, and Smoothed Rate of Change Worksheet

Momentum (Mtm:7) is today's closing price minus the closing price 7 days ago.

Rate of Change (RoC:7) is today's closing price divided by the closing price 7 days ago.

You can use closing prices for the day in these formulas or median prices (high plus low, divided by two). This also applies to most indicators described in this book. It is OK to use time windows that are wider or narrower than 7 days.

To create a Smoothed Rate of Change (S-RoC 13/21), calculate a 13-day exponential moving average of closing prices and apply a 21-day Rate of Change to it.

that bearish divergence gives a strong sell signal. The reverse holds true in downtrends.

There are times when Momentum and RoC act not as leading but as coincident indicators. Think what happens to a rocket when it hits an overhead obstacle. Its speed and momentum stop rising and fall together as the rocket crashes. This happens in the markets when the crowd gets hit by a major piece of bad news and this "overhead obstacle" sends RoC and prices down together.

Trading Rules

Leading indicators are like brake lights on a car ahead of you on a highway. When they light up, you do not know whether the other driver is tapping his breaks or slamming them. You have to be extra careful putting on trades using leading indicators (Figure 28-3).

1. When the trend is up, buy whenever RoC declines below its centerline and ticks up. It shows that the uptrend has slowed down — like a train that slows down to pick up passengers. When the trend is down, sell short whenever RoC rallies above its centerline and ticks down.

2. If you hold a long position and prices begin to slide, see whether RoC has reached a record peak before this pullback. A new peak in RoC shows a high level of bullish energy, which is likely to lift the market to its previous high or higher. Then it is relatively safe to hold long positions. On the other hand, a series of declining peaks in RoC is a sign of weakness — it is better to sell immediately. Reverse this approach in downtrends.

3. A break in a trendline of Momentum or RoC often precedes a break of a price trendline by a day or two. When you see a leading indicator break a trendline, prepare for a break in the price trend.

Smoothed Rate of Change

This oscillator, developed by Fred G. Schutzman, avoids the major flaw of RoC. It responds to each piece of data only once rather than twice. Smoothed Rate of Change (S-RoC) compares the values of an exponential moving average (EMA) instead of prices at two points in time. It gives fewer trading signals, and the quality of these signals is better.

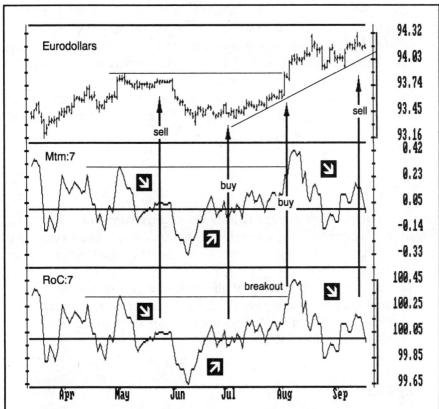

Figure 28–3.   Seven-day Momentum (Mtm:7) and Rate of Change (RoC:7)

When Momentum or RoC rises, it shows that a rally is accelerating. When it falls, it shows that a decline is accelerating. Peaks and bottoms of these indicators show when a trend has reached its maximum speed. Once Momentum or RoC turns, it is time to begin a countdown to a reversal. These indicators give their best signals when they diverge from prices (as marked by arrows on the chart).

Momentum and RoC can be analyzed using classical charting methods, which often give leading trading signals. Notice how RoC and Momentum have sliced through their resistance in August, several days prior to a price breakout. At the right edge of the chart, a bearish divergence shows that the uptrend has run out of steam. It is time to take profits on long positions and go short, with a protective stop a few ticks above the September top.

To create S-RoC you must first calculate an exponential moving average of closing prices (see Section 25). The next step is to apply Rate of Change to the EMA. S-RoC is not very sensitive to the length of its EMA or RoC parts. You can calculate a 13-day EMA of closing prices and then apply a 21-day Rate of Change to it (see worksheet, Figure 28-2).

Some traders calculate the Rate of Change of prices first and then smooth it with a moving average. Their method produces a much jumpier indicator, which is less useful than S-RoC.

Crowd Behavior

An exponential moving average reflects the average consensus of value of all market participants during the period of its window. It is like a composite photograph that reflects major features of the market crowd rather than its fleeting moods.

S-RoC compares each reading of an EMA to a past reading from your selected period of time. It compares the average mass consensus today to the average consensus in the past. S-RoC tracks major shifts in the bullishness and bearishness of the market crowd.

Trading Rules

Changes in the direction of S-RoC often identify important market turns. Upturns of S-RoC mark significant bottoms, and its downturns mark important tops (Figure 28-4). Divergences between S-RoC and prices give especially strong buy and sell signals.

1. Buy when S-RoC turns up from below its centerline.

2. Sell when S-RoC stops rising and turns down. Sell short when S-RoC turns down from above its centerline.

3. If prices reach a new high but S-RoC traces a lower peak, it shows that the market crowd is less enthusiastic even though prices are higher. A bearish divergence between S-RoC and price gives a strong signal to sell short.

4. If prices fall to a new low but S-RoC traces a higher bottom, it shows that the market crowd is less fearful, even though prices are lower. It

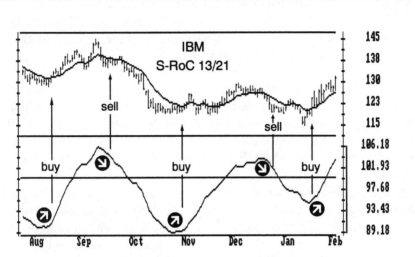

Figure 28–4.   Smoothed Rate of Change (S-RoC 13/21)

To create this indicator, calculate a 13-day exponential moving average of closing prices and apply a 21-day Rate of Change to it. S-RoC usually flows in smooth waves whose crests and bottoms identify many important turning points. This indicator works especially well in the stock market, with stock groups as well as with individual stocks.

shows that the downside pressure has lessened, even though the market has fallen deeper than before. A bullish divergence gives a strong signal to cover shorts and buy.

29. WILLIAMS %R

Williams %R (Wm%R) is a simple but effective oscillator described by Larry Williams in 1973. It measures the capacity of bulls and bears to close prices each day near the edge of the recent range. Wm%R confirms trends and warns of their upcoming reversals.

$$Wm\%R = 100 \cdot \frac{H_r - C}{H_r - L_r}$$

where r = the time window selected by a trader, such as 7 days.
H_r= the highest high of the selected period (i.e., a 7-day high).
L_r = the lowest low of the selected period (i.e., a 7-day low).
C = the latest close.

Wm%R measures the placement of each closing price in relation to the recent high-low range. It expresses the distance from the highest high to the lowest low in its time window as 100 percent. It expresses the distance from the latest closing price to the top of that window as a percentage of the range in its window (see worksheet, Figure 29-1). Williams %R is closely related to Stochastic (see Section 30).

Wm%R is designed to fluctuate between 0 and 100 percent. It equals 0 (plotted at the top of the chart) when bulls reach the peak of their power and close prices at the top of the range. It reaches 100 percent when bears are at the peak of their power and close prices at the bottom of the recent range.

A rule of thumb with all oscillators — when in doubt, make them shorter. This is the opposite of trend-following indicators — when in doubt make them longer. Oscillators with narrow windows help catch short-term reversals. If you work with cycles, make Wm%R equal half the cycle length. A 7-day window fits Wm%R fine. Wm%R works well with weekly charts — use a 7-week window.

Horizontal reference lines for Wm%R are drawn at 10 percent and 90 percent levels. When Wm%R closes above its upper reference line, it shows that bulls are strong but the market is overbought. When Wm%R closes below its lower reference line, it shows that bears are strong but the market is oversold.

Crowd Psychology

Each price is a momentary consensus of value among all market participants. The high of the recent range shows how high bulls can lift prices — it reflects their maximum power. The low of the range reflects the maximum power of bears during that period. Closing price is the most important consensus of the day because the settlement of trading accounts depends on it.

Wm%R compares each closing price to the recent range. It shows whether bulls can close the market near the top of the recent range or bears can close the market at the bottom of the range. Wm%R measures the balance of power between bulls and bears at closing time — the crucial money-counting time in the market.

Bulls may push prices higher during the day, or bears may push them

Gold

Date	High	Low	Close	Wm%R:7
8/14	362.2	358.2	361.2	
8/15	363.5	360.2	360.4	
8/16	361.6	360.3	361.3	
8/19	366.5	360.4	362.0	
8/20	362.0	355.3	359.3	
8/21	360.4	358.2	360.1	
8/22	359.9	357.4	357.5	80.36
8/23	357.2	355.3	356.7	87.50
8/26	358.6	357.1	358.5	71.43
8/27	358.8	356.9	357.8	77.68
8/28	359.5	356.1	357.3	70.15
8/29	356.4	353.7	354.1	94.03
8/30	351.5	348.5	351.4	74.56
9/03	352.0	349.4	351.6	71.82
9/04	352.3	351.6	351.8	70.00
9/05	350.7	349.8	350.3	83.64
9/06	352.5	349.8	352.3	65.45
9/09	355.9	353.4	354.3	26.58

Figure 29–1.   Williams %R Worksheet

Wm%R expresses the distance from the latest closing price to the top of the 7-day high–low range as a percentage of that range. Wm%R:7 is calculated here using a 7-day time window. You may choose a longer or a shorter window, depending on the trend you are trying to analyze.

lower. Wm%R shows which group is capable of closing the market in its favor. If bulls cannot close the market near the top during a rally, they are weaker than they seem. This is a shorting opportunity. If bears cannot close the market near the lows during a decline, they are weaker than they appear. This is a buying opportunity.

Trading Rules

Wm%R gives three types of trading signals. They are, in order of importance, bullish or bearish divergences, failure swings, and overbought–oversold readings (Figure 29-2).

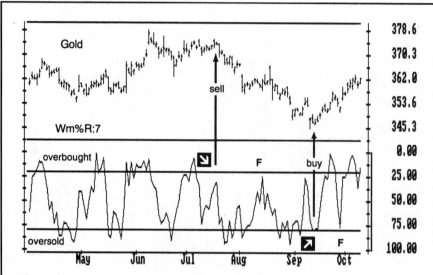

Figure 29–2.   Seven-Day Williams %R (Wm%R:7)

When Wm%R rises above its upper reference line, it shows that the market is overbought. When it falls below its lower reference line, it shows that the market is oversold. The best buy and sell signals are given by divergences (marked by arrows). A Class B bearish divergence in July gave a sell signal. A Class A bullish divergence in September gave a strong buy signal.

Failure swings (marked by the letter F) occur when Wm%R reverses without reaching its reference line. This happens during reactions against very strong trends–failure swings confirm those trends. A failure swing during a downtrend in August gave a strong sell signal. A failure swing during an uptrend in September gave a strong buy signal.

At the right edge of the chart, prices are surging. If Wm%R dips below its lower reference line, use that as a buying opportunity. Do not sell short unless a bearish divergence emerges.

Divergences

Divergences between prices and Wm%R rarely occur. They identify the best trading opportunities. When Wm%R rises above its upper reference line, falls, and then cannot rise above that line during the next rally, it creates a bearish divergence. It shows that bulls are losing their power and the market is likely to fall. A bullish divergence occurs when Wm%R falls below its lower reference line, rallies, and then cannot decline below that line when prices slide again. It shows that bears are losing power and a rally is in the offing.

1. When you identify a bullish divergence, go long and place a protective stop below the recent price low.

2. When you identify a bearish divergence, go short and place a protective stop above the recent price high.

Failure Swings

Crowds tend to swing from one extreme to the other. Wm%R seldom reverses in the middle of its range. Failure swings occur when Wm%R fails to rise above its upper reference line during a rally or fall below its lower reference line during a decline.

3. When Wm%R stops rising in the middle of a rally and turns down without reaching its upper reference line, it produces a failure swing. This shows that bulls are especially weak and gives a sell signal.

4. When Wm%R stops falling in the middle of a decline and turns up without reaching its lower reference line, that is a failure swing. It shows that bears are very weak and gives a buy signal.

Overbought and Oversold

When prices close near the upper edge of their range, Wm%R reaches its top and becomes overbought. When prices close near the bottom of their recent range, Wm%R falls and becomes oversold. Neither bulls nor bears are all-powerful. They seldom can close prices near the extreme of the recent range for too many days in a row.

5. When Wm%R rises above its upper reference line, it marks a potential market top and gives a sell signal.

6. When Wm%R falls below its lower reference line, it marks a potential market bottom and gives a buy signal.

These overbought and oversold signals tend to work well during flat trading ranges. They become premature and dangerous when the market enters a trend. Wm%R can stay near the top for a week or longer during a strong rally: Its overbought readings can identify strength rather than a shorting opportunity. Similarly, in a strong downtrend, Wm%R can stay oversold for weeks, indicating weakness rather than a buying opportunity.

Overbought and oversold readings of Wm%R should be used for trading only after you identify the major trend. Use long-term trend-following indicators for that purpose (see Section 43). If a weekly chart shows a bull market, take only buy signals from daily Wm%R, and do not go short when it gives a sell signal. If a weekly chart indicates a bear market, sell short whenever daily Wm%R gives you a sell signal, but do not go long when it becomes oversold.

30. STOCHASTIC

Stochastic is an oscillator popularized by George Lane. It is now included in many software programs and widely used by computerized traders. Stochastic tracks the relationship of each closing price to the recent high-low range.

Stochastic is more complex than Williams %R. It includes several steps for filtering out market noise and weeding out bad signals. Stochastic consists of two lines: a fast line called %K and a slow line called %D.

1. The first step in calculating Stochastic is to obtain "raw Stochastic" or %K:

$$\%K = \frac{C_{tod} - L_n}{H_n - L_n} \cdot 100$$

where C_{tod} = today's close.
L_n = the lowest point for the selected number of days.
H_n = the highest point for the selected number of days.
n = the number of days for Stochastic, selected by the trader.

The standard width of Stochastic's time window is 5 days, although some traders use much higher values. A narrow window helps catch more turning points, but a wider window helps identify major turning points.

2. The second step is to obtain %D. It is done by smoothing %K — usually over a three-day period. It can be done in several ways, such as:

$$\%D = \frac{\text{3-day sum of } (C_{tod} - L_n)}{\text{3-day sum of } (H_n - L_n)} \cdot 100$$

There are two ways to plot Stochastic—Fast and Slow. **Fast Stochastic** consists of two lines—%K and %D—plotted on the same chart. It is very sensitive to market turns but leads to many whipsaws. Many traders prefer a less sensitive **Slow Stochastic**. The %D of Fast Stochastic becomes the %K of Slow Stochastic and is smoothed by repeating step 2 to obtain %D of Slow Stochastic. Slow Stochastic does a better job of filtering out market noise and leads to fewer whipsaws. A 5-bar Slow Stochastic (smoothed over a 3-day period) is a popular choice among traders (see worksheet, Figure 30-1).

Swiss Franc

Date	High	Low	Close	% K:5	%D:5	Slow %D
9/16	68.07	67.24	67.83			
9/17	68.22	67.79	67.97			
9/18	67.61	66.81	67.36			
9/19	67.52	67.02	67.25			
9/20	67.57	66.87	67.50	48.94		
9/23	68.21	67.89	68.04	87.23		
9/24	68.53	67.48	67.64	48.26	60.57	
9/25	67.87	67.57	67.71	50.60	60.54	
9/26	67.97	67.48	67.58	42.77	47.22	56.11
9/27	68.30	67.37	68.23	74.14	53.79	53.85
9/30	68.49	68.25	68.37	86.21	64.57	55.20

Figure 30–1. Stochastic Worksheet

• The %K of Fast Stochastic is similar to Williams %R.
• The %D of Fast Stochastic is obtained by smoothing %K over a 3-day period.
• The %D of Fast Stochastic becomes the %K of Slow Stochastic and is smoothed once again to obtain %D of Slow Stochastic.

Most traders use computers to construct Stochastic. Choosing the width of the Stochastic window depends on a trend you are trying to identify. A very short-term Stochastic (5 days or so) helps catch short-term reversals. A longer Stochastic (14–21 days) helps identify more significant market turns.

Stochastic is designed to fluctuate between 0 and 100. Reference lines are drawn at 20 percent and 80 percent levels to mark overbought and oversold areas. Slow Stochastic seldom reaches the same extremes as raw Williams %R.

Crowd Psychology

Each price is the consensus of value of all market participants at the moment of transaction. Daily closing prices are important because the settlement of trading accounts depends on them. The high of any period marks the maximum power of bulls during that time. The low of that period shows the maximum power of bears during that time.

Stochastic measures the capacity of bulls or bears to close the market near the upper or lower edge of the recent range. When prices rally, markets tend to close near the high. If bulls can lift prices up during the day but cannot close them near the top, Stochastic turns down. It shows that bulls are weaker than they seem and gives a sell signal.

Daily closes tend to occur near the lows during downtrends. When a bar closes near its high, it shows that bears can only push prices down during the day but cannot hold them down. An upturn of Stochastic shows that bears are weaker than they appear and flashes a buy signal.

Trading Rules

Stochastic shows when bulls or bears become stronger or weaker. This information helps you decide whether bulls or bears are likely to win the current fight in the market. It pays to trade with the winners and against the losers.

Stochastic gives three types of trading signals, listed here in the order of importance: divergences, the level of Stochastic lines, and their direction (Figure 30-2).

Divergences

The most powerful buy and sell signals of Stochastic are given by divergences between this indicator and prices.

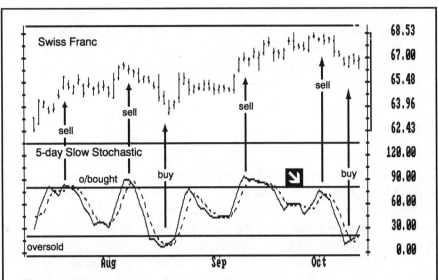

Figure 30–2. Five-Day Slow Stochastic

Stochastic lines help identify top and bottom areas when they move above or below their reference lines. These signals work well during trading ranges but are premature when a new trend begins (see early September). Stochastic gives its best signals when it diverges from prices. There is a Class A bearish divergence in early October, prior to a sharp price break.

Once you go long or short using Stochastic, place a protective stop immediately below the latest minor low or above the latest minor high. There is a buy signal at the right edge of the chart–it is time to cover shorts and buy.

1. A bullish divergence occurs when prices fall to a new low but Stochastic traces a higher bottom than during the previous decline. It shows that bears are losing strength and prices are falling out of inertia. As soon as Stochastic turns up from its second bottom, it gives a strong buy signal: Go long and place a protective stop below the latest low in the market. The best buy signals occur when the first bottom is below the lower reference line and the second is above it.

2. A bearish divergence occurs when prices rally to a new high but Stochastic traces a lower top than during its previous rally. It shows

that bulls are becoming weaker and prices are rising out of inertia. As soon as Stochastic turns down from its second top, it gives a sell signal: Go short and place a protective stop above the latest price peak. The best sell signals occur when the first top is above the upper reference line and the second is below.

Overbought and Oversold

When Stochastic rallies above its upper reference line, it shows that the market is overbought. Overbought means too high, ready to turn down. When Stochastic falls below its lower reference line, it shows that the market is oversold. Oversold means too low, ready to turn up.

These signals work fine during trading ranges but not when a market develops a trend. In uptrends, Stochastic quickly becomes overbought and keeps giving sell signals while the market rallies. In downtrends, Stochastic quickly becomes oversold and keeps giving premature buy signals. It pays to combine Stochastic with a long-term trend-following indicator (see Section 43). The Triple Screen trading system allows traders to take buy signals from daily Stochastic only when the weekly trend is up. When the weekly trend is down, it allows traders to take only sell signals from daily Stochastic.

3. When you identify an uptrend on a weekly chart, wait for daily Stochastic lines to decline below their lower reference line. Then, without waiting for their crossover or an upturn, place a buy order above the high of the latest price bar. Once you are long, place a protective stop below the low of the trade day or the previous day, whichever is lower.

The shape of Stochastic's bottom often indicates whether a rally is likely to be strong or weak. If the bottom is narrow and shallow, it shows that bears are weak and the rally is likely to be strong. If it is deep and wide, it shows that bears are strong and the rally is likely to be weak. It is better to take only strong buy signals.

4. When you identify a downtrend on a weekly chart, wait for daily Stochastic lines to rally above their upper reference line. Then, without waiting for their crossover or a downturn, place an order to sell short below the low of the latest price bar. By the time Stochastic lines cross over, the market is often in a free fall. Once you are short, place

a protective stop above the high of the trade day or the previous day, whichever is higher.

The shape of Stochastic's top often indicates whether a decline is likely to be steep or sluggish. A narrow top in Stochastic shows that bulls are weak and a severe decline is likely. A Stochastic top that is high and wide shows that bulls are strong — it is safer to pass up that sell signal.

5. Do not buy when Stochastic is overbought and do not sell short when it is oversold. This rule filters out most bad trades.

Line Direction

When both Stochastic lines are headed in the same direction, they confirm the short-term trend. When prices rise and both Stochastic lines rise, the uptrend is likely to continue. When prices slide and both Stochastic lines fall, the short-term downtrend is likely to continue.

More on Stochastic

Stochastic can be used in any timeframe, including weekly, daily, or intraday. **Weekly** Stochastic usually changes its direction one week prior to weekly MACD-Histogram. If weekly Stochastic turns, it warns you that trend-following MACD-Histogram is likely to turn the next week. It is a signal to tighten stops on existing positions or start taking profits.

Choosing **the width of the Stochastic window** is important. Short-term oscillators are more sensitive. Long-term oscillators turn only at important tops and bottoms. If you use Stochastic as a stand-alone oscillator, a longer Stochastic is preferable. If you use Stochastic as part of a trading system, combined with trend-following indicators, then a shorter Stochastic is preferable.

An ingenious way to use Stochastic, popularized by Jacob Bernstein, is called a **Stochastic pop**. When Stochastic crosses above its upper reference line, it indicates strength. You can buy for a quick rally and sell as soon as Stochastic turns down. This signal can help you catch the last splash of the bullish wave.

Stochastic is one of the favorite tools of automatic trading systems developers. These modern-day alchemists try to use Stochastic in a purely

mechanical manner, buying and selling when the two Stochastic lines cross. They discard Stochastic when it fails to deliver magic results. Trading the crossovers of Stochastic lines is not profitable, no matter how much you optimize them, because Stochastic works differently, depending on whether the market is in a trend or in a trading range.

31. RELATIVE STRENGTH INDEX

Relative Strength Index (RSI) is an oscillator developed by J. Welles Wilder, Jr. It is now included in most software packages. RSI measures the strength of any trading vehicle by monitoring changes in its closing prices. It is a leading or a coincident indicator—it is never a laggard.

$$RSI = 100 - \frac{100}{1 + RS}$$

$$RS = \frac{\text{average of net UP closing changes for a selected number of days}}{\text{average of net DOWN closing changes for the same number of days}}$$

The pattern of RSI peaks and valleys does not change in response to the width of its time window. Trading signals become more visible with shorter RSI, such as 7 or 9 days. Most traders use computers to calculate and plot RSI. Take these steps to calculate a 7-day RSI for any market:

1. Obtain closing prices for the past 7 days.

2. Find all days where the market closed higher than the day before and add up the amounts of increases. Divide the sum by 7 to obtain the average UP closing change.

3. Find all days when the market closed lower than the day before and add up the amounts of declines. Divide the sum by 7 to obtain the average DOWN closing change.

4. Divide the average UP closing change by the average DOWN closing change to obtain Relative Strength (RS). Insert RS in the formula above to arrive at RSI—Relative Strength Index.

5. Repeat the process daily (see worksheet, Figure 31-1).

Swiss Franc

Date	Close	UpAvg:7	DownAvg:7	RSI:7
10/29	77.34			
10/30	78.02			
10/31	77.71			
11/1	78.45			
11/2	79.15			
11/5	79.91			
11/6	79.63			
11/7	79.99	0.4629	0.0843	84.60
11/8	79.96	0.3967	0.0765	83.83
11/9	79.94	0.3401	0.0685	83.24
11/12	79.96	0.2943	0.0587	83.38
11/13	79.76	0.2523	0.0789	76.18
11/14	80.09	0.2634	0.0676	79.58
11/15	79.72	0.2258	0.1108	67.08
11/16	80.10	0.2478	0.0950	72.29

Figure 31–1. Seven-Day Relative Strength Index Worksheet

Begin by calculating average UP closing and average DOWN closing for the past 7 days. Insert the results in the RSI formula and then start using the calculation shortcut, as outlined in the text.

If you calculate RSI by hand, you can use a shortcut. Once you have 7 days' worth of data, replace steps 2 and 3 on all following days:

2. Multiply yesterday's average UP closing change by 6, add today's UP closing change, if any, and divide the total by 7. That is your new average UP closing change.

3. Multiply yesterday's average DOWN closing change by 6, add today's DOWN close if any, and divide the total by 7. That is your new average DOWN closing change. Then proceed to step 4 (opposite page).

RSI fluctuates between 0 and 100. When RSI reaches a peak and turns down, it identifies a top. When RSI falls and then turns up, it identifies a bottom. These turns come at different levels in different markets or even in the same market, during bull and bear periods.

Overbought and oversold levels vary from market to market and from year to year. There are no magical levels marking all tops and bottoms. Oversold and overbought signals are like hot and cold readings on a thermometer. The same temperature has a different meaning in summer or in winter.

Horizontal reference lines must cut across the highest peaks and the lowest valleys of RSI. They are often drawn at 30 and 70. Some traders use 40 and 80 levels in bull markets or 20 and 60 in bear markets. Use the 5 percent rule: Draw each line at a level beyond which RSI has spent less than 5 percent of its time in the past 4 to 6 months. Adjust reference lines once every three months.

Mass Psychology

Each price represents the consensus of value of all market participants at the moment of transaction. Closing price reflects the most important consensus of the day because the settlement of traders' accounts depends on it. When the market closes higher, bulls make money and bears lose. When the market closes lower, bears make money and bulls lose.

Most traders in all markets pay more attention to closing prices than to any other prices. In the futures markets, money is transferred from losers' to winners' accounts at the end of each trading day. RSI shows whether bulls or bears are stronger at closing time — the crucial money-counting time in the market.

Trading Rules

RSI gives three types of trading signals. They are, in order of importance, divergences, charting patterns, and the level of RSI.

Bullish and Bearish Divergences

Divergences between RSI and prices give the strongest buy and sell signals. They tend to occur at major tops and bottoms. They show when the trend is weak and ready to reverse (Figure 31-2).

1. Bullish divergences give buy signals. They occur when prices fall to a

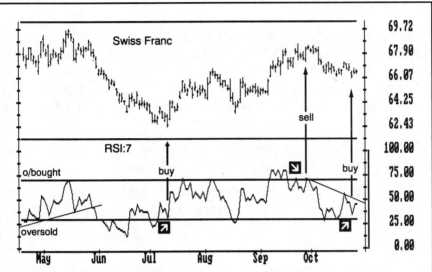

Figure 31-2. Seven-Day Relative Strength Index

RSI gives its best trading signals when it diverges from prices. Its strongest divergences are those in which prices rise to a new high or fall to a new low, while RSI fails to cross its reference line.

RSI tends to break its trendlines ahead of prices. In addition to the ones marked, you can find several other examples on this chart where the breaking of RSI trendlines identifies turning points in the Swiss Franc. At the right edge of the chart, as soon as RSI breaks above its trendline, it will confirm a bullish divergence and give a strong buy signal.

new low but RSI makes a more shallow bottom than during its previous decline. Buy as soon as RSI turns up from its second bottom, and place a protective stop below the latest minor price low. Buy signals are especially strong if the first RSI bottom is below its lower reference line and the second bottom is above that line.

2. Bearish divergences give sell signals. They occur when prices rally to a new peak but RSI makes a lower top than during the previous rally. Sell short as soon as RSI turns down from its second top, and place a protective stop above the latest minor high. Sell signals are especially strong if the first RSI top is above its upper reference line and the second top is below it.

Charting Patterns

Classical charting methods work better with Relative Strength Index than with other indicators. Trendlines, support and resistance, and head-and-shoulders patterns work well with RSI. RSI often completes these patterns a few days in advance of prices, providing hints of likely trend changes. For example, RSI trendlines are usually broken one or two days before price trendlines.

3. When RSI breaks its downtrendline, place an order to buy above the price trendline in order to catch an upside breakout.

4. When RSI breaks its uptrendline, place an order to sell short below the price trendline to catch a downside breakout.

RSI Levels

When RSI rises above its upper reference line, it shows that bulls are strong but the market is overbought and entering its sell zone. When RSI declines below its lower reference line, it shows that bears are strong but the market is oversold and entering its buy zone.

It pays to buy using overbought signals of daily RSI only when the weekly trend is up. It pays to sell short using sell signals of daily RSI only when the weekly trend is down (see Section 43).

5. Buy when RSI declines below its lower reference line and then rallies above it.

6. Sell short when RSI rises above its upper reference line and then crosses below it.

More on RSI

Some traders try to find deeper meaning in RSI patterns. Some analysts have described formations called **positive and negative reversals,** which they said forecasted the extent of any price move using RSI patterns. So far, there have been no reports of conspicuous success using these patterns from anyone but their promoters.

V

The Neglected Essentials

32. VOLUME

Volume represents the activity of traders and investors. Each unit of volume in the market reflects the action of two persons: One trader sells a share and another buys a share, or one buys a contract and another sells a contract. Daily volume is the number of contracts or shares traded in one day.

Traders usually plot volume as a histogram — vertical bars whose height reflects each day's volume (Figure 32-1). They usually draw it underneath prices. Changes in volume show how bulls and bears react to price swings. Changes in volume provide clues as to whether trends are likely to continue or to reverse.

Some traders ignore volume. They think that prices already reflect all information known to the market. They say, "You get paid on price and not on volume." Professionals, on the other hand, know that analyzing volume can help them understand markets deeper and trade better.

There are three ways to measure volume:

1. The actual number of shares or contracts traded. For example, the New York Stock Exchange reports volume this way. This is the most objective way of measuring volume.

2. The number of trades that took place. For example, the London Stock Exchange reports volume this way. This method is less objective because it does not distinguish between a 100-share trade and a 5000-share trade.

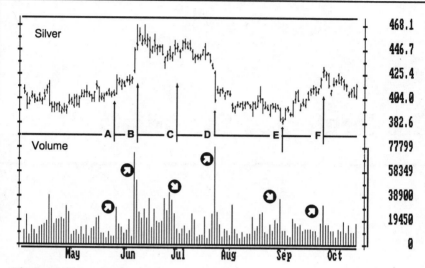

Figure 32–1. Volume

To interpret volume, you need to link its changes with changes in prices:

A. An increase in volume during an uptrend calls for higher prices ahead. Buy or add to longs.
B. Prices jump on more than double the average volume. It is a sign of a potential blow-off move. Tighten stops on long positions.
C. Prices rally near the level of their previous peak, but volume is much lower. This bearish divergence signals a top. Sell longs and go short.
D. Prices collapse on panicky volume. Such climax bottoms are usually retested. Tighten stops on short positions.
E. Silver falls to a new low, but volume is lower than it was at point D–a typical retest of a climax bottom. Cover shorts and go long.
F. A new high in price is accompanied by an increase in volume, similar to what happened at point A. Continue to hold long positions.

3. Tick volume is the number of price changes during a selected time, such as 10 minutes or an hour. It is called tick volume because most changes equal 1 tick. Most futures exchanges in the United States do not report intraday volume, and day-traders use tick volume as its proxy.

Volume reflects the activity of buyers and sellers. If you compare volume between two markets, it will show which one is more active or liquid. You are likely to suffer less slippage in liquid markets than in thin, low-volume markets.

Crowd Psychology

Volume reflects the degree of financial and emotional involvement, as well as pain, of market participants. A trade begins with a financial commitment by two persons. The decision to buy or sell may be rational, but the act of buying or selling creates an emotional commitment in most people. Buyers and sellers crave to be right. They scream at the market, pray, or use lucky talismans. Volume reflects the degree of emotional involvement among traders.

Each tick takes money away from losers and gives it to winners. When prices rise, longs make money and shorts lose. When prices fall, shorts gain and longs lose. Winners feel happy and elated, while losers feel depressed and angry. Whenever prices move, about half the traders are hurting. When prices rise, bears are in pain, and when prices fall, bulls suffer. The greater the increase in volume, the more pain in the market.

Traders react to losses like frogs to hot water. If you throw a frog into a boiling kettle, it will jump in response to sudden pain, but if you put a frog into cool water and heat it slowly, you can boil it alive. If a sudden price change hits traders, they jump from pain and liquidate losing positions. The same losers can be very patient if their losses increase gradually.

You can lose a great deal of money in a sleepy market, such as corn, where a one-cent move costs only $50. If corn goes against you just a few cents a day, the pain is easy to tolerate. If you hang on, those pennies can add up to thousands of dollars in losses. Sharp moves, on the other hand, make losers cut their losses in a panic. Once weak hands get shaken out, the market is ready to reverse. Trends can last for a long time on moderate volume but can expire after a burst of volume.

Who buys from a trader who sells his losing long position? It may be a short seller taking profits and covering shorts. It may be a bargain hunter who steps in because prices are "too low." That bottom-picker assumes the position of a loser who washed out—and he either catches the bottom or becomes the new loser.

Who sells to a trader who buys to cover his losing short position? It may be a savvy investor who takes profits on his long position. It also may be a top-picker who sells short because he thinks that prices are "too high." He assumes the position of a loser who covered his shorts, and only the future will tell whether he is right or wrong.

When shorts give up during a rally, they buy to cover and push the market higher. Prices rise, flush out even more shorts, and the rally feeds on itself. When longs give up during a decline, they sell and push the market lower. Falling prices flush out even more longs, and the decline feeds on itself. Losers who give up propel trends. A trend that moves on steady volume is likely to continue. Steady volume shows that new losers replace those who wash out. Trends need a fresh supply of losers the way builders of the ancient pyramids needed a fresh supply of slaves.

Falling volume shows that the supply of losers is running low and a trend is ready to reverse. It happens after enough losers catch on to how wrong they are. Old losers keep bailing out, but fewer new losers come in. Falling volume gives a sign that the trend is about to reverse.

A burst of extremely high volume also gives a signal that a trend is nearing its end. It shows that masses of losers are bailing out. You can probably recall holding a losing trade longer than you should have. Once the pain becomes intolerable and you get out, the trend reverses and the market goes the way you expected, but without you! This happens time and again because most amateurs react to stress similarly and bail out at about the same time. Professionals do not hang in while the market beats them up. They close out losing trades fast and reverse or wait on the sidelines, ready to re-enter.

Volume usually stays low in trading ranges because there is relatively little pain. People feel comfortable with small price changes, and trendless markets seem to drag on forever. A breakout is often marked by a dramatic increase in volume because losers run for the exits. A breakout on low volume shows little emotional commitment to a new trend. It indicates that prices are likely to return into their trading range.

Rising volume during a rally shows that more buyers and short sellers are pouring in. Buyers are eager to buy even if they have to pay up, and shorts are eager to sell to them. Rising volume shows that losers who leave are being replaced by a new crop of losers.

When volume shrinks during a rally, it shows that bulls are becoming less eager, while bears are no longer running for cover. The intelligent bears have left long ago, followed by weak bears who could not take the pain. Falling volume shows that fuel is being removed from the uptrend and it is ready to reverse.

When volume dries up during a decline, it shows that bears are less eager to sell short, while bulls are no longer running for the exits. The intelligent bulls have sold long ago, and the weak bulls have been shaken out. Falling volume shows that the remaining bulls have a higher level of pain tolerance. Perhaps they have deeper pockets or bought later in the decline, or both. Falling volume identifies an area in which a downtrend is likely to reverse.

This reasoning applies to long and short timeframes. As a rule of thumb, if today's volume is higher than yesterday's volume, then today's trend is likely to continue.

Trading Rules

The terms "high volume" and "low volume" are relative. What is low for IBM is high for Apple Computer, while what is low for gold is high for platinum, and so on. As a rule of thumb, "high volume" for any given market is at least 25 percent above average for the past two weeks, and "low volume" is at least 25 percent below average.

1. High volume confirms trends. If prices rise to a new peak and volume reaches a new high, then prices are likely to retest or exceed that peak.

2. If the market falls to a new low and the volume reaches a new high, that bottom is likely to be retested or exceeded. A "climax bottom" is almost always retested on low volume, offering an excellent buying opportunity.

3. If volume shrinks while a trend continues, that trend is ripe for a reversal. When a market rises to a new peak on lower volume than its previous peak, look for a shorting opportunity. This technique does not work as well at market bottoms because a decline can persist on low volume. There is a saying on Wall Street: "It takes buying to put stocks up, but they can fall of their own weight."

4. Watch volume during reactions against the trend. When an uptrend is punctuated by a decline, volume often picks up in a flurry of profit taking. When the dip continues but volume shrinks, it shows that bulls are no longer running or that selling pressure is spent. When volume dries up, it shows that the reaction is nearing an end and the uptrend is ready to resume. This identifies a good buying opportunity. Major downtrends are often punctuated by rallies which begin on heavy vol-

ume. Once weak bears have been flushed out, volume shrinks and gives a signal to sell short.

More on Volume

You can use **a moving average** to define the trend of volume. The slope of a 5-day exponential moving average of volume can define volume's trend. You can also draw **trendlines** of volume and watch for their breakouts (see Section 21). Volume breakouts confirm price breakouts.

Volume-based indicators provide more precise timing signals than volume alone. Traders' Index, Herrick Payoff Index, Force Index, and others include volume data (see Chapters 6 and 8).

33. VOLUME-BASED INDICATORS

Traders can use several technical indicators to help them analyze volume. Some traders track a 5-day exponential moving average of volume. Its slope identifies the trend of volume (see Sections 25 and 32). Others use On-Balance Volume and Accumulation/Distribution.

On-Balance Volume

On-Balance Volume (OBV) is an indicator designed by Joseph Granville and described in his book, *New Strategy of Daily Stock Market Timing*. Granville used OBV as a leading indicator of the stock market, but other analysts have applied it to the futures markets.

OBV is a running total of volume. It rises or falls each day, depending on whether prices close higher or lower than on the previous day. When a stock closes higher, it shows that bulls won the day's battle; its volume on that day is added to OBV. When a stock closes lower, it shows that bears won the day, and that day's volume is subtracted from OBV. If prices close unchanged, OBV stays unchanged.

On-Balance Volume often rises or falls before prices — it acts as a leading indicator. As Granville put it, "Volume is the steam that makes the choo-choo go."

Crowd Psychology

Prices represent the consensus of value, while volume represents the emotions of market participants. It reflects the intensity of traders' financial and emotional commitments, as well as pain among losers (see Section 32). OBV is a running total of volume. It tracks changes in traders' involvement in the market and the intensity of their pain.

A new high in OBV shows that bulls are powerful, bears are hurting, and prices are likely to rise. A new low in OBV shows that bears are powerful, bulls are hurting, and prices are likely to fall. When the pattern of OBV deviates from the pattern of prices, it shows that mass emotions are not in gear with mass consensus. A crowd is more likely to follow its heart than its mind. This is why changes in volume often precede changes in prices.

Trading Signals

The patterns of OBV tops and bottoms are more important than the absolute levels of this indicator. Those levels depend on when you start to calculate On-Balance Volume. When OBV rises or falls together with prices, the trend is confirmed. If prices reach a new high and OBV reaches a new high, the uptrend is likely to continue. If prices reach a new low and OBV falls to a new low, the downtrend is likely to continue. It is safer to trade in the direction of a trend that is confirmed by OBV (Figure 33-1).

1. When OBV reaches a new high, it confirms the power of bulls, indicates that prices are likely to rise even higher, and gives a buy signal. When OBV reaches a new low, it confirms the power of bears, calls for lower prices ahead, and gives a signal to sell short.

2. OBV gives its strongest buy and sell signals when it diverges from prices. If prices rally, sell off, and then rise to a new high, but OBV rallies to a lower high, it creates a bearish divergence and gives a strong sell signal. If prices decline, rebound, and then fall to a new low, but OBV falls to a more shallow bottom, it traces a bullish divergence and gives a buy signal. Long-term divergences are more important than short-term divergences. Divergences that develop over the course of several weeks give stronger signals than those that last only a few days.

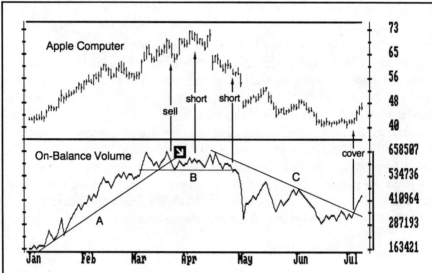

Figure 33–1.   On-Balance Volume

When OBV moves in gear with a trading vehicle, it confirms its trend. The uptrend A of OBV confirms the stock rally. Its break in March gives a sell signal. There are two shorting signals at the top. The first, in early April, is given by a bearish divergence between OBV and price. Two weeks later, OBV breaks its support B, giving another signal to sell short. The downtrendline C of OBV confirms the slide of Apple Computer–hold shorts. An upside breakout in July gives a signal to cover shorts.

   3. When prices are in a trading range and OBV breaks out to a new high, it gives a buy signal. When prices are in a trading range and OBV breaks down and falls to a new low, it gives a signal to sell short.

More on OBV

One of the reasons for Granville's success in his heyday (see Section 6) was that he combined OBV with two other indicators – the **Net Field Trend indicator** and the **Climax indicator**. Granville calculated OBV for each stock in the Dow Jones Industrial Average and rated its OBV pattern as rising, falling, or neutral. He called that a Net Field Trend of a stock: It could be +1, –1, or 0. Climax indicator was a sum of the Net Field Trends of all 30 Dow stocks.

When the stock market rallied and the Climax indicator reached a new high, it confirmed strength and gave a buy signal. If the stock market rallied but the Climax indicator made a lower top, it gave a sell signal.

You can view the Dow Jones Industrial Average as a team of 30 horses pulling the market wagon. The Climax indicator shows how many horses are pulling uphill, downhill, or standing still. If 24 out of 30 horses pull up, 1 down and 5 are resting, then the market wagon is likely to move up. If 9 horses pull up, 7 pull down, and 14 are resting, then the wagon is ready to roll downhill.

OBV, the Net Field Trend indicator, and the Climax indicator can be easily programmed on a computer. It would be worthwhile to apply them to a database which includes all stocks of the S&P 500 index. That may produce good signals for trading S&P 500 futures or options.

Accumulation/Distribution

This indicator was developed by Larry Williams and described in his 1972 book, *How I Made a Million Dollars.* It was designed as a leading indicator for stocks, but several analysts have applied it to futures. The unique feature of Accumulation/Distribution (A/D) is that it tracks the relationship between opening and closing prices, along with volume.

If prices close higher than they opened, then bulls won the day and A/D is positive. If prices close lower than they opened, then the bears won and A/D is negative. If prices close where they opened, then nobody won and A/D is zero. A running total of each day's A/D creates a cumulative Accumulation/Distribution indicator.

A/D credits bulls or bears with only a fraction of each day's volume. That fraction depends on the day's range and the distance from opening to closing price. The greater the spread between opening and closing price relative to daily range, the greater the change in Accumulation/Distribution.

$$A/D = \frac{\text{Close} - \text{Open}}{\text{High} - \text{Low}} \cdot \text{Volume}$$

For example, if the distance from today's high to low is 5 points but the distance from the open to the close is 2 points, then only 2/5 of today's volume is credited to the winning camp. The pattern of A/D highs and lows is more important than its absolute level, which depends on the starting date.

When the market rises, most people focus on new highs. But if prices open higher and close lower, then A/D, which tracks their relationship, turns down. It warns that the uptrend is weaker than it appears. If A/D ticks up while prices are down, it shows that bulls are gaining strength.

Crowd Behavior

Opening and closing prices are among the most important prices of the day. The opening price reflects all the pressures that have gathered while the market was closed. Openings are often dominated by amateurs who read their newspapers in the evening and trade in the morning.

Professional traders are active throughout the day. They often trade against the amateurs. As the day goes on, waves of buying and selling by amateurs and slow-moving institutions gradually subside. Professionals usually dominate the markets at closing time. Closing prices are especially important because the settlement of trading accounts depends on them.

A/D tracks the outcomes of daily battles between amateurs and professionals. It ticks up when prices close higher than they opened—when professionals are more bullish than amateurs. It ticks down when prices close lower than they opened—when professionals are more bearish than amateurs. It pays to bet with the professionals and against the amateurs.

Trading Rules

When the market opens low and closes high, it moves from weakness to strength. A/D then rises and shows that market professionals are more bullish than amateurs. This means that the market is likely to move higher the following day. When A/D falls, it shows that market professionals are more bearish than amateurs. When the market moves from strength to weakness, it is likely to reach a lower low the following day.

The best trading signals are given by divergences between A/D and prices.

1. If prices rally to a new high but A/D reaches a lower peak, it gives a signal to sell short. This bearish divergence shows that market professionals are selling into the rally (Figure 33-2).

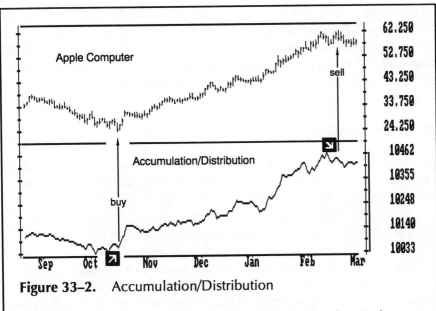

Figure 33–2. Accumulation/Distribution

Accumulation/Distribution gives its strongest signals when it diverges from prices. A bullish divergence gives a buy signal at the October bottom. Four months later and $30 higher, a bearish divergence gives a sell signal. Take profits on long positions and go short.

2. A bullish divergence occurs when prices fall to a new low but A/D stops at a higher low than during its previous decline. It shows that market professionals are using the decline for buying, and a rally is coming.

More on Accumulation/Distribution

When you go long or short, following a divergence between A/D and price, remember that even market professionals can go wrong. Use stops and protect yourself by following the **Hound of the Baskervilles** rule (see Section 23).

Volume Accumulator, designed by Marc Chaikin, is an indicator very similar to A/D. Volume Accumulator uses a mean price for the day instead of the opening price. It is especially useful for those analysts who do not have access to opening prices. Its trading signals and rules are similar to Accumulation/Distribution.

There are important parallels between A/D and Japanese **Candlestick charts**. Both focus on the differences between opening and closing prices. A/D goes further than candlesticks by taking volume into account.

34. OPEN INTEREST

Open interest is the number of contracts held by buyers or owed by short sellers in a given market on a given day. It shows the number of existing contracts. Open interest equals either a total long or a total short position.

Stock market shares are traded for as long as a company stays in business as a separate unit. Futures and options traders, on the other hand, deal in contracts for a future delivery that expire at a set time.

A futures or options buyer who wants to accept delivery and a seller who wants to deliver have to wait until the first notice day. This waiting period ensures that the numbers of contracts that are long and short are always equal.

In any case, very few futures and options traders plan to deliver or to accept delivery. Most traders close out their positions before the first notice day.

Open interest rises or falls depending on whether new traders enter the market or old traders exit it. Open interest rises only when a new buyer and a new seller enter the market. Their trade creates a new contract. For example, if open interest in April COMEX gold is 8500 contracts, then 8500 contracts are held by bulls and 8500 contracts are owed by short sellers at the close of that day. If open interest rises to 8600, it means that the net of 100 new contracts have been bought and sold short.

Open interest falls when a trader who is long trades with someone who is short. When both of them close out their positions, open interest falls by one contract because one contract disappears. If a new bull buys from an old bull who is getting out of his long position, open interest remains unchanged. Open interest also does not change when a new bear sells to an old bear who needs to buy because he is closing out his short position.

Buyer	Seller	Open Interest
New buyer	New seller	Increases
New buyer	Former buyer sells	Unchanged
Former seller buys to cover	New seller	Unchanged
Former seller buys to cover	Former buyer sells	Decreases

Most futures and options exchanges release open interest data one day later than prices. Some exchanges provide phone numbers to call for preliminary figures on open interest.

Technicians usually plot open interest as a line below price bars (Figure 34-1). Some chart services also plot average open interest for the past several years. Open interest gives important messages when it deviates from its seasonal norm. Open interest varies from season to season in many markets because of massive hedging by commercial interests at different stages in production cycles.

Open interest in currency futures tends to drop four times a year, at the time of a contract rollover. If open interest does not drop during a rollover, it shows a strong commitment among traders to the existing trend, which is likely to accelerate.

Crowd Psychology

It takes one bull and one bear to create a futures or options contract. A bull buys a contract if he is convinced that prices are going higher. A bear sells short a contract if he is convinced that prices are going lower. When the two trade, open interest rises by one contract. A single trade between one bull and one bear is unlikely to move the markets. But when thousands of traders make their trades, they propel or reverse market trends.

Open interest reflects the intensity of conflict between bulls and bears. It reflects the willingness of longs to maintain long positions and the willingness of shorts to maintain short positions. When bulls and bears do not expect the market to move in their favor, they close out their positions and open interest shrinks.

There are two people on opposite sides of every trade. One of them gets hurt when prices change. If prices rally, bears get hurt. If prices fall, bulls get hurt. As long as the losers hope, they hang on, and open interest does not change.

A rise in open interest shows that a crowd of confident bulls is facing down a crowd of equally confident bears. It points to a growing disagreement between the two camps. One group is sure to lose, but as long as potential losers keep pouring in, the trend will continue. These ideas have been clearly put forth in L. Dee Belveal's classic book, *Charting Commodity Market Price Behavior.*

Bulls and bears keep adding to their positions as long as they strongly dis-

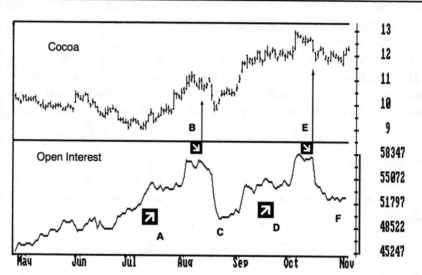

Figure 34–1. Open Interest

Open interest (OI) reflects the number of all short or long positions in any futures or options market. Open interest depends on the intensity of conflict between bulls and bears.

Rising OI shows that the conflict between bulls and bears is becoming more intense and confirms the existing trend. Rising OI during uptrends shows it is safe to add to long positions (A and D). Flat OI shows that fewer losers are entering the market. This means that a mature trend is nearing its end and it is time to take profits or tighten stops (B and E). Falling OI shows that losers are leaving the market and winners are cashing in–that a trend is nearing its end. A fire cannot continue when fuel is withdrawn, and a sharp drop in OI during a trend signals that a reversal is near (C and F).

At the right edge of the chart, cocoa prices have stabilized after falling in October and open interest is flat. It shows that the decline in cocoa has shaken out weak bulls and the uptrend is ready to resume. It is time to go long, with a protective stop below the recent lows.

agree about the future course of prices. It takes conviction and disagreement to maintain a trend. Rising open interest shows that the supply of losers is growing and the current trend is likely to persist. If open interest increases during an uptrend, it shows that longs are buying while bears are shorting because they believe that the market is too high. They are likely to run for cover when the uptrend puts a squeeze on them — and their buying will propel prices higher.

If open interest rises during a downtrend, it shows that shorts are aggressively selling while bottom-pickers are buying. Those bargain hunters are likely to bail out when falling prices hurt them, and their selling will push prices even lower. An increase in open interest gives a green light to the existing trend.

When a bull is convinced that prices are going higher and decides to buy, but a bear is afraid to sell short, that bull can buy only from another bull who bought earlier and now wants to get out. Their trade creates no new contract, and open interest stays unchanged. When open interest stays flat during a rally, it shows that the supply of losers has stopped growing.

When a bear is convinced that prices are going lower, he wants to sell short. If a bull is afraid to buy from him, that bear can only sell to another bear who shorted earlier and now wants to cover and leave. Their trade creates no new contract, and open interest does not change. When open interest stays flat during a decline, it shows that the supply of bottom-pickers is not growing. Whenever open interest flattens out, it flashes a yellow light — a warning that the trend is aging and the best gains are probably behind.

Falling open interest shows that losers are bailing out while winners are taking profits. When their disagreement decreases, the trend is ripe for a reversal. Open interest falls when losers abandon hope and get out of the market without being replaced by new losers. When a bull decides to get out of his long position and a bear decides to cover his short position, the two may trade with one another. When they do, a contract disappears, and open interest shrinks by one contract. Falling open interest shows that winners are cashing in and losers are giving up hope. It flashes a red light — it signals the end of a trend.

Trading Rules

A 10 percent change in open interest deserves serious attention, while a 25 percent change often gives major trading messages. The meaning of rising, falling, or flat open interest depends on whether prices are rallying, falling, or flat at the time of change in open interest.

1. When open interest rises during a rally, it confirms the uptrend and gives a signal that it is safe to add to long positions. It shows that more

short sellers are coming into the market. When they bail out, their short covering is likely to push the rally higher.

2. When open interest rises while prices fall, it shows that bottom-pickers are active in the market. It is safe to sell short because these bargain hunters are likely to push prices lower when they throw in the towel.

3. When open interest rises while prices are in a trading range, it is a bearish sign. Commercial hedgers are more likely to sell short than speculators. A sharp increase in open interest while prices are flat shows that savvy hedgers are probably shorting the market.

4. When open interest falls sharply while prices are in a trading range, it identifies short covering by major commercial interests and gives a buy signal. When commercials start covering shorts, they show that they expect the market to rise.

5. When open interest falls during a rally, it shows that both winners and losers are getting "cold feet." Longs are taking their profits, and shorts are covering. Markets discount the future, and a trend that is accepted by the majority is ready to reverse. If open interest falls during a rally, sell and get ready to sell short.

6. When open interest falls during a decline, it shows that shorts are covering and buyers are taking their losses and bailing out. If open interest falls during a slide, cover shorts and get ready to buy.

7. When open interest goes flat during a rally, it warns that the uptrend is getting old and the best gains have already been made. This gives you a signal to tighten stops on long positions and avoid new buying. When open interest goes flat during a decline, it warns you that the downtrend is mature and it is best to tighten stops on short positions. Flat open interest in a trading range does not contribute any new information.

More on Open Interest

The higher the open interest, the more active the market, and the less **slippage** you risk while getting in and out of positions. Short-term traders should focus on the markets with the highest open interest. In the futures markets, it pays to trade the delivery months with the highest open interest.

Tracking **Commitments of Traders** reports can help you find out whether new buying or selling is primarily done by small or large speculators or by hedgers (see Chapter 7).

Very few technical indicators use open interest. The **Herrick Payoff Index** is the best-known indicator that utilizes it.

35. HERRICK PAYOFF INDEX

The Herrick Payoff Index (HPI) is an indicator developed by John Herrick, a technical market analyst from California. He taught it privately, but the indicator became more popular after it was included in CompuTrac software in the early 1980s.

The Herrick Payoff Index helps detect accumulation and distribution. Most indicators measure only prices, some measure volume, but HPI tracks open interest as well as prices and volume. HPI confirms valid trends and helps catch their reversals.

How to Construct HPI

The Herrick Payoff Index may be calculated using several types of daily data. You may use a single contract with its own price, volume, and open interest. It is more practical to combine volume and open interest from all contracts and apply them to the prices of the most active delivery month.

HPI uses daily high and low prices, volume, and open interest. It requires data for at least three weeks before it begins producing meaningful numbers. Its complex formula makes using a computer almost a necessity (see worksheet, Figure 35-1).

$$\text{HPI} = K_y + (K' - K_y)$$

where K_y = yesterday's HPI.

$$K = [(M - M_y) \cdot C \cdot V] \cdot [1 \pm \{(I \cdot 2)/G\}]$$

and M = mean price — i.e., (High + Low)/2.

   M_y = yesterday's mean price.

   C = the value of a 1-cent move (or use the same constant for all contracts).

   V = volume.

Copper

Date	High	Low	Close	Vol.	OI	Mean	HPI
12/27	106.80	104.58	104.65	4552	30343	105.69	
12/28	105.19	104.11	105.13	3208	30195	104.65	
12/29	105.50	104.57	105.43	1770	29987	105.04	-29.0
1/02	105.17	103.60	104.97	4146	30249	104.38	-28.8
1/03	108.17	105.61	108.02	9940	30028	106.89	-0.6
1/04	109.09	105.96	106.51	10036	28944	107.52	6.3
1/05	107.97	107.03	107.55	4262	29015	107.50	5.5
1/08	109.46	108.01	109.15	8030	30125	108.74	15.6
1/09	110.00	108.00	108.05	6107	30162	109.00	15.7
1/10	108.00	105.86	106.16	5841	29814	106.93	2.3
1/11	107.41	106.52	107.17	3033	29996	106.96	2.2
1/12	105.77	103.71	104.20	9053	30850	104.74	-17.1

Figure 35–1. Herrick Payoff Index Worksheet

HPI measures changes in prices, volume, and open interest. It is based on mean rather than closing prices–the average consensus of value for the day. The complexity of HPI makes using a computer almost a necessity.

I = absolute value of today's minus yesterday's open interest.

G = today's or yesterday's open interest, whichever is less.

The "+" or "–" sign in the right brackets is determined as follows: If $M > My$, the sign is "+"; if $M < My$, the sign is "–".

Traders can apply HPI only to daily data and not to weekly or intraday data. There is no such thing as weekly open interest. Weekly volume can be obtained by adding up daily volume for five days, but open interest cannot be added up.

Crowd Psychology

The Herrick Payoff Index measures mean prices rather than closing prices. Daily mean prices represent the average consensus of value for the day.

Volume represents the degree of financial commitment in a given market. When volume increases, the absolute value of HPI for that day increases.

Daily changes in open interest represent the flow of funds into and out of the market. Rising open interest is bullish in an uptrend and bearish in a downtrend. Falling open interest is bearish in an uptrend and bullish in a downtrend. Flat open interest is essentially neutral.

Trading Rules

The Herrick Payoff Index gives several types of trading signals, listed here in the order of importance. Divergences between HPI and prices identify some of the best trading opportunities (Figure 35-2). When HPI breaks its trendline, it gives an early warning that a price trendline is likely to be broken. When HPI crosses its centerline, it confirms new price trends.

1. When prices fall to a new low but HPI makes a higher bottom than during the previous decline, it creates a bullish divergence and gives a buy signal. When HPI turns up from its second bottom, buy and place a protective stop below the latest price low.

2. A bearish divergence occurs when prices rally to a new high but HPI makes a lower top. The signal to sell short is flashed when HPI turns down from its second top. Place a protective stop above the latest high price.

Important divergences develop over the course of several weeks. A divergence that takes two months to develop is more powerful than the one in which two weeks passed between the tops or bottoms. Pay attention to the differences in the height of the adjacent HPI tops or bottoms. If the first top or bottom is far away from the centerline and the second top or bottom is near that line, that divergence is likely to lead to a greater move.

Bullish and bearish divergences of HPI often have long lead times. Once you have identified a potential turning point using an HPI divergence, lean on short-term oscillators for more precise timing. If a divergence between HPI and price aborts, and you get stopped out, watch closely — you may get an even better trading opportunity if a regular divergence turns into a triple bullish or triple bearish divergence. Triple bullish divergences consist of three lower bottoms in prices and three higher bottoms in HPI. Triple bearish divergences consist of three higher tops in prices and three lower tops in HPI. They occur at some of the major turning points in the markets.

3. HPI lends itself well to classical charting methods, especially trendlines. When trendlines of prices and HPI point in the same direction,

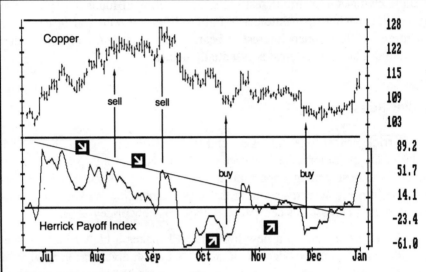

Figure 35–2.   Herrick Payoff Index

HPI tracks the flow of funds into or out of the market by measuring changes in prices, volume, and open interest. HPI gives its best signals when its patterns diverge from price patterns. HPI identified market tops in August and September by tracing lower peaks while prices rose to new highs. HPI called market bottoms in October and November when it stopped declining and bottomed out at more shallow levels while copper slid to new lows.

The bullish divergence in November was followed by a breaking of a downtrendline of HPI and a rally above HPI's centerline. This combination gave an especially strong signal to buy copper. The best signals develop slowly and give traders plenty of time to get aboard a new trend.

they confirm trends. HPI often breaks its trendline before prices break theirs. When HPI breaks below its uptrend, it gives a sell signal. When it breaks above a downtrend, it gives a buy signal. Then it pays to either take profits or to tighten stops.

4. The position of HPI above or below its centerline shows whether bulls or bears dominate the market. When HPI is above its centerline, it shows that bulls are in control—it is better to be long. When HPI is below its centerline, it is better to be short. Bulls may buy or add to

their long positions when HPI rises above its centerline. When HPI declines below its centerline, it confirms downtrends.

36. TIME

Most people conduct their lives as if they intend to live forever — with no review of the past, no real planning for the future, and minimal learning from past mistakes. Freud showed that the unconscious mind does not have a notion of time. Our deep-seated wishes remain largely unchanged throughout life.

When people join crowds, their behavior becomes even more primitive and impulsive than when they are alone. Crowds pay no attention to time even though they are affected by its passage. Individuals are ruled by the calendar and the clock, but crowds have no notion of time. Crowds act out their emotions as if they had all the time in the world.

Most traders focus only on changes in prices and pay little attention to time. This is just another sign of being caught up in mass mentality.

The awareness of time is a sign of civilization. A thinking person is aware of time, while someone who is acting impulsively is not. A market analyst who pays attention to time is aware of a dimension hidden from the market crowd.

Cycles

Long-term price cycles are a fact of economic life. For example, the U.S. stock market tends to run in four-year cycles. They exist because the ruling party inflates the economy going into the presidential election once every four years. The party that wins the election deflates the economy when voters cannot take revenge at the polls. Flooding the economy with liquidity lifts the stock market, and draining liquidity pushes it down. This is why the 2 years before a presidential election tend to be bullish, and the first 12 to 18 months following an election tend to be bearish.

Major cycles in agricultural commodities are due to fundamental production factors, coupled with the mass psychology of producers. For example, when livestock prices rise, farmers breed more animals. When those animals reach the market, prices fall and producers cut back. When the supply is absorbed, scarcity pushes prices up, breeders go to work again, and the bull/bear cycle repeats. This cycle is shorter in hogs than in cattle because pigs breed faster than cows.

Long-term cycles can help traders identify market tides. Instead, most traders get themselves in trouble by trying to use short-term cycles for precision timing and predicting minor turning points.

Price peaks and valleys on the charts often seem to follow in an orderly manner. Traders reach for a pencil and a ruler, measure distances between neighboring peaks, and project them into the future to forecast the next top. Then they measure distances between recent bottoms and extend them into the future to forecast the next low.

Cycles put bread and butter on the tables of several experts who sell services forecasting highs and lows. Few of them realize that what appears like a cycle on the charts is often a figment of the imagination. If you analyze price data using a mathematically rigorous program such as John Ehlers' MESA (Maximum Entropy Spectral Analysis), you will see that approximately 80 percent of what appears like cycles is simply market noise. A human mind needs to find order in chaos—and an illusion of order is better than no order for most people.

If you look at any river from the air, it appears to have cycles, swinging right and left. Every river meanders in its valley because water flows faster in its middle than near the shores, creating turbulences that force the river to turn.

Looking for market cycles with a ruler and a pencil is like searching for water with a divining rod. Profits from an occasional success are erased by many losses due to unsound methods. If you are serious about trading with cycles, you need a mathematical method for finding them, such as MESA or Fourier analysis.

Fourier analysis searches for cycles in very large data samples, but MESA takes a different tack. It searches for evidence of orderly cyclical movement in a relatively short data window (Figure 36-1). Unlike other packages, which give nonstop trading signals, MESA tells traders that no valid cycles are present about 80 percent of the time. It aims to recognize cycles as they emerge from market noise and tells you when a cycle begins to fade.

Indicator Seasons

A farmer sows in spring, harvests in late summer, and uses the fall to get ready for winter. There is a time to sow and a time to reap, a time to bet on a warm trend and a time to get ready for a cold spell. The concept of seasons

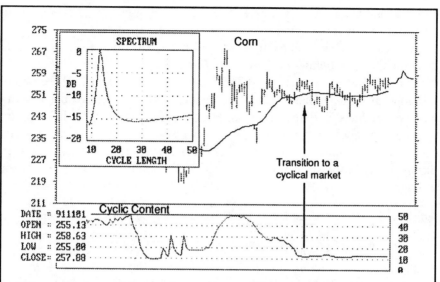

Figure 36–1. Price Cycles–Maximum Entropy Spectral Analysis (MESA)

MESA (a method and a software package) shows that cycles are prone to shift and disappear. The narrow window at the bottom of the chart keeps track of cyclic content. When it is near its upper edge it shows that the market is chaotic, and when it nears its lower edge it shows that the market is cycling. A vertical arrow marks a transition from a chaotic to a cyclical market.

The square window in the upper left corner shows cyclic content for any date selected by the analyst. It currently shows that a 13-day cycle is rising above the market noise. The jagged line at the right edge of the chart projects the current cycle several days into the future.

can be applied to the financial markets. A trader can use a farmer's approach. He should look to buy in spring, sell in summer, go short in the fall, and cover in winter.

Martin Pring developed the model of seasons for prices, but this concept works even better with technical indicators. Indicator seasons show you where you are in the market cycle. This simple but effective concept helps you buy when prices are low and sell short when they are high. It tells you when an indicator signal is likely to be strong or weak. It helps you stand apart from the market crowd.

The season of any indicator is defined by two factors: its slope and its position above or below the centerline. For example, we can apply the concept of indicator seasons to MACD-Histogram (see Section 26). We define the slope of MACD-Histogram as the relationship between two neighboring bars. When MACD-Histogram rises from below its centerline, it is spring; when it rises above its centerline, it is summer; when it falls from above its centerline, it is autumn; and when it falls below its centerline, it is winter. Spring is the best season for going long, and autumn is the best season for selling short (Figure 36-2).

Indicator Slope	Position Relative to Centerline	Season	Action
Rising	Below	Spring	Go long
Rising	Above	Summer	Start selling
Falling	Above	Fall	Go short
Falling	Below	Winter	Start covering

When MACD-Histogram is below its centerline but its slope is rising, it is spring in the market. The weather is cool but turning warmer. Most traders expect the winter to return and are afraid to buy. Emotionally, it is hard to buy because the memories of a downtrend are still fresh. In fact, spring is the best time for buying, with the highest profit potential. Risk is low because a protective stop can be placed slightly below the market.

When MACD rises above its centerline, it is summer in the market—and most traders recognize the uptrend. It is emotionally easy to buy in summer because bulls have plenty of company. In fact, profit potential in summer is lower than in spring and risks are higher because stops have to be farther away from the market.

When MACD-Histogram is above its centerline but its slope turns down, it is autumn in the market. Few traders recognize the change and they keep buying, expecting summer to return. Emotionally, it is hard to sell short in autumn—it requires you to stand apart from the crowd, which is still bullish. In fact, autumn is the best time for selling short. The profit potential is high, while risks can be limited by placing a stop above the recent highs or using options.

When MACD-Histogram falls below its centerline, it is winter in the market. By then, most traders recognize the downtrend. It is emotionally easy to sell short in winter, joining many vocal bears. In fact, the risk/reward ratio is rapidly shifting against bears. Potential rewards are getting smaller and risks are high because stops have to be placed relatively far away from prices.

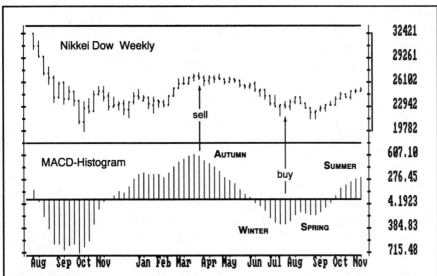

Figure 36-2.   Indicator Seasons

The concept of seasons can be applied to almost any indicator, even though this example focuses on the weekly MACD-Histogram. It helps you trade in gear with the markets.

Autumn–the indicator is above its centerline but falling. This is the best season for establishing short positions.

Winter–the indicator drops below its centerline. Use weakness to take profits on short positions.

Spring–the indicator turns up from below its centerline. It is the best time to establish long positions. Notice "a cold spell" in spring when prices fell to a new low and MACD-Histogram ticked down temporarily. Do not sell short when MACD-Histogram turns down from below its centerline. Do not buy when it turns up from above its centerline. A bullish divergence when prices fall to a new low while the indicator makes a more shallow bottom gives a powerful buy signal.

Summer–the indicator rises above its centerline. When the weather gets hot, use strength to take profits on long positions.

Just as a farmer pays attention to the vagaries of weather, a trader needs to pay attention to the vagaries of the markets. An autumn on the farm can be interrupted by an Indian summer, and a market can stage a strong rally in autumn. A sudden freeze can hit the fields in spring, and the market can drop early in a bull move. A trader needs to use his judgment and apply several indicators and techniques to avoid getting whipsawed (see Section 43).

The concept of indicator seasons focuses a trader's attention on the passage of time in the market. It helps you plan for the season ahead instead of jumping in response to other people's actions.

Retracements

Many traders watch price retracements. For example, if a market rallies 120 points, traders try to add to long positions when the market retraces 50 percent of the preceding move and declines 60 points from the top.

Many floor traders look for a trend to reverse after it retraces 61.8 percent of the previous move. This number is based on the Fibonacci number series.

This idea of measuring retracements can also be applied to time. It pays to measure how long each rally and decline have lasted. For example, rallies in a bull market are often interrupted by declines that last approximately half as long as the preceding rallies. If you discover that rallies tend to last 8 days and declines 5 days, that knowledge encourages you to look for a buying opportunity 4 days into a decline.

The Factor of Five

Analysts often feel confused when they look at charts in different timeframes and see that the market is going in several directions at once. The trend may be up on the daily charts but down on the weeklies, and vice versa. Which of these trends will you follow? This becomes even more complex if you look at intraday charts. Most traders pick one timeframe and close their eyes to others — until a sudden move outside of "their" timeframe hits them.

The factor of 5 links all timeframes. If you start with monthly charts and proceed to the weeklies, you will notice that there are 4.5 weeks to a month. As you switch to daily charts, you will see 5 trading days to a week. As your timeframe narrows, you will look at hourly charts — and there are approximately 5–6 hours to a trading day. Day-traders can proceed even further and look at 10-minute charts, followed by 2-minute charts. All are related by the factor of 5.

The proper way to analyze any market is to analyze it in at least two time-frames. They should be related by the factor of 5. When you analyze the market in two timeframes, the shorter of them has to be five times shorter than the longer one. If you want to analyze daily charts, you must first examine weekly charts, and if you want to day-trade using 10-minute charts, you first need to analyze hourly charts. This is one of the key principles of the Triple Screen trading system (see Section 43).

VI

Stock Market Indicators

---

37. NEW HIGH–NEW LOW INDEX

Stock and futures traders used to live like two separate tribes. They traded different markets and used different analytic tools. The wall between them began to crumble after stock index futures were created in 1982. Both tribes rushed to trade them. An astute trader owes it to himself to master the tools of both tribes.

Shrewd stock traders use Stochastic, moving averages, and other tools of futures analysts. Futures and options traders can time their stock index trades better by using stock market indicators. They include the New High–New Low Index (probably the best leading indicator of the stock market), the Traders' Index (TRIN), and several others.

How to Construct NH-NL

The New High–New Low Index (NH-NL) tracks the numbers of market leaders. It measures the number of stocks that have reached new highs or lows for the year on any given day. The stocks on the list of new highs are the leaders in strength, and the stocks on the list of new lows are the leaders in weakness. NH-NL confirms trends when it rallies or falls in gear with prices. It identifies tops and bottoms in the stock market when it diverges from prices.

The New High–New Low Index measures daily differences between new

194

highs and new lows. The New High–New Low Index is easy to calculate by hand, using information from the Market Diary section of most major newspapers.

NH-NL = New Highs – New Lows

New highs and new lows are reported by most data services in the United States. Make sure that your data vendor calculates new highs and lows over a 52-week period. Some use the ancient "calendar method" and calculate new highs and lows going back only to January.

Plot the New High–New Low Index as a histogram, with a horizontal reference line at zero level. On the days when there are more new highs than new lows, NH-NL is positive and plotted above the centerline. On the days when there are more new lows than new highs, NH-NL is negative and plotted below the centerline. If the numbers of new highs and new lows are equal, NH-NL is zero.

Crowd Psychology

A stock appears on the list of new highs when it is the strongest it has been in a year. This shows that a herd of eager bulls is chasing its shares. A stock appears on the list of new lows when it is the weakest it has been in a year. This shows that a crowd of aggressive bears is dumping its shares.

The New High–New Low Index tracks the strongest and the weakest stocks on the exchange and compares their numbers. It measures the balance of power between the leaders in strength and the leaders in weakness. This is why NH-NL is a leading indicator of the stock market. The broad indexes, such as the S&P 500, tend to follow the trend of NH-NL (Figure 37-1).

You can visualize the 2000 stocks on the New York Stock Exchange as a regiment of 2000 men. If each stock is a soldier, then new highs and new lows are the officers. New highs are the officers who lead the attack up a hill, and new lows are the officers who are deserting and running downhill. There are no bad soldiers, only bad officers, say the military experts. The New High–New Low Index shows whether more officers lead the attack uphill or run downhill.

When NH-NL rises above its centerline, it shows that bullish leadership is stronger. When NH-NL falls below its centerline, it shows that bearish leadership is stronger. If the market rallies to a new high and NH-NL rises to a new peak, it shows that bullish leadership is growing and the uptrend is likely to

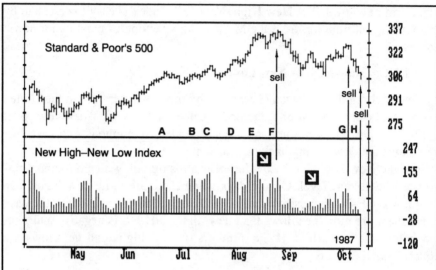

Figure 37–1.   New High–New Low Index

Stocks making new highs for the year are the leaders in strength, and stocks making new lows are the leaders in weakness. NH-NL measures the direction and intensity of market leadership by comparing the number of new highs and new lows.

In the summer of 1987, mass bullishness rose to a high pitch, as the bull market roared into its final peak. It was safe to hold stocks as long as each new high in the stock market was confirmed by a new peak in the New High–New Low Index (A, B, C, D, and E). The August peak in the stock market was accompanied by a bearish divergence (E–F) in the NH-NL Index, giving a sell signal.

When the stock market declined in September, many traders went bargain hunting. Five years of rising prices had trained them to use declines for buying. NH-NL, meanwhile, pointed to a severe weakness. It peaked out at only 100 (G), indicating weakness. NH-NL turned negative in October (H). It gave repeated sell signals in advance of the historic crash.

continue. If the market rallies but NH-NL shrinks, it shows that the uptrend is in trouble. A regiment whose officers are deserting is likely to turn and run.

A new low in NH-NL shows that the downtrend is likely to persist. If officers are running faster than men, the regiment is likely to be routed. If stocks fall but NH-NL turns up, it shows that officers are no longer running.

When officers regain their morale, the whole regiment is likely to rally (Figures 37-2 and 37-3).

Trading Rules

Traders need to pay attention to three aspects of NH-NL, listed here in the order of their importance: divergences between the peaks and bottoms of NH-NL and prices, the trend of NH-NL, and the level of NH-NL above or below its centerline.

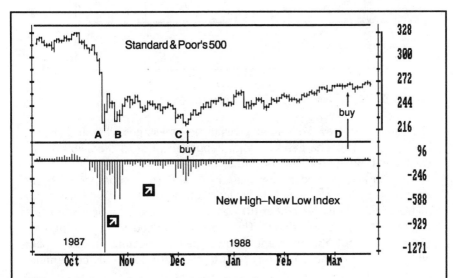

Figure 37–2. New High–New Low Index

The stock market crashed in October 1987, and the number of new lows exploded, reaching nearly 1300 (A). The stock market bounced ("a dead cat bounce") and fell back to its lows (B). The newspapers were filled with alarmist articles, wondering whether this was the end of the Western financial system as we knew it. NH-NL flashed a much more optimistic message. It showed that new lows were shrinking–the officers were refusing to run. The market retested its lows in December (C), and NH-NL traced an even stronger bullish divergence, giving a buy signal. It was confirmed when NH-NL crossed into positive territory (D). This was the beginning of a 2-year bull market.

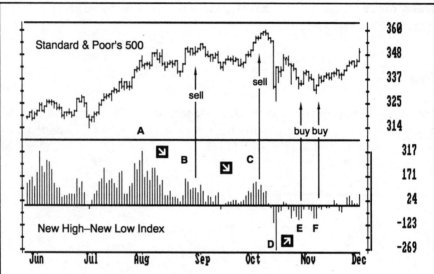

Figure 37–3.   New High–New Low Index

The New High–New Low Index gives its best messages when it diverges from prices. This chart shows what happened prior to the 1989 mini-crash and how the recovery began.

The market reached a new peak in August (A), accompanied by a new peak in NH-NL, which indicated that the market was likely to go higher. The rally in September (B) was accompanied by a bearish divergence that gave a sell signal. The market struggled to a new high in October (C), but NH-NL made a lower peak, repeating its sell signal. NH-NL turned negative one day prior to the crash, forcefully confirming its sell signal.

The October low (D) was followed by a reflex rally ("a dead cat bounce"), and then prices twice retested their October lows (E, F). On both occasions, NH-NL made more shallow bottoms than in October. These bullish divergences gave buy signals, and a new uptrend began.

As long as a price peak is confirmed by a new high in NH-NL, the rally is likely to continue, even if it is punctuated by a decline. When low prices are accompanied by new lows in NH-NL, it means that bears are in control and the downtrend is likely to continue. Divergences between NH-NL and broad market averages provide the best trading signals. A trend that loses its leaders is likely to reverse.

1. If NH-NL traces a lower peak while the market rallies to a new high, it creates a bearish divergence. This shows that bullish leadership is weakening even though the broad market is higher. Bearish divergences mark the ends of uptrends. If the last peak in NH-NL is about +100 or less, then a major reversal is probably at hand and it is time to get short. If the latest peak is much higher than +100, then the upside leadership is strong enough to prevent the market from collapsing.

2. If NH-NL traces a more shallow bottom while the market declines to a new low, it creates a bullish divergence. This shows that bearish leadership is shrinking, even though the market is lower. If the latest low in NH-NL is near −100, it shows that the bearish leadership is exhausted and a major upside reversal is near. If the latest low is much lower than −100, then bears still have some strength, and the downtrend may pause but not reverse. Keep in mind that bullish divergences at stock market bottoms tend to develop faster than bearish divergences at market tops: Buy fast and sell slowly.

The slope of NH-NL on any given day is defined by the trend of its bars for the last few days. When the market rallies and NH-NL rises, it confirms uptrends. When NH-NL declines together with the market, it confirms downtrends.

3. A rise in NH-NL shows that it is safe to hold long positions and add to them. If NH-NL declines while the broad market stays flat or rallies, it is time to take profits on short-term long positions. When NH-NL falls, it shows that the bearish leadership is strong and it is safe to hold short positions and even add to them. If the market continues to fall but NH-NL rises, the downtrend is in question — it is time to cover shorts.

4. If NH-NL rises on a flat day, it flashes a bullish message and gives a buy signal. It shows that officers are going over the top while the soldiers are still crouching in their foxholes. When NH-NL falls on a flat day, it gives a signal to sell short. It shows that officers are deserting while the troops are still holding their positions. Soldiers are not stupid — if the officers run, they will not stay and fight.

The position of NH-NL in relation to its centerline shows whether bulls or bears are in control. When NH-NL is above its centerline, it shows that more market leaders are bullish than bearish. Then it is better to trade the stock market from the long side. When NH-NL is below its centerline, it shows that bearish leadership is stronger, and it is better to trade from the short side. NH-NL can stay above its centerline for months at a time in bull markets and below its centerline for months at a time in bear markets.

5. If NH-NL stays negative for several months but then rallies above its centerline, it signals that a bull move is likely to begin. Then it is time to look for buying opportunities, using oscillators for precise timing. If NH-NL stays positive for several months but then falls below its centerline, it shows that a bear move is likely to begin. Then it is time to look for shorting opportunities using oscillators for precise timing.

More on NH-NL

Old analysts used to **smooth NH-NL** using 10-day and 30-day simple moving averages. When a 10-day MA of NH-NL crossed above a 30-day MA, it gave a buy signal. When a 10-day MA crossed below a 30-day MA, it gave a sell signal. Raw NH-NL gives clearer signals, but if you still want to smooth NH-NL, it is better to use exponential moving averages.

The number of new highs and new lows is reported daily by the New York Stock Exchange, the American Stock Exchange, the Over-the-Counter Exchange, and the London Stock Exchange. Most **overseas stock exchanges** do not report these numbers, but a computer-equipped analyst should have no difficulty creating NH-NL for any market. Traders who use NH-NL outside of the United States get an edge over competitors who lack this indicator. You need to obtain one year's worth of daily data for every stock on the exchange you follow and update that file daily. Program your computer to examine your database each day and flag those stocks that have reached a new high or a new low for the past 52 weeks.

NH-NL does not work in the **stock markets dominated by a handful of stocks.** For example, hundreds of stocks are listed on the Milan Stock Exchange in Italy, but only 2 of them—FIAT and Generale—represent nearly 70 percent of total market capitalization. These two giants can override the rest of the market.

38. TRADERS' INDEX AND OTHER STOCK MARKET INDICATORS

The Traders' Index (TRIN) is a leading stock market indicator. It shows when major rallies and declines get ready to reverse by measuring the intensity of optimism of the dominant market group. Excessive optimism is associated with market tops and excessive pessimism with bottoms.

TRIN measures the ratio of advancing to declining stocks and compares it to the ratio of advancing to declining volume. This indicator was popularized by Richard Arms and is included in most quote systems. Any broker with a terminal on his desk can punch a few keys and see the latest TRIN. It is easy to calculate TRIN by hand or by using a computer at the end of each trading day.

New market developments have changed TRIN over the years: listed stock options, index arbitrage, dividend recapture plays, and so on. The original interpretation of TRIN had to be adjusted, but TRIN continues to stand out as one of the best stock market indicators. It helps in timing stock trades as well as trades in stock index futures and options.

How to Construct TRIN

You need four pieces of data to calculate the Traders' Index: the number and volume of advancing and declining stocks as well as the volume of both groups. These figures are released by the New York Stock Exchange and several other exchanges throughout each trading session.

$$\text{TRIN} = \frac{\text{Adv Issues}}{\text{Decl Issues}} \bigg/ \frac{\text{Adv Volume}}{\text{Decl Volume}}$$

TRIN compares the relationship between the ratio of advancing and declining stocks and the ratio of advancing and declining volume (see worksheet, Figure 38-1). If 1000 stocks rally on a volume of 100 million shares, and 1000 stocks decline on a volume of 100 million shares, then TRIN equals 1. If 1500 stocks go up on a volume of 150 million shares and 500 stocks go down on a volume of 50 million shares, TRIN remains 1.

TRIN falls when the volume of advancing stocks is disproportionately high, compared to their number. TRIN rises when the volume of declining stocks is disproportionately high, compared to their number.

S&P 500

Date	Adv	Decl	Adv Vol	Decl Vol	TRIN:1	TRIN: 13-EMA
6/04	784	765	8374	7107	.87	
6/05	661	895	7162	9418	.97	
6/06	681	861	6339	8783	1.10	
6/07	445	1113	3251	11771	1.45	
6/10	648	905	4230	6644	1.12	
6/11	868	680	9371	4831	.66	
6/12	356	1237	2049	12906	1.81	
6/13	765	734	6787	5420	.83	
6/14	1036	531	11529	4123	.70	
6/17	645	851	4518	6916	1.16	
6/18	622	895	5261	8177	1.08	
6/19	399	1159	2453	11567	1.62	
6/20	655	854	6305	7734	.94	1.10
6/21	841	684	11192	5239	.58	1.02
6/24	298	1322	1202	11592	2.17	1.18
6/25	612	888	5216	8171	1.08	1.17

Figure 38–1.   Traders' Index (TRIN) Worksheet

TRIN tracks the ratio of advancing to declining stocks and compares it with the ratio of advancing to declining volume. It works best when it is smoothed with an exponential moving average, such as a 13-day EMA.

The volume of advancing stocks often swells out of proportion to their number during rallies. If the ratio of advancing to declining issues is 2:1, but the ratio of advancing to declining volume is 4:1, then TRIN equals 0.50 (2/1 ÷ 4/1). A low TRIN shows that bulls are highly optimistic, a rally is being overdone, and a top is near.

When the market falls, the volume of declining stocks often swells out of proportion to their number. If the ratio of advancing to declining issues is 1:2, but the ratio of advancing to declining volume is 1:4, then TRIN equals 2 (1/2 ÷ 1/4). A high TRIN shows that bears are too optimistic, too much volume goes into the declining stocks, a decline is being overdone, and the market is nearing a bottom.

TRIN can change sharply from day to day. TRIN gives better signals when it is smoothed with a moving average. You can use a 13-day exponential moving average of daily TRIN (see Section 25). It filters out the noise of daily swings and shows the true trend of this indicator. For the rest of this chapter, the term TRIN is used as shorthand for 13-day EMA of daily TRIN.

Plot TRIN on an inverted vertical scale. Low numbers on the top identify market peaks, and high numbers at the bottom identify market lows. Two horizontal reference lines mark overbought and oversold levels. When TRIN rises above its upper reference line, it shows that the stock market is overbought and nearing a top. When TRIN falls below its lower reference line, it shows that the market is oversold and nearing a bottom.

The level of reference lines depends on whether the stocks are in a bull or bear market or a neutral trading range. The overbought line is usually placed at 0.65 or 0.70 in bull markets, 0.70 or 0.75 in bear markets. The oversold line is placed at 0.90 or 0.95 in bull markets, 1.00 or 1.10 in bear markets. These levels may shift by the time you read this book—use them as a starting point for your own research.

The best way to draw reference lines is to examine a chart of an index such as the S&P 500 for the past six months, along with TRIN. Mark all important tops and bottoms of the S&P 500 and draw two reference lines that cut across the corresponding tops and bottoms of TRIN. When TRIN enters those extreme areas again, you will know that the market has entered a reversal zone. Adjust oversold and overbought lines every three months.

Crowd Psychology

The stock market is a manic-depressive beast—it swings from expansive mania to fearful depression. The mood of a manic-depressive patient goes through cycles. When he reaches the bottom of depression, his mood starts to improve. When he rises to the height of mania, he starts to slow down. Traders can use TRIN to diagnose manic and depressive episodes in the stock market and bet on their reversals (see Figure 38-2).

Crowds are emotional and short-term oriented. Trends often go farther than you expect because crowds act out their feelings and run instead of acting rationally. Trends reverse when masses of traders get tired of running. TRIN shows when they become exhausted.

If bulls become greedy during a rally, they buy so many shares that advancing volume swells out of proportion with the number of advancing stocks. When TRIN rises above its upper reference line it shows that mass optimism has risen to a level associated with tops.

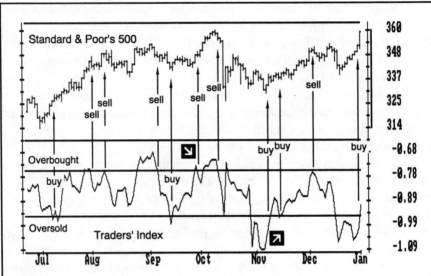

Figure 38–2.   Traders' Index (TRIN)

When the volume of rising stocks rises out of proportion to their number, it reflects bullish enthusiasm, and TRIN becomes overbought. It rises and then flashes a sell signal when it leaves its overbought zone. When the volume of declining stocks becomes too large relative to their number, TRIN becomes oversold. It gives a buy signal when it leaves its oversold zone.

TRIN gives its best buy and sell signals when it diverges from the pattern of the S&P 500 index. The market rose higher in October than in September, but TRIN reached a lower top, giving a strong sell signal. After the October fall, the market retested its bottom in November, but a much higher bottom in TRIN showed that bears were out of breath. This bullish divergence gave a strong buy signal. At the right edge of the chart, the market is strong but TRIN is nowhere near overbought—hold longs.

If bears dump shares during a decline, then downside volume swells out of proportion with the number of declining stocks. When TRIN falls below its lower reference line, it shows that bearishness is being overdone and an upside reversal is near.

Changes of TRIN are similar to what happens during rush hours at a suburban commuter train station. In the morning, the departure platform gets overcrowded, while at night there is a crowd at the arriving platform. The biggest crowd identifies the peak of the trend — either into the city or back home. You can identify traffic reversals by measuring the number of commuters crowding a platform. That is what TRIN does in the stock market.

TRIN identifies rush hours in uptrends and downtrends. It flags bullish extremes at stock market tops and bearish extremes at market bottoms. TRIN identifies mood swings of the stock market crowd. Professionals use this information because they tend to trade against deviations and for a return to normalcy.

Trading Rules

TRIN is plotted on an inverted scale. High numbers mark the bottoms and low numbers signal market tops. TRIN hovers between 0.75 to 0.85 in neutral markets. It is less than 1.0 because the volume of advancing stocks normally exceeds the volume of declining stocks. People are normally more bullish than bearish.

TRIN cannot be used mechanically — the same readings mean different things under different market conditions. Overbought and oversold readings are lower during bear markets and higher during bull markets. For example, TRIN of 0.60 marks great bullish strength at an early stage of a bull market. It tells you to look for every opportunity to add to long positions. The same reading of 0.60 during a rally in a bear market marks a major shorting opportunity. This is why it pays to adjust overbought and oversold lines every three months.

1. Buy when TRIN leaves its oversold zone. When it crosses above its lower reference line, it shows that bears have run out of steam. Buying at this time is like betting on a traffic reversal after the rush hour.

2. Sell when TRIN leaves its overbought zone. When TRIN sinks below its upper reference line, it shows that bulls are running out of breath. Selling short at this time is safer than trying to pick the exact top.

3. TRIN works best when combined with the New High–New Low Index (see Section 37). If TRIN becomes oversold while NH-NL reaches a new low, it shows that bearish leadership is strong and the downtrend is likely to continue. If TRIN becomes oversold but NH-

NL traces a bullish divergence, it marks an important low. The combined signals of TRIN and NH-NL give traders confidence to buy a larger position.

4. If TRIN becomes overbought but NH-NL rises to a new high, it shows that the upside leadership is strong and the uptrend is likely to continue. If TRIN becomes overbought while NH-NL traces a bearish divergence, it often marks an important stock market top. Then you can short a larger position.

TRIN gives its strongest buy and sell signals when it diverges from prices.

5. When the stock market rises to a new high but TRIN traces a lower peak than it did during its previous rally, it shows that bulls are losing power. When bulls cannot purchase as many shares as before, the uptrend is in trouble. A bearish divergence between TRIN and the stock market gives a strong sell signal.

6. When the stock market falls to a new low but TRIN flattens out at a more shallow level than during its previous decline, it shows that bears have fewer stocks to sell. When bears start losing power, the market is ready to rally. A bullish divergence between TRIN and the stock market gives a strong buy signal.

More on TRIN

The New York Stock Exchange releases information on advancing and declining stocks and their volume throughout each trading session. **Intraday TRIN** can be used by day-traders.

TRIN can be applied to any stock exchange that reports the numbers of advancing and declining stocks and their volume. When that data becomes available for **overseas exchanges**, the first traders to use it will have a competitive advantage.

Advance/Decline

The Advance/Decline line (A/D line) measures mass participation in rallies and declines. If New Highs and New Lows are the officers, and the Dow

Jones Industrials are the generals, then the A/D line shows whether or not the soldiers are following their leaders. A rally or decline is more likely to persist when the A/D line rises to a new high or falls to a new low in gear with the Dow.

To calculate A/D for each day, subtract the number of declining stocks from the number of advancing stocks and ignore unchanged stocks. The result is positive or negative, depending on whether more stocks advanced or declined. For example, if 1900 stocks were traded, 900 advanced, 700 declined, and 300 were unchanged, then Advance/Decline equals +200 (900 – 700). Each day's Advance/Decline figures are added to the previous day's total, creating a cumulative A/D line.

Traders should keep an eye on new peaks and valleys in the A/D line because its absolute level depends mostly on its starting date. Broadly based rallies and declines have greater staying power. If a new high in the stock market is accompanied by a new high in the A/D line, it shows that the rally has broad support and is likely to continue. If the stock market reaches a new peak but the A/D line reaches a lower peak than during the previous rally, it shows that fewer stocks are participating, and the rally may be near its end. When the market falls to a new low but the A/D line traces a more shallow bottom than during the previous decline, it shows that the decline is narrowing down and the bear move is nearing an end. These signals tend to precede reversals by weeks if not months.

Most Active Stocks

The Most Active Stocks indicator (MAS) is an advance/decline line of the 15 most active stocks on the New York Stock Exchange. They are listed daily in many newspapers. Several large capitalization stocks, such as IBM, frequently appear on this list. Other stocks make the list only when they catch the public's eye due to an extremely positive or negative piece of news. MAS is a big money indicator — it shows whether big money is bullish or bearish.

MAS for each day equals the number of the most active stocks that advanced minus the number of the most active stocks that declined. For example, if 9 of the most active stocks went up, 4 fell, and 2 were unchanged, then MAS for that day is 5 (9 – 4). Each day's MAS is added to the previous day's total, creating a cumulative MAS line.

When MAS moves in the same direction as the broad stock market, it shows that big money supports the trend and it is likely to continue. When the market goes one way and MAS goes the other way, it shows that big money is betting on a reversal. When the trend of MAS diverges from the price trend, the market is especially likely to reverse.

Other Stock Market Indicators

Only a few stock market indicators have withstood the test of time. The New High–New Low Index and TRIN are probably the best stock market indicators, followed by Advance/Decline and Most Active Stocks.

Old stock market books are full of fascinating indicators, but you have to be very careful using them today. Changes in the market over the years have killed many indicators.

Indicators based on **volume of low-priced stocks** lost their usefulness when the average volume of the U.S. stock market soared tenfold and the Dow rose sixfold. The **Member Short Sale Ratio** and the **Specialist Short Sale Ratio** stopped working after options became popular. Member and specialist short sales are now tied up in the intermarket arbitrage. **Odd-lot statistics** lost value when conservative odd-lotters bought mutual funds. The **Odd-lot Short Sale Ratio** stopped working when gamblers discovered puts.

VII

Psychological Indicators

---

39. CONSENSUS INDICATORS

Many private traders keep their market opinions to themselves, but financial journalists and market letter writers spew them forth like open fire hydrants. Some writers are very bright, but both groups as a whole have poor trading records.

Financial journalists and letter writers overstay important trends and miss major turning points. When these groups become bullish or bearish, it pays to trade against them. The behavior of groups is more primitive than individual behavior.

Consensus indicators, also known as contrary opinion indicators, are not as exact as trend-following indicators or oscillators. They simply draw your attention to the fact that a trend is ready to reverse. When you get that message, use technical indicators for more precise timing.

As long as the market crowd remains in conflict, the trend can continue. When the crowd reaches a strong consensus, the trend is ready to reverse. When the crowd becomes highly bullish, it pays to get ready to sell. When the crowd becomes strongly bearish, it pays to get ready to buy.

The foundations of the contrary opinion theory were laid by Charles Mackay, a Scottish barrister. He described in his book, *Extraordinary Popular Delusions and the Madness of Crowds*, crowd behavior during the Dutch Tulip Mania and the South Seas Bubble in England. Humphrey B. Neill applied the theory of contrary opinion to stocks and other financial markets. He explained in his book, *The Art of Contrary Thinking*, why the majority must be wrong at the market's major turning points. Prices are established by crowds, and by the time the majority turns bullish, there are not enough new buyers left to support a bull market.

Abraham W. Cohen, a New York lawyer, came up with the idea of polling market advisors and using their responses as a proxy for the entire body of traders. Cohen was a skeptical man who spent many years on Wall Street and saw that the advisors as a group performed no better than the market crowd. In 1963, he established a service called *Investors Intelligence* for tracking market letter writers. When the majority of them became bearish, Cohen identified a buying opportunity. Selling opportunities were marked by strong bullishness among letter writers. James H. Sibbet applied this theory to commodities. In 1964, he set up an advisory service called *Market Vane*. He studied the opinions of advisors and also weighed them in proportion to the numbers of their subscribers.

Tracking Advisory Opinion

Some letter writers are very smart, but taken as a group they are no better than average traders. They become very bullish at major tops and very bearish at major bottoms. Their consensus is similar to that of the trading crowd.

Most letter writers follow trends because they are afraid to appear foolish and lose subscribers by missing a major move. The longer a trend continues, the louder letter writers bay at it. The advisors are most bullish at market tops and most bearish at market bottoms. When most letter writers become strongly bullish or bearish, it is a good idea to trade against them.

Several rating services track the percentage of bulls and bears among advisors. The main rating services are *Investors Intelligence* in the stock market and *Market Vane* in the futures markets. Some advisors are very skilled at doubletalk. The man who speaks from both sides of his mouth can later claim that he was right regardless of the market's direction. Editors of *Investors Intelligence* and *Market Vane* have plenty of experience pinning down such lizards. As long as the same editor does the ratings, they remain internally consistent.

Investors Intelligence

Investors Intelligence was founded by Abe Cohen in 1963. He died in 1983, and his work is being continued by Michael Burke, the new editor and publisher. *Investors Intelligence* monitors about 130 stock market letters. It tabulates the percentage of bulls, bears, and fence-sitters among letter writers. The percentage of bears is especially important because it is emotionally hard for stock market writers to be bearish.

When the percentage of bears among stock market letter writers rises above 55, the market is near an important bottom. When the percentage of bears falls below 15 and the percentage of bulls rises above 65, the stock market is near an important top.

Market Vane

Market Vane rates about 70 newsletters covering 32 markets. It rates each writer's degree of bullishness in each market on a 9-point scale. It multiplies these ratings by an estimated number of subscribers to each service (most advisors wildly inflate those numbers to appear more popular). A consensus report on a scale from 0 (most bearish) to 100 (most bullish) is created by adding the ratings of all advisors. When bullish consensus approaches 70 percent to 80 percent, it is time to look for a downside reversal, and when it nears 20 percent to 30 percent, it is time to look to buy.

The reason for trading against the extremes in consensus is rooted in the structure of the futures markets. The number of contracts bought long and sold short is always equal. For example, if open interest in gold is 12,000 contracts, then 12,000 contracts are long and 12,000 contracts are short.

While the number of long and short contracts is always equal, the number of individuals who hold them keeps changing. If the majority is bullish, then the minority, those who are short, has more contracts per person than the longs. If the majority is bearish, then the bullish minority has bigger positions per person. The following example illustrates what happens when the consensus changes among 1000 traders who hold 12,000 contracts in one market.

Open Interest	Bullish Consensus	Number of Bulls	Number of Bears	Contracts per Bull	Contracts per Bear
12,000	50	500	500	24	24
12,000	80	800	200	15	60
12,000	20	200	800	60	15

1. If bullish consensus equals 50 percent, then 50 percent of traders are long and 50 percent are short. An average trader who is long holds as many contracts as an average trader who is short.

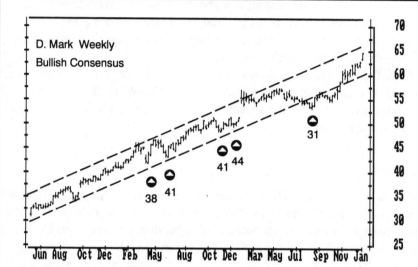

Figure 39–1.   Bullish Consensus

The opinions of market advisors serve as a proxy for the opinions of the entire market crowd. The best time to buy is when the crowd is bearish, and the best time to go short is when the crowd is bullish. The levels of bullishness at which to buy or sell short vary from market to market. They need to be adjusted every few months.

This weekly chart shows a bull market in the D. Mark, steadily moving up between a trendline and a parallel channel line. Whenever bullish consensus fell below 45 percent during this bull market, it gave a buy signal. The lower the bullish consensus, the more explosive the subsequent rally!

2. When bullish consensus reaches 80 percent, it shows that 80 percent of traders are long and 20 percent are short. Since the sizes of total long and total short positions are always equal, an average bear is short four times as many contracts as are held long by an average bull. This means that an average bear has four times more money than an average bull. The big money is on the short side of the market.

3. When bullish consensus falls to 20 percent, it means that 20 percent of

traders are long and 80 percent are short. Since the numbers of long and short contracts are always equal, an average bull holds four times more contracts than are held by an average bear. It shows that big money is on the long side of the market.

Big money did not grow big by being stupid. Big traders tend to be more knowledgeable and successful than average — otherwise they stop being big traders. When big money gravitates to one side of the market, think of trading in that direction.

To interpret bullish consensus in any market, obtain at least twelve months of historical data on consensus and note the levels at which the market has turned in the past (Figure 39-1). Update these levels once every three months. The next time the market consensus becomes highly bullish, look for an opportunity to sell short using technical indicators. When the consensus becomes very bearish, look for a buying opportunity.

Advisory opinion sometimes begins to change a week or two in advance of major trend reversals. If bullish consensus ticks down from 78 to 76, or if it rises from 25 to 27, it shows that the savviest advisors are abandoning what looks like a winning trend. This means that the trend is ready to reverse.

Signals from the Press

To understand any group of people, you must know what its members want and what they fear. Financial journalists want to appear serious, intelligent, and informed; they are afraid of appearing ignorant or flaky. It is normal for financial journalists to straddle the fence and present several sides of every issue. A journalist is safe as long as he writes something like "monetary policy is about to push the market up, unless unforeseen factors push it down."

Internal contradiction is the normal state of affairs in financial journalism. Many financial editors are even bigger cowards than their writers. They print contradictory articles and call this "presenting a balanced picture."

For example, a recent issue of *Business Week* had an article headlined "The Winds of Inflation Are Blowing a Little Harder" on page 19. The article stated that the end of a war was likely to push oil prices up. Another article on page 32 of the same issue was headlined "Why the Inflation Scare Is Just That." It stated that the end of a war was going to push oil prices down.

Only a powerful and long-lasting trend can lure journalists and editors

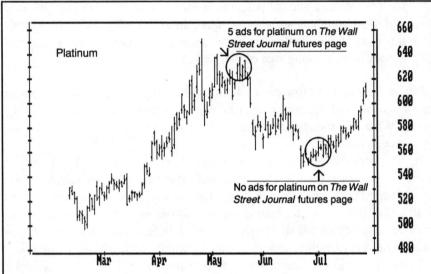

Figure 39–2.   Advertising as a Contrary Indicator

By the time several firms prepare ads for the same product and place them in the same newspaper, the trend is ready to reverse. More than three ads for the same market on the same page is a bearish warning.

down from their fences. This happens when a wave of optimism or pessimism sweeps the market at the end of a major trend. When journalists climb down from the fence and express strongly bullish or bearish views, the trend is ripe for a reversal.

This is also the reason why the front covers of major business magazines are good contrarian indicators. When *Business Week* puts a bull on its cover, it is usually a good time to take profits on long positions in stocks, and when a bear graces the front cover, a bottom cannot be too far away.

Signals from the Advertisers

A group of three or more ads touting the same "opportunity" on the same page of a major newspaper often warns of a top (Figure 39-2). Only a well-established uptrend can break through the inertia of several brokerage firms. By the time all of them recognize a trend, come up with trading recommendations, produce ads, and place them in a newspaper, that trend is very old.

The ads on the commodities page of the *Wall Street Journal* appeal to the bullish appetites of the least-informed traders. Those ads almost never recommend selling; it is hard to get amateurs excited about going short. When three or more ads on the same day day tout opportunities in the same market, it is time to look at technical indicators for shorting signals.

40. COMMITMENT INDICATORS

Several government agencies and exchanges collect data on buying and selling by several groups of investors and traders. They publish summary reports of actual trades—commitments of money as well as ego. It pays to trade with those groups that have a track record of success and bet against those with poor track records.

For example, the Commodity Futures Trading Commission (CFTC) reports long and short positions of hedgers and big speculators. Hedgers— the commercial producers and consumers of commodities—are the most successful participants in the futures markets. The Securities and Exchange Commission (SEC) reports purchases and sales by corporate insiders. Officers of publicly traded companies know when to buy or sell their company shares. The New York Stock Exchange reports the number of shares bought, sold, and shorted by its members and by odd-lot traders. Members are more successful than small-time speculators.

Commitments of Traders

Traders must report their positions to the CFTC after they reach certain levels, called **reporting levels**. At the time of this writing, if you are long or short 100 contracts of corn or 300 contracts of the S&P 500 futures, the CFTC classifies you as a big speculator. Brokers send reports on positions that reach reporting levels to the CFTC. It compiles them and releases summaries once every two weeks.

The CFTC also sets up the maximum number of contracts, called **position**

limits, that a speculator is allowed to hold in any given market. At this time, a speculator may not be net long or short more than 2400 contracts of corn or 500 contracts of the S&P 500 futures. These limits are set to prevent very large speculators from accumulating positions that are big enough to bully the markets.

The CFTC divides all market participants into three groups: commercials, small speculators, and large speculators. **Commercials,** also known as **hedgers,** are firms or individuals who deal in actual commodities in the normal course of business. In theory, they trade futures to hedge business risks. For example, a bank trades interest rate futures to hedge its loan portfolio, or a food processing company trades wheat futures to offset the risks of buying grain. Hedgers post smaller margins and are exempt from speculative position limits.

Large speculators are those traders whose positions reach reporting levels. The CFTC reports buying and selling by commercials and large speculators. To find the positions of **small traders,** you need to subtract the holdings of the first two groups from the open interest.

The divisions between hedgers, big speculators, and small speculators are somewhat artificial. Smart small traders grow into big traders, dumb big traders become small traders, and many hedgers speculate. Some market participants play games that distort the CFTC reports. For example, an acquaintance who owns a brokerage firm sometimes registers his wealthy speculator clients as hedgers, claiming they trade stock index and bond futures to hedge their stock and bond positions.

The commercials can legally speculate in the futures markets using inside information. Some of them are big enough to play futures markets against cash markets. For example, an oil firm may buy crude oil futures, divert several tankers, and hold them offshore in order to tighten supplies and push futures prices up. They can take profits on long positions, go short, and deliver several tankers at once to refiners in order to push crude futures down and cover shorts. This manipulation is illegal, and most firms hotly deny that it takes place.

As a group, the commercials have the best track record in the futures markets. They have inside information and are well-capitalized. It pays to follow them because they are successful in the long run. The few exceptions, such as orange juice hedgers, only confirm this rule.

Big speculators used to be highly successful as a group until a decade or so ago. They used to be wealthy individuals who took careful risks with their own money. Today's big traders are commodity funds. These trend-following behemoths do poorly as a group. The masses of small traders are the proverbial "wrong-way Corrigans" of the markets.

It is not enough to know whether a certain group is short or long. Commercials are often short futures because many of them own physical commodities. Small traders are usually long, reflecting their perennial optimism. To draw valid conclusions from the CFTC reports, you need to compare current positions to their historical norms.

The modern approach to analyzing commitments of traders has been developed by Curtis Arnold and popularized by Stephen Briese, publisher of the *Bullish Review* newsletter. These analysts measure deviations of current commitments from their historical norms. *Bullish Review* uses the following formula:

$$\text{COT Index} = \frac{\text{Current Net} - \text{Minimum Net}}{\text{Maximum Net} - \text{Minimum Net}}$$

where   COT Index   = commitments of Traders Index.
        Current Net = the difference between commercial and speculative net positions.
        Minimum Net = the smallest difference between commercial and speculative net positions.
        Maximum Net = the largest difference between commercial and speculative net positions.
        Net Position = long contracts minus short contracts of any given group.

When the COT Index rises above 90 percent, it shows that commercials are uncommonly bullish and gives a buy signal. When the COT Index falls below 10 percent, it shows that commercials are uncommonly bearish and gives a sell signal.

Insider Trading

Officers and investors who hold more than 5 percent of the shares in publicly traded companies must report their buying and selling to the Securities and Exchange Commission. The SEC tabulates insider buying and selling and releases this data to the public once a month.

Corporate insiders have a record of buying stocks cheap and selling dear. Insider buying emerges after severe market drops, and insider selling accelerates when the market rallies and becomes overpriced.

Buying or selling by a single insider matters little. For example, an executive may sell shares in his firm to meet major personal expenses or may buy
shares to exercise stock options. Analysts who researched legal insider trading found that insider buying or selling was meaningful only if more than
three executives or large stockholders bought or sold within a month. These
actions reveal that something very positive or negative is about to happen to
the firm. A stock is likely to rise if three insiders buy in one month and to
fall if three insiders sell within a month.

Stock Exchange Members

Membership in a stock exchange — particularly as a specialist — is a license
to mint money. An element of risk does not deter generations of traders from
paying hundreds of thousands of dollars for the privilege of planting their
feet on a few square inches of a crowded floor.

The **Member Short Sale Ratio** (MSSR) is the ratio of shorting by members to total shorting. The **Specialist Short Sale Ratio** (SSSR) is the ratio of
shorting by specialists to shorting by members. These indicators used to
serve as the best tools of stock market technicians. High readings of MSSR
(over 85 percent) and SSSR (over 60 percent) showed that savvy traders
were selling short to the public and identified stock market tops. Low readings of MSSR (below 75 percent) and SSSR (below 40 percent) showed that
members were buying from the bearish public and identified stock market
bottoms. These indicators became erratic in the 1980s. They were done in by
the options markets, which gave exchange members more opportunities for
arbitrage. Now it is impossible to tell when their shorting is due to bearishness or to arbitrage plays.

Odd-Lot Activity

Odd-lotters are people who trade less than 100 shares of stock at a time — the
small fry of the stock exchange. They remind us of a more bucolic time on
Wall Street. Odd-lotters transacted one quarter of the exchange volume a
century ago, and 1 percent as recently as two decades ago. Odd-lotters as a
group are value investors. They buy when stocks are cheap and sell when
prices rise.

The indicators for tracking the behavior of odd-lotters were developed in the 1930s. The **Odd-Lot Sales Ratio** measured the ratio of odd-lot sales to purchases. When it fell, it showed that odd-lotters were buying and the stock market was near the bottom. When it rose, it indicated that odd-lotters were selling and the stock market was near the top.

The **Odd-Lot Short Sale Ratio** was a very different indicator. It tracked the behavior of short-sellers among odd-lotters, many of whom were gamblers. Very low levels of odd-lot short sales indicated that the market was near the top, and high levels of odd-lot short sales showed that the stock market was at a bottom.

These indicators lost value as the financial scene changed in the 1970s and 1980s. The intelligent small investors moved their money into well-run mutual funds, and gamblers discovered that they could get more bang for their money in options. Now the New York Stock Exchange has a preferential mechanism for filling odd-lot orders, and many professionals trade in 99-share lots.

VIII

New Indicators

41. ELDER-RAY

Elder-ray is a new technical indicator. It was developed in 1989 by this author and named for its similarity to X-rays. Doctors use X-rays to see bone structure below the surface of the skin. Traders can use Elder-ray to see the power of bulls and bears below the surface of the markets.

To be a successful trader, you do not have to forecast the future. You need to find when bulls or bears are in control and trade with the dominant group. Elder-ray helps you see when bulls and bears become stronger or weaker.

How to Construct Elder-ray

Elder-ray combines the best features of trend-following indicators and oscillators (see Section 24). It includes an exponential moving average, which is a trend-following indicator. Its Bull Power and Bear Power components are oscillators.

To create Elder-ray, divide your computer screen or chart paper into three horizontal windows. Plot a bar chart and an exponential moving average (EMA) in the upper window. Plot Bull Power in the middle window and Bear Power in the bottom window.

It takes four steps to construct Elder-ray (see worksheet, Figure 41-1).

Gold

Date	High	Low	Close	13-EMA	Bull Power	Bear Power
09/19	353.5	351.4	351.6	351.34	2.16	0.06
09/20	352.1	350.9	351.7	351.39	0.71	−0.49
09/23	354.2	352.2	354.1	351.78	2.42	0.42
09/24	357.9	354.9	357.1	352.54	5.36	2.36
09/25	356.8	355.3	356.2	353.06	3.74	2.24
09/26	355.9	355.3	354.1	353.21	2.69	0.09
09/27	352.6	350.9	352.5	353.11	−0.51	−2.21
09/30	359.6	355.2	357.4	353.72	5.88	1.48
10/01	357.8	356.8	357.4	345.25	3.55	2.55
10/02	360.8	357.9	358.8	354.90	5.90	3.00

Figure 41–1.   Elder-ray Worksheet

Bull Power = High of the bar – 13-day EMA.
Bear Power = Low of the bar – 13-day EMA

It is normal for Bull Power to be positive and for Bear Power to be negative. The higher the Bull Power, the stronger the bulls, and the deeper the Bear Power, the stronger the bears. When Bull Power turns negative, it shows that the bears are so strong they completely over-power the bulls. If Bear Power turns positive, it shows that bulls are uncommonly strong, completely overpowering the bears.

1. Draw a bar chart of any trading vehicle in the top window of your screen.

2. Plot an EMA of closing prices in the same window. A 13-day EMA is a good choice.

   Bull Power = High – EMA

   Bear Power = Low – EMA

3. Calculate Bull Power according to the above formula. Plot it as a histogram in the middle window. Bull Power of any day equals the high of that day minus the EMA of that day. Normally, the high of a bar is above the EMA, Bull Power is positive, and the histogram is above

the centerline. The entire bar may sink below the EMA during a sharp break. When the high is below the EMA, Bull Power turns negative and its histogram falls below the centerline.

4. Calculate Bear Power and plot it as a histogram in the bottom window. Bear Power of any bar equals the low of that bar minus the EMA. Normally, the low of a bar is below the EMA, Bear Power is negative, and the histogram is below the centerline. If the entire bar rises above the EMA during a sharp rally, then Bear Power turns positive and its histogram rises above the centerline (Figure 41-2).

Trading Psychology

Elder-ray combines several pieces of information: price, a moving average, the high of each bar, and the low of each bar. We need to understand their meaning in order to understand Elder-ray.

Each price is a momentary consensus of value (see Section 12). Buyers are buying because they expect prices to rise. Sellers are selling because they expect them to fall. The undecided traders are standing aside, but their presence puts pressure on bulls and bears. A trade takes place when a buyer is willing to buy and a seller is willing to sell, both prompted by fear that an undecided trader may step in and snap away an opportunity. The price of every trade reflects the latest consensus of value of any trading vehicle.

A moving average shows the average consensus of value during its time window. A 10-day MA represents the average consensus of value for the past 10 days, a 20-day MA for the past 20 days, and so on. An exponential moving average is more reliable than a simple MA (see Section 25). The most important message of a moving average is its slope. When it rises, it shows that the crowd is becoming more bullish. When it declines, it shows that the crowd is becoming more bearish. Trade in the direction of the slope of a moving average.

The high of any bar reflects the maximum power of bulls during that bar. Bulls make money when prices rise. They keep buying until they cannot lift prices any higher. Bulls would love to raise prices one more tick—but they are out of breath. The high point of a daily bar represents the maximum power of bulls during the day, the high point of a weekly bar represents the maximum power of bulls during the week, and so on.

The low of any bar represents the maximum power of bears during that

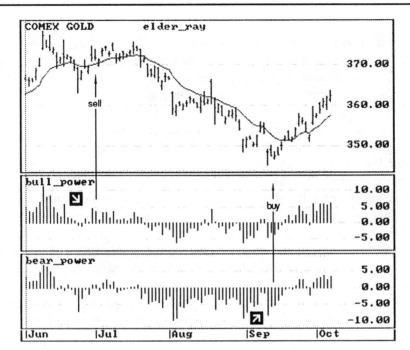

Figure 41-2. Elder-ray

The 13-day EMA reflects the average consensus of value; its slope identifies the market trend. Bull Power reflects the ability of bulls to lift prices above the average consensus of value. Bear Power reflects the ability of bears to push prices below the average consensus of value.

The best buy signals are given by bullish divergences–when prices fall to a new low, but Bear Power stops at a more shallow bottom. The best shorting signals are given by bearish divergences–when prices rise to or above the previous high, but Bull Power reaches a lower peak.

A bearish divergence in June and July gave a sell signal–a double top in price, accompanied by a lower peak in Bull Power. The sell signal was confirmed when the 13-day EMA turned down. Bull Power became positive several times during the downtrend, showing where to add to short positions. When Bull Power turns positive during a downtrend and then ticks down, place an order to sell short below the last day's low.

A bullish divergence developed in September when gold fell to a new low, but Bear Power made a more shallow low. The buy signal was confirmed when the 13-day EMA of gold turned up. At the right edge of the chart, the new peak in Bull Power confirms that the rally is strong and likely to continue.

bar. Bears make money when prices fall. They keep selling and shorting until they cannot push prices down another tick. The lowest point of a daily bar reflects the maximum power of bears during the day, the low of a weekly bar shows the maximum power of bears during the week, and so on.

Elder-ray compares the maximum power of bulls and bears to the average consensus of value. It does this by measuring the spread between the high and the low of every bar and an exponential moving average.

Bull Power reflects the bulls' ability to push prices above the average consensus of value. It measures the distance from the bar's high to the EMA. Bull Power is normally positive. It rises when bulls become stronger and falls when they stumble. Bear Power turns negative when bulls' heads are under water.

Bear Power reflects the bears' ability to push prices below the average consensus of value. It measures the distance from the bar's low to the EMA. Bear Power is normally negative. It deepens when bears grow stronger and rises when they become weaker. If Bear Power turns positive, it shows that very strong bulls are holding bears up in the air by the scruff of their necks.

To summarize the key points of Elder-ray:

1. Price is a consensus of value, expressed in action.

2. A moving average is an average consensus of value.

3. The highest point of each bar represents the maximum power of bulls during that bar.

4. The lowest point of each bar represents the maximum power of bears during that bar.

5. Bull Power is the difference between the raw power of bulls and the average consensus of value.

6. Bear Power is the difference between the raw power of bears and the average consensus of value.

Trading Rules

Elder-ray can work as a stand-alone trading method, but it pays to combine it with another method, such as the Triple Screen trading system (see Section 43). If you use Elder-ray alone, remember that the slope of its EMA identifies the trend, and trade only in that direction. Use Bull Power and Bear Power to find entry and exit points for your trades in the direction of that trend.

Triple Screen, on the other hand, identifies the trend using weekly charts. It then uses Bull Power and Bear Power on the daily charts to find trades in the direction of the weekly trend. If the weekly trend is up, Triple Screen takes only buy signals from daily Elder-ray. If the weekly trend is down, it takes only shorting signals from daily Elder-ray.

Buying and Selling

There are two essential conditions for buying:

1. The trend is up (identified by EMA or a weekly trend-following indicator).

2. Bear Power is negative but rising.

The third and fourth conditions are desirable but not essential:

3. The latest peak in Bull Power is higher than the previous peak.

4. Bear Power is rising from a bullish divergence.

Do not buy when Bear Power is positive. This occurs in runaway uptrends, when the entire bar rises above the EMA. If you buy when bears are being held up in the air, you are betting on the greater fool theory—paying a high price and hoping to meet a greater fool down the road willing to buy from you at an even higher price.

The best time to buy is when Bear Power is negative but rising—when bears regain their footing but are starting to slip again. When Bear Power ticks up, place a buy order above the high of the last two days. If the rally continues, your stop will be touched and you will go long. Once long, place a protective stop below the latest minor low.

The strongest buy signals are given by bullish divergences between Bear Power and price. If prices fall to a new low but Bear Power traces a higher bottom, it shows that prices are falling out of inertia and bears are becoming weaker. When Bear Power ticks up from the second bottom, buy a larger than usual position.

Bear Power is useful for deciding when to pyramid. As the uptrend continues, you can add to your long position whenever Bear Power dips below its centerline and then ticks up again.

If you buy using indicators, use them to decide when to sell. Do not be distracted by every uptick and downtick of Bull Power — its normal breathing process. You can monitor the power of bulls by tracking the pattern of peaks and valleys in Bull Power. As long as every new peak in price is accompanied by a new peak in Bull Power, the uptrend is safe. Sell when bulls start losing power. A sell signal is given when prices reach a new high but Bull Power reaches a lower peak than it reached during its previous rally.

Shorting and Covering

There are two essential conditions for shorting:

1. The trend is down (identified by EMA or weekly trend-following indicator).

2. Bull Power is positive but falling.

The third and fourth conditions are desirable but not essential:

3. The latest bottom in Bear Power is deeper than its previous bottom.

4. Bull Power is falling from a bearish divergence.

Do not sell short if Bull Power is already negative. This happens when the whole price bar is below the EMA — during a waterfall decline. If you sell short when bears already have bulls' heads under water, you are betting that bears can push bulls' heads even deeper. This is another version of the greater fool theory.

The best time to sell short is when Bull Power is positive but falling. It shows that bulls have come up for air but are starting to sink again. Place an order to sell short below the low of the last two days. If the decline continues, you will be stopped in automatically. Once short, place a protective stop above the latest minor high.

The strongest shorting signals are given by bearish divergences between Bull Power and prices. If prices rally to a new high but Bull Power reaches a lower top, it shows that bulls are weaker than before and prices are rising out of inertia. When Bull Power ticks down from a lower top, sell short a bigger position.

Bull Power shows when to pyramid short positions. As a downtrend continues, you can add to your shorts whenever Bull Power rallies above its centerline and then ticks down again.

If you sell short using indicators, use them also for deciding when to cover. When the trend is down, monitor Bear Power to see whether bears are becoming stronger or weaker. The pattern of peaks and valleys in Bear Power is much more important than its single upticks and downticks. If a new low in price is accompanied by a new low in Bear Power, the downtrend is safe.

A bullish divergence occurs when prices fall to a new low but Bear Power traces a more shallow bottom. It shows that bears are running out of steam and prices are falling out of inertia. This is a signal to cover shorts and get ready to go long.

Divergences between Bull and Bear Power and prices mark the best trading opportunities. X-rays show broken bones under healthy skin — and Elder-ray shows when the dominant group is broken below the surface of a trend.

42. FORCE INDEX

Force Index is an oscillator developed by this author. It measures the force of bulls behind every rally and of bears behind every decline.

Force Index combines three essential pieces of market information — the direction of price change, its extent, and trading volume. It provides a new, practical way of using volume to make trading decisions.

Force Index can be used raw, but it works better if you smooth it with a moving average. Force Index smoothed with a short MA helps pinpoint entry and exit points. Force Index smoothed with a long MA reveals major changes in the force of bulls and bears.

How to Construct Force Index

The force of every move is defined by its direction, distance, and volume. If prices close higher than the previous bar, the force is positive. If prices close lower than the previous bar, the force is negative. The greater the change in prices, the greater the force. The bigger the volume, the greater the force of the move (see worksheet, Figure 42-1).

$$\text{Force Index} = \text{Volume}_{today} \cdot (\text{Close}_{today} - \text{Close}_{yesterday})$$

Raw Force Index is plotted as a histogram, with a horizontal centerline at

Nikkei Dow

Date	Close	Volume	Force Index	FI: 2-ema	FI: 13-ema
10/29	25329	3834			
10/30	25242	4495	−391065		
10/31	25194	1372	−65856	−130807	
11/01	24295	2547	−2289753	−1570105	
11/02	24195	2891	−289100	−716102	
11/05	24385	1448	275120	−55287	
11/06	23966	2796	−1171524	−799445	
11/07	23500	3675	−1712550	−1408182	
11/08	22970	3167	−1678510	−1588400	
11/09	22932	2880	−109440	−602426	
11/13	23974	2484	2588328	1524743	
11/14	23937	1827	−67599	463181	
11/15	23487	2212	−995400	−509206	
11/16	23172	2741	−863415	−745345	−338231
11/19	23519	1931	670057	198256	−261590
11/20	23205	1405	−441170	−228027	−256796
11/21	22816	2259	−878751	−661843	−314660
11/22	23400	2163	1263192	621514	−180921

Figure 42–1.   Force Index Worksheet

Force Index = Volume$_{today}$ • (Close$_{today}$ − Close$_{yesterday}$)

Short-term Force Index is smoothed with a 2-day exponential moving average. Intermediate-term Force Index is smoothed with a 13-day exponential moving average. You can use a programming trick to reduce very large Force Index numbers–simply divide Force Index by the latest closing price.

a zero level. If the market closes higher, Force Index is positive and is plotted above the centerline. If the market closes lower, Force Index is negative and plotted below the centerline. If the market closes unchanged, Force Index equals zero.

The histogram of raw Force Index appears very jagged. This indicator gives better trading signals after being smoothed with a moving average (see Section 25). A 2-day EMA of Force Index provides a minimal degree of smoothing. It is useful for finding entry points into the markets. It pays to buy when the 2-day EMA is negative and sell when it is positive, as long as you trade in the direction of the 13-day EMA of prices.

A 13-day EMA of Force Index tracks longer-term changes in the force of bulls and bears. When it crosses above its centerline, it shows that bulls are in control. When it turns negative, it shows that bears are in control. Divergences between a 13-day EMA of Force Index and prices identify important turning points.

Trading Psychology

When the market closes higher, it shows that bulls won the day's battle, and when it closes lower, it shows that bears carried the day. The distance between today's and yesterday's closing prices reflects the margin of victory by bulls or bears. The greater this distance, the more important the victory.

Volume reflects the degree of commitment by the mass of market participants (see Section 32). Prices moving at high volume are like an avalanche that gathers mass as it rolls. High-volume rallies and declines have more inertia and are more likely to continue. Low volume, on the other hand, shows that the supply of losers is running low and a trend is nearing an end.

Prices reflect what market participants think, while volume reflects their feelings. Force Index combines price and volume—it shows whether the head and the heart of the market are in gear with each other.

When Force Index rallies to a new high, it shows that the force of bulls is high and the uptrend is likely to continue. When Force Index falls to a new low, it shows that the force of bears is big and the downtrend is likely to persist. If the change in prices is not confirmed by volume, Force Index flattens out and warns that a trend is about to reverse. It also flattens out and warns that a trend reversal is near if high volume generates only a small price move.

Trading Rules

Short-Term Force Index

A 2-day EMA of Force Index is a highly sensitive indicator of the short-term force of bulls and bears. When it swings above its centerline, it shows that bulls are stronger, and when it falls below its centerline, it shows that bears are stronger.

A 2-day EMA of Force Index is so sensitive that it is best used to fine-tune signals of other indicators. When a trend-following indicator identifies

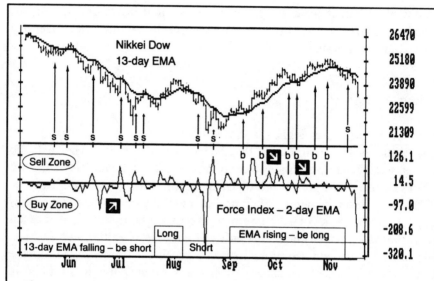

Figure 42-2   Force Index—2-Day EMA

This sensitive short-term indicator pinpoints buying opportunities in uptrends and shorting opportunities in downtrends. It helps traders buy weakness and sell strength. When the trend, identified by the slope of the 13-day EMA, is up and Force Index declines below zero, it gives a buy signal. When the trend is down and Force Index rallies above zero, it gives a signal to sell short.

The decision when to take profits depends on whether you are a short-term or a long-term trader. If you are a short-term trader, sell longs when Force Index becomes positive or cover shorts when Force Index becomes negative. A long-term trader has to wait until the exponential moving average changes its direction or until there is a divergence between Force Index and price (marked by slanted arrows on this chart). When you are trading with the trend, you can add to your positions (pyramid) whenever Force Index gives additional signals in the direction of the trend.

an uptrend, the declines of the 2-day EMA of Force Index spot the best buying points. When a trend-following tool identifies a downtrend, a 2-day EMA of Force Index pinpoints the best shorting areas (Figure 42-2).

1. Buy when a 2-day EMA of Force Index turns negative during uptrends.

No matter how fast and furious an uptrend, there are always pullbacks. If you delay buying until the 2-day EMA of Force Index turns negative, you will buy closer to a short-term bottom.

When a 2-day EMA of Force Index turns negative during an uptrend, place a buy order above the high price of that day. If the uptrend resumes and prices rally, you will be stopped in on the long side. If prices continue to decline, your order will not be executed. Then lower your buy order to within one tick of the high of the latest bar. Once your buy stop is triggered, place a protective stop below the low of the trade day or the previous day, whichever is lower. This tight stop is seldom touched in a strong uptrend, but it gets you out early if the trend is weak.

2. Sell short when a 2-day EMA of Force Index turns positive in downtrends.

When trend-following indicators identify a downtrend, wait until the 2-day EMA of Force Index turns positive. It indicates a quick splash of bullishness — a shorting opportunity. Place an order to sell short below the low of the latest price bar.

If the 2-day EMA of Force Index continues to rally after you place your sell order, raise it daily to within a tick of the latest bar's low. Once prices slide and you go short, place a protective stop above the high of the latest price bar or the previous bar, whichever is higher. Move your stop down to a break-even level as early as possible.

A 2-day EMA of Force Index helps you decide when to pyramid your positions. You can add to longs in uptrends each time Force Index turns negative and add to shorts in downtrends whenever Force Index turns positive.

Force Index even provides a glimpse into the future. When a 2-day EMA of Force Index falls to its lowest low in a month, it shows that bears are strong and prices are likely to fall even lower. When a 2-day EMA of Force Index rallies to its highest level in a month, it shows that bulls are strong and prices are likely to rise even higher.

A 2-day EMA of Force Index helps decide when to close out a position. A short-term trader who buys when this indicator is negative should sell when it turns positive. A short-term trader who goes short when this indicator is positive should cover when it turns negative. A longer-term trader should get out of his position only if a trend changes (as identified by the slope of a 13-day EMA of price) or if there is a divergence between 2-day EMA of Force Index and the trend.

3. Bullish divergences between 2-day EMA of Force Index and price give strong buy signals. A bullish divergence occurs when prices fall to a new low while Force Index makes a more shallow bottom.

4. Bearish divergences between 2-day EMA of Force Index and price give strong sell signals. A bearish divergence occurs when prices rally to a new high while Force Index traces a lower second top.

A 2-day EMA of Force Index fits well into the Triple Screen trading system (see Section 43). Its ability to find short-term buying and selling points is especially useful when it is combined with a longer-term trend-following indicator.

Intermediate-Term Force Index

A 13-day EMA of Force Index identifies longer-term changes in the strength of bulls and bears. Its position relative to its centerline shows which group is in control. Its divergences from prices identify major turning points (Figure 42-3).

5. When a 13-day EMA of Force Index is above the centerline, bulls are in control of the market, and when it is below the centerline, bears are in control. When this indicator flutters near its centerline, it identifies a trendless market — a warning not to use trend-following trading methods.

When a rally begins, prices often jump on heavy volume. When a 13-day EMA of Force Index reaches a new high, it confirms the uptrend. When the uptrend ages, prices rise more slowly or volume becomes thinner. Then a 13-day EMA of Force Index starts tracing lower tops and eventually drops below its centerline. It signals that the back of the bull has been broken.

6. A new peak in the 13-day EMA of Force Index shows that a rally is likely to continue. A bearish divergence between a 13-day EMA of Force Index and price gives a strong signal to sell short. If prices reach a new high but this indicator traces a lower peak, it warns that bulls are losing power and bears are ready to take control.

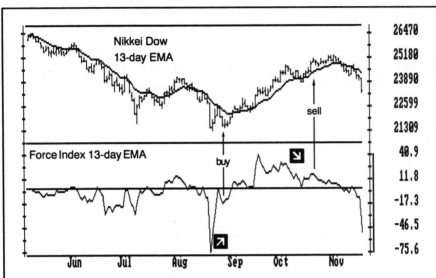

Figure 42-3   Force Index—13-Day EMA

Divergences between a 13-day EMA of Force Index and prices identify important turning points in the markets. A bullish divergence between a 13-day EMA of Force Index and the Nikkei Dow in August pointed to a buying opportunity. The Nikkei Dow retested its lows, but Force Index traced a much more shallow second bottom, giving a buy signal.

A spike low in Force Index, like the one seen in August, gives two trading messages. In the long run, it usually marks the end of an important decline. In the short run, it tells traders that the latest price bottom is likely to be retested or exceeded.

The Nikkei Dow surged higher in October, but Force Index kept tracing lower tops. Its bearish divergence showed that bulls were growing weak and prices neared a top. There was plenty of time to position short. The spike low at the right edge of the chart indicates that the latest price low is likely to be retested or exceeded.

7. A new low in 13-day EMA of Force Index shows that a downtrend is likely to continue. If prices fall to a new low but this indicator traces a more shallow low, it warns that bears are losing power. This bullish divergence gives a strong buy signal.

When a downtrend begins, prices usually drop on heavy volume. When a 13-day EMA of Force Index falls to new lows, it confirms the decline. As the downtrend grows old, prices fall more slowly or volume dries up. Then the 13-day EMA of Force Index starts tracing more shallow bottoms and finally rallies above its centerline. It shows that the back of the bear has been broken.

IX

Trading Systems

---

43. TRIPLE SCREEN TRADING SYSTEM

The Triple Screen trading system was developed by this author and has been used for trading since 1985. It was first presented to the public in April 1986, in an article in *Futures* Magazine.

Triple Screen applies three tests or screens to every trade. Many trades that seem attractive at first are rejected by one or another screen. Those trades that pass the Triple Screen test have a higher degree of profitability.

Triple Screen combines trend-following methods and counter-trend techniques. It analyzes all potential trades in several timeframes. Triple Screen is more than a trading system, it is a method, a style of trading.

Trend-Following Indicators and Oscillators

Beginners often look for a magic bullet — a single indicator for making money. If they get lucky for a while, they feel as if they discovered the royal road to profits. When the magic dies, amateurs give back their profits with interest and go looking for another magic tool. The markets are too complex to be analyzed with a single indicator.

Different indicators give contradictory signals in the same market. Trend-following indicators rise during uptrends and give buy signals, while oscillators become overbought and give sell signals. Trend-following indicators turn down in downtrends and give signals to sell short but oscillators become oversold and give buy signals.

Trend-following indicators are profitable when markets are moving but lead to whipsaws in trading ranges. Oscillators are profitable in trading ranges, but give premature and dangerous signals when the markets begin to trend. Traders say: "The trend is your friend," and "Let your profits run." They also say: "Buy low, sell high." But why sell if the trend is up? And how high is high?

Some traders try to average out the votes of trend-following indicators and oscillators. It is easy to rig this vote. If you use more trend-following tools, the vote will go one way, and if you use more oscillators, it will go the other way. A trader can always find a group of indicators telling him what he wants to hear.

The Triple Screen trading system combines trend-following indicators with oscillators. It is designed to filter out their disadvantages while preserving their strengths.

Choosing Timeframes—The Factor of Five

Another major dilemma is that the trend can be up and down at the same time, depending on what charts you use. A daily chart may show an uptrend while a weekly chart shows a downtrend, and vice versa (see Section 36). A trader needs to handle conflicting signals in different timeframes.

Charles Dow, the author of the venerable Dow theory, stated at the turn of the century that the stock market had three trends. The long-term trend lasted several years, the intermediate trend several months, and anything shorter than that was a minor trend. Robert Rhea, the great market technician of the 1930s, compared the three market trends to a tide, a wave, and a ripple. He believed that traders should trade in the direction of the market tide and take advantage of the waves but ignore the ripples.

Times have changed, and the markets have become more volatile. Traders need a more flexible definition of timeframes. The Triple Screen trading system is based on the observation that every timeframe relates to the larger and shorter ones by approximately a factor of five (see Section 36).

Each trader needs to decide which timeframe he wants to trade. Triple Screen calls that the **intermediate** timeframe. The **long-term** timeframe is one order of magnitude longer. The **short-term** timeframe is one order of magnitude shorter.

For example, if you want to carry a trade for several days or weeks, then your intermediate timeframe will be defined by the daily charts. Weekly charts are one order of magnitude longer, and they determine the long-term timeframe. Hourly charts are one order of magnitude shorter, and they determine the short-term timeframe.

Day-traders who hold their positions for less than an hour can use the same principle. For them, a 10-minute chart may define the intermediate timeframe, an hourly chart the long-term timeframe, and a 2-minute chart the short-term timeframe.

Triple Screen demands that you examine the long-term chart first. It allows you to trade only in the direction of the tide — the trend on the long-term chart. It uses the waves that go against the tide for entering positions. For example, daily declines create buying opportunities when the weekly trend is up. Daily rallies provide shorting opportunities when the weekly trend is down.

First Screen—Market Tide

Triple Screen begins by analyzing the long-term chart, one order of magnitude greater than the one you plan to trade. Most traders pay attention only to the daily charts, with everybody watching the same few months of data. If you begin by analyzing weekly charts, your perspective will be five times greater than that of your competitors.

The first screen of Triple Screen uses trend-following indicators to identify long-term trends. The original system uses the slope of weekly MACD-Histogram (see Section 26) to identify the market tide. The slope is defined as the relationship between the two latest bars. When the slope is up, it shows that bulls are in control — it is time to trade from the long side. When the slope is down, it shows that bears are in control and tells you to trade only from the short side (Figure 43-1).

A single uptick or a downtick of weekly MACD-Histogram indicates a change of a trend. The upturns that occur below the centerline give better buy signals than those above the centerline (See "Indicator Seasons" in Section 36). The downturns that occur above the centerline give better sell signals than the downturns below the centerline.

Some traders use other indicators to identify major trends. Steve Notis wrote an article in *Futures* magazine showing how he used the Directional System as the first screen of Triple Screen. Even a simpler tool, such as the

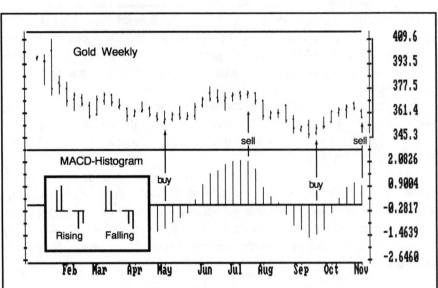

Figure 43–1. Weekly MACD-Histogram—The First Screen of Triple Screen

The slope of MACD-Histogram is defined by the relationship between its two latest bars (see inset). Triple Screen tells traders to examine weekly charts before looking at the dailies. When the weekly trend is up, it allows us to trade only from the long side or stand aside. When the weekly trend is falling, it allows us only to trade from the short side or stand aside.

Weekly MACD-Histogram gives a buy signal when its slope turns up. The best buy signals are given when this indicator turns up below its centerline. When MACD-Histogram turns down, it gives a sell signal. The best sell signals are given when it turns down from above its center-line (see "Indicator Seasons," Section 36). Once you find the trend of the weekly MACD-Histogram, turn to daily charts and look for trades in the same direction.

slope of a 13-week exponential moving average, can serve as the first screen of the Triple Screen trading system. The principle is the same. You can use most trend-following indicators, as long as you analyze the trend on the weekly charts first and then look for trades on the daily charts only in that direction.

Screen One: Identify the weekly trend using a trend-following indicator and trade only in its direction.

A trader has three choices: buy, sell, or stand aside. The first screen of the Triple Screen trading system takes away one of those choices. It acts as a censor who permits you only to buy or stand aside during major uptrends. It allows you only to sell short or stand aside during major downtrends. You have to swim with the tide or stay out of the water.

Second Screen—Market Wave

The second screen identifies the wave that goes against the tide. When the weekly trend is up, daily declines point to buying opportunities. When the weekly trend is down, daily rallies point to shorting opportunities.

The second screen applies oscillators to the daily charts in order to identify deviations from the weekly trend. Oscillators give buy signals when markets decline and sell signals when markets rise. The second screen of the Triple Screen trading system allows you to take only those daily signals that point in the direction of the weekly trend.

Screen Two: Apply an oscillator to a daily chart. Use daily declines during weekly uptrends to find buying opportunities and daily rallies during weekly downtrends to find shorting opportunities.

When the weekly trend is up, Triple Screen takes only buy signals from daily oscillators and ignores their sell signals. When the weekly trend is down, Triple Screen takes only shorting signals from oscillators and ignores their buy signals. Force Index and Elder-ray are good oscillators to use with Triple Screen, but Stochastic and Williams %R also perform well.

When the weekly MACD-Histogram rises, the 2-day EMA of Force Index (see Chapter 8) gives buy signals when it falls below its centerline, as long as it does not fall to a new multiweek low. When the weekly MACD-Histogram declines, Force Index gives shorting signals when it rallies above its centerline, as long as it does not rise to a new multiweek high (Figure 43-2).

When the weekly trend is up, daily Elder-ray (see Section 41) gives a buy signal when Bear Power declines below zero and then ticks back up toward

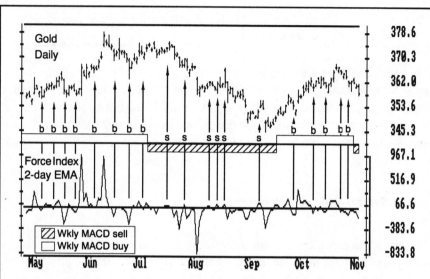

Figure 43–2. Daily Force Index—The Second Screen of Triple Screen

The 2-day EMA of Force Index is one of several oscillators that can work as the second screen of the Triple Screen trading system. Force Index marks buying opportunities when it falls below its centerline. It marks selling opportunities when it rallies above its centerline.

When the weekly trend is up, take only buy signals from the daily oscillator for entering long positions. When the weekly trend is down, take only sell signals for entering short positions. At the right edge of the chart, the weekly trend has turned down. Wait for a rise in Force Index in order to sell short.

the centerline. When the weekly trend is down, daily Elder-ray signals to go short when Bull Power rallies above zero and then ticks back down.

Stochastic (see Section 30) gives trading signals when its lines enter a buy or a sell zone. When weekly MACD-Histogram rises but daily Stochastic falls below 30, it identifies an oversold area, a buying opportunity. When the weekly MACD-Histogram declines but daily Stochastic rises above 70, it identifies an overbought area, a shorting opportunity.

Williams %R (see Section 29) needs a 4- or 5-day window to work with Triple Screen. It is interpreted similarly to Stochastic. The Relative Strength

Index does not react to price changes as fast as other oscillators. It helps with overall market analysis, but is too slow for Triple Screen.

Third Screen—Intraday Breakout

The first screen of the Triple Screen trading system identifies market tide on a weekly chart. The second screen identifies a wave that goes against that tide on a daily chart. The third screen identifies the ripples in the direction of the tide. It uses intraday price action to pinpoint entry points.

The third screen does not require a chart or an indicator. It is a technique for entering the market after the first and second screens gave a signal to buy or sell short. The third screen is called a trailing buy-stop technique in uptrends and a trailing sell-stop technique in downtrends (Figure 43-3).

When the weekly trend is up and the daily trend is down, trailing buy-stops catch upside breakouts. When the weekly trend is down and the daily trend is up, trailing sell-stops catch downside breakouts.

Triple Screen Summary

Weekly Trend	Daily Trend	Action	Order
Up	Up	Stand aside	None
Up	Down	Go long	Trailing buy-stop
Down	Down	Stand aside	None
Down	Up	Go short	Trailing sell-stop

When the weekly trend is up and a daily oscillator declines, it activates a trailing buy-stop technique. Place a buy order one tick above the high of the previous day. If prices rally, you will be stopped in long automatically when the rally takes out the previous day's high. If prices continue to decline, your buy-stop will not be touched. Lower your buy order the next day to the level one tick above the latest price bar. Keep lowering your buy-stop each day until stopped in or until the weekly indicator reverses and cancels its buy signal.

When the weekly trend is down, wait for a rally in a daily oscillator to activate a trailing sell-stop technique. Place an order to sell short one tick below the latest bar's low. As soon as the market turns down, you will be stopped in on the short side. If the rally continues, keep raising your sell order daily. The aim of a trailing sell-stop technique is to catch an intraday downside breakout from a daily uptrend in the direction of a weekly down-trend.

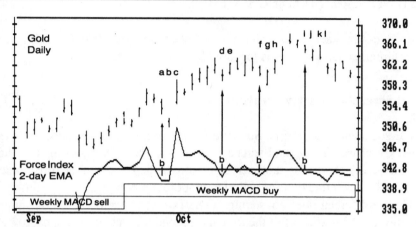

Figure 43–3. Trailing Buy-Stop—The Third Screen of Triple Screen

Weekly MACD-Histogram has turned up in mid-September. When the first screen points up, every decline of the second screen–the 2-day EMA of Force Index–marks a buying opportunity.

a. Force Index falls below its centerline. Place a buy order for tomorrow 1 tick above the high of day *a*.
b. The decline continues. Lower the buy order to 1 tick above the high of bar *b*.
c. Bought at the opening. Place a stop at the low of bar *b*. The new high in Force Index shows that the rally is strong, likely to continue.
d. Force Index falls below its centerline. Place a buy order at the bar's high.
e. Bought when prices rallied above the high of *d*. Place a stop at the low of bar *d*.
f. Force Index falls below its centerline. Place a buy order at the bar's high.
g. Decline continues. Lower the buy-stop to within 1 tick of the high of bar *g*.
h. Bought when prices rallied above the high of *g*. Place a stop at the low of bar *g*.
i. Force Index falls below its centerline. Place a buy order at the bar's high.
j. Decline continues. Lower the buy-stop to within 1 tick of the high of bar *j*.
k. Bought at the opening. Place a stop at the low of bar *j*.
l. Gold opens lower and hits the protective stop. It is important to use stops because no indicator is perfect.

Screen Three: Use the trailing buy-stop technique when the weekly trend is up and the daily oscillator is down. Use the trailing sell-stop technique when the weekly trend is down and the daily oscillator is up.

Stop-Loss

Proper money management is essential for successful trading. A disciplined trader cuts his losses short and outperforms a loser who keeps hanging on and hoping. The Triple Screen trading system calls for placing very tight stops.

As soon as you buy, place a stop-loss order one tick below the low of the trade day or the previous day, whichever is lower. Once you sell short, place a protective stop-loss one tick above the high of the trade day or the previous day, whichever is higher. Move your stop to a break-even level as soon as the market moves in your favor. Afterwards, the rule of thumb is to move your stop to protect approximately 50 percent of paper profits (see Section 48).

The reason for using such tight stops is that Triple Screen trades only in the direction of the tide. If a trade does not work out fast, it is a sign that something is fundamentally changing below the surface of the market. Then it is better to run fast. The first loss is the best loss — it allows you to re-examine the market from the safety of the sidelines.

Conservative traders should go long or short on the first signal of the Triple Screen trading system and stay with that position until the major trend reverses or until stopped out. Active traders can use each new signal from the daily oscillator for pyramiding the original position.

A position trader should try and stay with a trade until the weekly trend reverses. A short-term trader may take profits using signals from the second screen. For example, if a trader is long and Force Index becomes positive or Stochastic rises to 70 percent, he may sell and take profits, then look for another buying opportunity.

The Triple Screen trading system combines different timeframes and several types of indicators. It uses a trend-following indicator with the long-term charts and a short-term oscillator with the intermediate charts. It uses special entry techniques for buying or selling short. It also uses tight money management rules.

44. PARABOLIC TRADING SYSTEM

The Parabolic trading system was described in 1976 by J. Welles Wilder, Jr. It was named after the pattern of its stops during runaway moves, which resembled a parabola. The Parabolic system is now included in many software packages.

Parabolic aims to catch trends and to reverse positions when trends reverse. Its unique feature is that it responds to the passage of time as well as to changing prices. Most traders focus on prices but ignore time (see Section 36).

How to Construct Parabolic

Parabolic is a reversal system, designed to keep a trader in the market all the time. When Parabolic stops you out of a long position, it tells you to go short at the same price. If it stops you out of a short position, it tells you to go long at the same price and time. This method worked well during the inflationary markets of the 1970s, but has led to many whipsaws in later years. Now Parabolic should be used selectively, only when markets are trending.

Parabolic is based on a good old rule — move your stops only in the direction of the trade and never against it. If you are long, you may raise your stops but never lower them. If you are short, you may only lower your stops.

Parabolic stops are set daily, using a formula:

$$Stop_{tomorrow} = Stop_{today} + AF \cdot (EP_{trade} - Stop_{today})$$

where $Stop_{today}$ = the current stop.
  $Stop_{tomorrow}$ = the stop for the next trading day.
  EP_{trade} = the extreme point reached by the market in the current trade. If a trader is long, EP is the highest high reached since the day he bought. If a trader is short, EP is the lowest low reached since the day he went short.
  AF = the acceleration factor. This unique tool determines how fast to move a stop in the direction of a trend. AF depends on the number of new highs since the entry into a long trade or the number of new lows since the entry into a short trade.

On the first day in a trade, Acceleration Factor equals 0.02. This means that the stop is moved by 2 percent of the distance between the extreme point and the original stop. AF increases by 0.02 each day the rally reaches a new high or a decline reaches a new low, up to the maximum of 0.20.

If the market reaches 3 higher highs during a long trade, AF equals 0.08 [0.02 + (0.02 • 3)], and if the market reaches 9 new highs, AF rises to its maximum of 0.20, or 0.02 + (0.02 • 9). In the latter case, the daily stop gets moved by 20 percent of the distance between the extreme point of the trade and the latest stop.

In the beginning of a trade, Acceleration Factor is small and stops move slowly. As the market reaches new highs or new lows, AF increases and stops move fast. If the market does not reach new highs or lows, AF keeps moving stops in the direction of the trade. By doing so, Parabolic forces traders to get out of trades that go nowhere.

Many traders change the Acceleration Factor. They adjust the size of the basic 0.02 step and the 0.20 maximum size of AF. Some increase them to make the system more sensitive, others decrease them to make the system react slower. The size of a step often varies from 0.015 to 0.025 and the maximum size of AF from 0.18 to 0.23.

Trading Psychology

Losers go broke by hanging onto losing positions and hoping for a reversal. The Parabolic system protects traders from indecision and imposes an iron discipline on them. It sets a stop the moment you enter a trade and tells you to move it in the direction of the trade.

If you go long or short but prices remain flat, it gives you a message that your timing was wrong. You would not have bought or shorted unless you expected prices to move right after you put on a trade! Parabolic does not let you hang onto a trade that goes nowhere. It moves stops in the direction of the trade, saying in effect "Put up or shut up."

The Parabolic system is extremely useful during runaway trends. When prices soar or crash without a pullback, it is hard to place stops using normal chart patterns or indicators. Parabolic is the best tool for placing stops under those conditions.

Trading Rules

When you begin using Parabolic in any given market, go back several weeks to calculate its stops. Adjust Parabolic stops daily, with one exception: If it tells you to move the stop into the previous day's range, don't do it. Stops should be kept outside of the previous day's range.

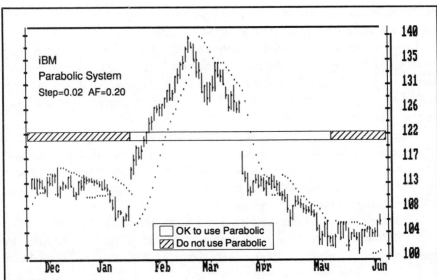

Figure 44–1.   Parabolic System

Parabolic works well when the markets are moving, but not when the markets are flat. If you get whipsawed twice in a row, it signals a flat market. Stop using Parabolic, but continue to track it on paper until you get two good signals.

Parabolic shines in fast-moving markets. Here it took most of the profit out of a 30+ point run in IBM and its subsequent decline, with a single whipsaw in April. Two whipsaws in a row in May gave a signal to stop using Parabolic.

The Parabolic system works well in trending markets but leads to whipsaws in trendless markets. It can generate spectacular profits during price trends but chop up an account in a trading range. Do not use it as an automatic trading method.

The original Parabolic was a true reversal system. When a trader was long one contract, it told him to place an order to sell two contracts if his stop was hit. Then he sold his long position and automatically went short. When a trader was short one contract, Parabolic told him to place an order to buy two if his stop was hit. Then he covered his short position and went long.

A trader is better off entering the market using some other trading method, such as the Triple Screen trading system, and then switching to

Parabolic only if he finds himself riding a dynamic uptrend or a downtrend (Figure 44-1).

1. When you find yourself in a strong uptrend, go over the past several weeks of data and apply the Parabolic system. Having updated Parabolic to the current day, begin calculating stops daily and use them to protect profits on your long position.

2. When you find yourself short in a fast downtrend, apply Parabolic to the past several weeks of data and update it to the present day. From that day on, calculate its stops daily to protect profits on your short position.

The Parabolic system ties together price and time and moves stops in the direction of the trade. The faster the trend, the faster Parabolic moves its stops. Parabolic is an excellent tool for getting the most out of a strong trend that was entered using any method.

45. CHANNEL TRADING SYSTEMS

Prices often flow in channels, the way rivers flow in valleys. When a river touches the right edge of its valley, it turns left. When a river touches the left rim of its valley, it turns right. When prices rally, they often seem to stop at an invisible ceiling. When they fall, they often seem to hit an invisible floor.

Channels help traders identify buying and selling opportunities and avoid bad trades. The original research into trading channels was conducted by J. M. Hurst and described in his 1970 book, *The Profit Magic of Stock Transaction Timing*.

Four Ways to Construct a Channel

Channels help traders because their boundaries show where to expect support or resistance to come into the market. There are four main ways to construct a channel:

1. By drawing a channel line parallel to a trendline (see Section 21).

2. By plotting two lines parallel to a moving average: one above it and another below.

3. Same as above, only the distance between each line and the moving average changes depending on the market's volatility (Bollinger bands).

4. By drawing a moving average of the highs and another of the lows.

Channels parallel to trendlines are useful for long-term analysis, especially on the weekly charts. Channels around moving averages are useful for short-term analysis, especially on daily and intraday charts. Channels whose width depends on volatility are good for catching early stages of major new trends.

Support is where buyers buy with greater intensity than sellers sell. Resistance is where sellers sell with greater intensity than buyers buy (see Section 19). Channels show where to expect support and resistance in the future.

A channel's slope identifies a market's trend. When a channel lies flat, you may trade all swings within its walls. When a channel rises, it pays to trade only from the long side, buying at the lower wall and selling at the upper wall. When a channel declines, it pays to trade only from the short side, shorting at the upper channel wall and covering at the lower wall.

Moving Average Channels

A 13-day exponential moving average can serve as the backbone of a channel (see Section 25). Draw upper and lower channel lines parallel to it. The width of a channel depends on the coefficient selected by the trader.

Upper Channel Line = EMA + Channel Coefficient • EMA

Lower Channel Line = EMA − Channel Coefficient • EMA

You need to adjust channel coefficients until a channel contains 90 percent to 95 percent of the price action. A channel shows the boundaries between normal and abnormal price action. It is normal for prices to be inside a channel, and only unusual events push them outside. The market is undervalued below its lower channel line and overvalued above its upper channel line.

For example, in 1992, the channel coefficient on the daily chart of the S&P 500 futures was 1.5 percent. If the 13-day EMA stood at 400, then the upper channel line was 406 [400 + (400 • 1.5/100)] and the lower channel line was 394 [400 − (400 • 1.5/100)].

Adjust channel coefficients at least once every three months to make a channel contain 90 percent to 95 percent of prices. If prices keep blowing out of a channel and staying outside for more than a few days, that channel should be widened. Too many reversals within the channel without reaching its walls indicate falling volatility, and that channel should be tightened.

Volatile markets require wider channels, and quieter markets require narrow channels. Long-term charts require wider channels. As a rule of thumb, weekly channel coefficients are twice as wide as daily ones.

Mass Psychology

An exponential moving average reflects the average consensus of value during the time covered by that average (see Section 25). When prices rise above the average consensus of value, sellers see an opportunity to take profits on long positions or go short. When they overpower the bulls, prices decline. When prices fall below the moving average, bargain hunters step in. Their buying and short covering by bears lift prices, and the cycle repeats.

When prices are near their moving average, the market is fairly valued. When prices are at or below the lower channel line, the market is undervalued. When prices are at or above the upper channel line, the market is overvalued. Channels help traders find buying opportunities when the market is cheap and shorting opportunities when the market is dear.

The market is like a manic-depressive person. When he reaches the height of mania, he is ready to calm down, and when he reaches the bottom of his depression, his mood is ready to improve. A channel marks the limits of mass optimism and pessimism. Its upper line shows where bulls run out of steam, and its lower line shows where bears become exhausted.

Every animal fights harder closer to home. The upper channel line shows where bears have their backs against the wall and fight off the bulls. The lower channel line shows where bulls have their backs against the wall and fight off the bears.

When a rally fails to reach the upper channel line, it is a bearish sign. It shows that bulls are becoming weaker. If a rally shoots out of a channel and prices close above it, it shows that the uptrend is strong. The reverse rules apply in downtrends.

Channels help traders who use them remain objective when others get swept up in bullish or bearish hysteria. If prices touch the upper channel line, you see that mass bullishness is being overdone and it is time to think about selling. When everyone turns bearish but prices touch the lower channel line, you know that it is time to think about buying instead of selling.

Trading Rules

Amateurs and market professionals handle channels differently. Amateurs bet on long shots — they tend to buy upside breakouts and sell short downside breakouts. When an amateur sees a breakout from a channel, he hopes that a major new trend is about to begin and make him rich quick.

Professionals trade against deviations and for a return to normalcy. It is normal for prices to remain within channels. Most breakouts are exhaustion moves that are quickly aborted. Professionals like to fade them — trade against them. They sell short as soon as an upside breakout stalls and buy when a downside breakout stops reaching new lows.

Breakouts can produce spectacular gains for amateurs when a major new trend blows out of a channel. Amateurs occasionally win, but it pays to trade with the professionals. Most breakouts are false and are followed by reversals.

Moving average channels can be used as a stand-alone trading method or combined with other techniques. Gerald Appel has recommended the following rules for trading with channels:

1. Draw a moving average and build a channel around it. When a channel is relatively flat, the market is almost always a good buy near the bottom of its trading channel and a good sell near the top.

2. When the trend turns up and a channel rises sharply, an upside penetration of the upper channel line shows very strong bullish momentum. It indicates that you will probably have one more chance to sell in the area of the highs that are being made. It is normal for the market to return to its moving average after an upside penetration, offering an excellent buying opportunity. Sell your long position when the market returns to the top of the channel.

3. The above rule works in reverse during sharp downtrends. A breakout below the lower channel boundary indicates that a pullback to the moving average is likely to occur, offering another opportunity to sell short. When prices return to the lower channel line, it is time to cover shorts.

The best trading signals are given by a combination of channels and technical indicators. Indicators give their strongest signals when they diverge from prices (see Figure 45-1). A method for combining channels and divergences has been described by Manning Stoller in an interview with this author.

4. A sell signal is given when prices reach the upper channel line while an indicator, such as Stochastic or MACD-Histogram, traces a lower top and creates a bearish divergence. It shows that bulls are becoming weak when prices are overextended.

5. A buy signal is given when prices reach the lower channel line while an indicator traces a higher bottom and creates a bullish divergence. It shows that bears are becoming weak when prices are already low.

We must analyze markets in more than one timeframe. Go long when prices are rising from the bottom to the top of the channel on both weekly and daily charts. Sell short when prices are sinking from the top to the bottom of the channel on both weekly and daily charts.

6. Go long below the moving average when the channel is rising, and take profits at the upper channel line. Go short when the channel is falling, and take profits at the lower channel line.

Standard Deviation Channels (Bollinger Bands)

Standard Deviation Channels have been proposed by Perry Kaufman in his book, *The New Commodity Trading Systems and Methods,* and popularized by analyst John Bollinger. The unique feature of Bollinger bands is that their width changes in response to market volatility. Trading rules for them differ from those for other channels.

1. Calculate a 21-day EMA.

2. Subtract the 21-day EMA from each closing price to obtain all the deviations from the average.

3. Square each of the deviations and get their sum to obtain the total squared deviation.

4. Divide the total squared deviation by the EMA length to obtain the average squared deviation.

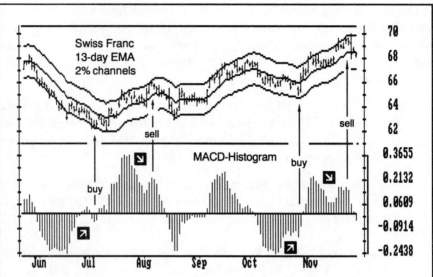

Figure 45–1. Trading with Channels and Indicators

A moving average reflects the average consensus of value. A channel or an envelope must be adjusted until it contains 90 percent–95 percent of all data. The upper channel line shows where the market is overvalued. The lower channel line shows where it is undervalued. It pays to buy in the lower half of a rising channel and to sell short in the upper half of a falling channel. Channels work best when their signals are combined with indicator divergences.

Bullish divergences in July and October occurred when the Swiss Franc was undervalued, near its lower channel line. These buy signals led to strong rallies. Bearish divergences occurred in August and November, when the Swiss Franc was overvalued, near its upper channel line. These sell signals were followed by sharp breaks. Combining channels with divergences allows you to trade against the market crowd at key turning points.

5. Take the square root of the average squared deviation to obtain the standard deviation.

These steps, outlined by John Bollinger, can be performed by many software packages for technical analysis. A Bollinger band becomes wider when volatility increases and narrows down when it decreases. A narrow Bollinger band identifies a sleepy, quiet market. Major market moves ted to erupt from flat bases. Bollinger bands help find transitions from quiet to active markets.

When prices rally outside a very narrow Bollinger band, they give a buy signal. When they drop out of a very narrow Bollinger band, they give a signal to go short. When prices pull back to their channel from the outside, it is time to close out positions.

Bollinger bands are especially useful for options traders. Options prices depend heavily on the swings in volatility. Bollinger bands help you buy when volatility is low and options are relatively cheap. They help you sell options when volatility is high and options are expensive.

More on Channels

Some traders use channels whose upper line is **a moving average of the highs** and whose lower line is **a moving average of the lows.** They appear more ragged than other channels. A trader has to choose a smoothing period for these channels. Here, as elsewhere, a 13-day EMA is a safe bet. A 13-day EMA of the highs creates the upper channel line, and a 13-day EMA of the lows creates the lower channel line.

One of the popular technical indicators is the **Commodity Channel Index** (CCI). It is based on the same principles as channels — it measures deviations from the moving average. If you use channels in trading, you may dispense with the CCI. Channels are better because they keep you visually closer to prices.

X

Risk Management

---

46. EMOTIONS AND PROBABILITIES

Trading is so exciting that it often makes amateurs feel high. A trade for them is like a ticket to a movie or a professional ballgame. Trading is a much more expensive entertainment than the cinema.

Nobody can get high and make money at the same time. Emotional trading is the enemy of success. Greed and fear are bound to destroy a trader. You need to use your intellect instead of trading on gut feeling.

A trader who gets giddy from profits is like a lawyer who starts counting cash in the middle of a trial. A trader who gets upset at losses is like a surgeon who faints at the sight of blood. A real professional does not get too excited about wins or losses.

The goal of a successful professional in any field is to reach his personal best — to become the best doctor, the best lawyer, or the best trader. Money flows to them almost as an afterthought. You need to concentrate on trading right — and not on the money. Each trade has to be handled like a surgical procedure — seriously, soberly, without sloppiness or shortcuts.

Why Johnny Can't Sell

A loser cannot cut his losses quickly. When a trade starts going sour, he hopes and hangs on. He feels that he cannot afford to get out, meets his mar-

254

gin calls, and keeps hoping for a reversal. His paper loss grows until what seemed like a bad loss starts looking like a bargain. Finally, his broker forces him to bite the bullet and take his punishment. As soon as he gets out of a trade, the market comes roaring back.

The loser is ready to smash his head against the wall — had he hung on, he would have made a small fortune on the reversal. Trends reverse when they do because most losers are alike. They act on their gut feelings instead of using their heads. The emotions of people are similar, regardless of their cultural backgrounds or educational levels. A frightened trader with sweaty palms and a pounding heart feels the same whether he grew up in New York or Hong Kong and whether he had 2 years or 20 years of schooling.

Roy Shapiro, a New York psychologist from whose article this subtitle is borrowed, writes:

> With great hope, in the private place where we make our trading decisions, our current idea is made ready. . . . one difficulty in selling is the attachment experienced toward the position. After all, once something is ours, we naturally tend to become attached to it. . . . This attachment to the things we buy has been called the "endowment effect" by psychologists and economists and we all recognize it in our financial transactions as well as in our inability to part with that old sports jacket hanging in the closet.
>
> The speculator is the parent of the idea. . . . the position takes on meaning as a personal extension of self, almost as one's child might. . . . Another reason that Johnny does not sell, even when the position may be losing ground, is because he wants to dream. . . . For many, at the moment of purchase critical judgment weakens and hope ascends to govern the decision process.

Dreaming in the markets is a luxury that nobody can afford. If your trades are based on dreams, you are better off putting your money into psychotherapy.

Dr. Shapiro describes a test that shows how people conduct business involving a chance. First, a group of people are given a choice: a 75 percent chance to win $1000 with a 25 percent chance of getting nothing — or a sure $700. Four out of five subjects take the second choice, even after it is explained to them that the first choice leads to a $750 gain over time. The majority makes the emotional decision and settles for a smaller gain.

Another test is given: People have to choose between a sure loss of $700 or a 75 percent chance of losing $1000 and a 25 percent chance of losing nothing. Three out of four take the second choice, condemning themselves to lose $50 more than they have to. In trying to avoid risk, they maximize losses!

Emotional traders want certain gains and turn down profitable wagers that involve uncertainty. They go into risky gambles to avoid taking certain losses. It is human nature to take profits quickly and postpone taking losses. Irrational behavior increases when people feel under pressure. According to Dr. Shapiro, "bets on long shots increase in the last two races of the day."

Emotional trading destroys losers. If you review your trading records, you will see that the real damage to your account was done by a few large losses or by long strings of losses while trying to trade your way out of a hole. Good money management would have kept you out of the hole in the first place.

Probability and Innumeracy

Losing traders look for "a sure thing," hang on to hope, and irrationally avoid accepting small losses. Their trading is based on emotions. Losers do not understand the key concepts of probability. They have no grasp of odds or random processes and have many superstitions about them.

Innumeracy—not knowing the basic notions of probability, chance, and randomness—is a fatal intellectual weakness in traders. Those simple ideas can be learned from many basic books.

The lively book *Innumeracy* by John Allen Paulos is an excellent primer on the concepts of probability. Paulos describes being told by a seemingly intelligent person at a cocktail party: "If the chance of rain is 50 percent on Saturday and 50 percent on Sunday, then it is 100 percent certain it will be a rainy weekend." Someone who understands so little about probability is sure to lose money trading. You owe it to yourself to develop a basic grasp of mathematical concepts involved in trading.

Ralph Vince begins his important book *Portfolio Management Formulas* with a delightful paragraph: "Toss a coin in the air. For an instant you experience one of the most fascinating paradoxes of nature—the random process. While the coin is in the air there is no way to tell for certain whether it will land heads or tails. Yet over many tosses the outcome can be reasonably predicted."

Mathematical expectation is an important concept for traders. It is called the player's edge (a positive expectation) or the house advantage (a negative expectation), depending on who the odds in a game favor. If you and I flip a coin, neither of us has an edge—each has a 50 percent chance of winning. But if you flip a coin in a casino that skims 10 percent from every pot, you will win only 90 cents for every dollar you lose. This "house advantage" creates a negative mathematical expectation for you. No system for money management can beat a negative expectation game over a period of time.

A Positive Expectation

If you know how to count cards in blackjack, you can have an edge against a casino (unless they detect you and throw you out. Casinos love drunk gamblers but hate card counters). An edge lets you win more often than you lose over a period of time. Good money management can help you make more money from your edge and minimize losses. Without an edge, you might as well give money to charity. In trading, the edge comes from a system that delivers greater profits than losses, slippage, and commissions. No money management method can rescue a bad trading system.

You can win only if you trade with a positive mathematical expectation — a sensible trading system. Trading on hunches leads to disasters. Many traders act like drunks wandering through a casino, going from game to game. Slippage and commissions destroy those who overtrade.

The best trading systems are crude and robust. They are made of a few elements. The more complex the systems, the more elements that can break. Traders love to optimize their systems using past data. The trouble is, your broker won't let you trade the past. Markets change, and the ideal parameters from the past may be no good today. Try to de-optimize your system instead — check how it would have performed under bad conditions. A robust system holds up well when markets change. It is likely to beat a heavily optimized system in real world trading.

Finally, when you develop a good system, don't mess with it. Design another one if you like to tinker. As Robert Prechter put it: "Most traders take a good system and destroy it by trying to make it into a perfect system." Once you have your trading system, it is time to set the rules for money management.

47. MONEY MANAGEMENT

Suppose you and I bet a penny on a coin flip: Tails, you win, heads, you lose. Suppose you have $10 of risk capital and I have $1. Even though I have less money, I have little to fear — it would take a string of 100 losses to wipe me out. We can play for a long time, unless two brokers get between us and drain our capital by commissions and slippage.

The odds will dramatically change if you and I raise our bet to a quarter. If I have only $1, then a string of only four losses will destroy me. If you have $10, you can afford to lose a quarter 40 times in a row. A series of four losses is likely to come much sooner than forty. All other factors being equal, the poorer of two traders is the first to go broke.

Most amateurs think that "other factors" are far from equal. They consider themselves brighter than the rest of us. The trading industry works hard to reinforce that delusion, telling traders that winners get the money lost by losers. They try to hide the fact that trading is a minus-sum game (see Section 3). Cocky amateurs take wild risks, producing commissions for brokers and profits for floor traders. When they blow themselves out of the market, new suckers come in because hope springs eternal.

Survival First

The first goal of money management is to ensure survival. You need to avoid risks that can put you out of business. The second goal is to earn a steady rate of return, and the third goal is to earn high returns—but survival comes first.

"Do not risk thy whole wad" is the first rule of trading. Losers violate it by betting too much on a single trade. They continue to trade the same or even a bigger size during a losing streak. Most losers go bust trying to trade their way out of a hole. Good money management can keep you out of the hole in the first place.

The deeper you fall, the more slippery your hole. If you lose 10 percent, you need to gain 11 percent to recoup that loss, but if you lose 20 percent, you need to gain 25 percent to come back. If you lose 40 percent, you need to make a whopping 67 percent, and if you lose 50 percent, you need to make 100 percent simply to recover. While losses grow arithmetically, the profits that are required to recoup them increase geometrically.

You have to know in advance how much you can lose—when and at what level you will cut your loss. Professionals tend to run as soon as they smell trouble and re-enter the market when they see fit. Amateurs hang on and hope.

Get Rich Slowly

An amateur trying to get rich quick is like a monkey out on a thin branch. He reaches for a ripe fruit but crashes when the branch breaks under his weight.

Institutional traders as a group tend to be more successful than private traders. They owe it to their bosses, who enforce discipline (See Section 14). If a trader loses more than his limit on a single trade, he is fired for insubordination. If he loses his monthly limit, his trading privileges are suspended for the rest of the month and he becomes a gofer, fetching other traders coffee. If he loses his monthly limit several times in a row, the company either fires or transfers him. This system makes institutional traders avoid losses. Private traders have to be their own enforcers.

An amateur who opens a $20,000 trading account and expects to run it into a million in two years is like a teenager who runs away to Hollywood to become a pop singer. He may succeed, but the exceptions only confirm the rule. Amateurs try to get rich quick but destroy themselves by taking wild risks. They may succeed for a while but hang themselves, given enough rope.

Amateurs often ask me what percentage profit they can make annually from trading. The answer depends on their skills or lack of such and market conditions. Amateurs never ask a more important question: "How much will I lose before I stop trading and re-evaluate myself, my system, and the markets?" If you focus on handling losses, profits will take care of themselves.

A person who makes 25 percent profit annually is a king of Wall Street. Many top-flight money managers would give away their firstborn child to be able to top this. A trader who can double his money in a year is a star — as rare as a pop musician or a top athlete.

If you set modest goals for yourself and achieve them, you can go very far. If you can make 30 percent annually, people will beg you to manage their money. If you manage $10 million — not an outlandish amount in today's markets — your management fee alone can run 6 percent of that, or $600,000 a year. If you make a 30 percent profit, you will keep 15 percent of it as an incentive fee — another $450,000. You will earn over a million dollars a year trading, without taking big risks. Keep these numbers in mind when you plan your next trade. Trade to establish the best track record, with steady gains and small drawdowns.

How Much to Risk

Most traders get killed by one of two bullets: ignorance or emotion. Amateurs act on hunches and stumble into trades that they should never take due to negative mathematical expectations. Those who survive the stage of virginal ignorance go on to design better systems. When they become more confident, they lift their heads out of the foxholes — and the second bullet hits them! Confidence makes them greedy, they risk too much money on a trade, and a short string of losses blows them out of the market.

If you bet a quarter of your account on each trade, your ruin is guaranteed. You will be wiped out by a very short losing streak, which happens even with excellent trading systems. Even if you bet a tenth of your account on a trade, you will not survive much longer.

A professional cannot afford to lose more than a tiny percentage of his equity on a single trade. An amateur has the same attitude toward trading as an alcoholic has toward drinking. He sets out to have a good time, but winds up destroying himself.

Extensive testing has shown that the maximum amount a trader may lose on a single trade without damaging his long-term prospects is 2 percent of his equity. This limit includes slippage and commissions. If you have a $20,000 account, you may not risk more than $400 on any trade. If you have a $100,000 account, you may not risk more $2000 on a trade, but if you have only $10,000 in your account, then you can risk no more than $200 on a trade.

Most amateurs shake their heads when they hear this. Many have small accounts and the 2 percent rule throws a monkey wrench into the dreams of quick profits. Most successful professionals, on the other hand, consider the 2 percent limit too high. They do not allow themselves to risk more than 1 percent or 1.5 percent of their equity on any single trade.

The 2 percent rule puts a solid floor under the amount of damage the market can do to your account. Even a string of five or six losing trades will not cripple your prospects. In any case, if you are trading to create the best track record, you will not want to show more than a 6 percent or 8 percent monthly loss. When you hit that limit, stop trading for the rest of the month. Use this cooling-off period to reexamine yourself, your methods, and the markets.

The 2 percent rule keeps you out of riskier trades. When your system gives an entry signal, check to see where to place a logical stop. If that would expose more than 2 percent of your account equity — pass up that trade. It pays to wait for trades that allow very close stops (see Chapter 9). Waiting for them reduces the excitement of trading but enhances profit potential. You choose which of the two you really want.

The 2 percent rule helps you decide how many contracts to trade. For example, if you have $20,000 in your account, you may risk up to $400 per trade. If your system flags an attractive trade with a $275 risk, then you may trade only one contract. If the risk is only $175, then you can afford to trade two contracts.

What about pyramiding—increasing the size of your trading positions as a trade moves in your favor? The 2 percent rule helps here too. If you show profit on a trend-following position, you may add to it, as long as your existing position is at a break-even level or better and the risk on the additional position does not exceed 2 percent of your equity.

Martingale Systems

Once you set your maximum risk per trade, you have to decide whether to risk the same amount on every trade. Most systems vary the amount of money at risk from trade to trade. One of the oldest money management systems is the martingale, originally developed for gambling. It has you bet a greater amount after a loss, in order to "come back." Needless to say, this approach has a great emotional appeal to losers.

A martingale player in a casino keeps betting $1 as long as he wins, but if he loses, he doubles up and bets $2. If he wins, he ends up with a $1 profit (–$1 + $2) and goes back to betting $1. If he loses, he doubles up again and bets $4. If he wins, he gets a $1 profit (–$1, –$2, +$4), but if he loses, he doubles up and bets $8. As long as he keeps doubling up, his very first win will cover all his losses and return a profit equal to his original bet.

A martingale system sounds like a no-lose proposition, until you realize that a long run of bad trades will wipe out every gambler, no matter how rich. At the extreme, a gambler who starts betting $1 and has 46 losses in a row, has to bet $70 trillion on his 47th bet—more than the net worth of the entire world (about $50 trillion). He is sure to run out of money or hit the house limit much sooner than that. A martingale system is futile if you have a negative or even-money expectation. It is self-defeating if you have a winning system and a positive expectation.

Amateurs love martingale systems because of their emotional appeal. There is a common superstition that you can get unlucky only up to a point and that bad luck is bound to change. Losers often trade more heavily after a drawdown. A loser fighting to come back often doubles his trading size after a loss. This is a very poor method of money management.

If you want to vary your trading size, logic requires you to trade more when your system is in gear with the market and making money. As your account grows, the 2 percent rule allows you to trade larger amounts. You should trade less when your system is out of sync with the market and losing money.

Optimal *f*

Some traders who develop computerized trading systems believe in trading what they call the optimal *f*— an "optimal fixed fraction" of the account. The fraction of capital they risk on any trade depends on a formula that is based on the performance of their trading system and their account size. It is a complex method, but whether you use it or not, you can borrow several sound ideas from it.

Ralph Vince has shown in his book, *Portfolio Management Formulas*, that: (1) optimal *f* keeps changing; (2) if you trade more than optimal *f*, you gain no benefit and are virtually certain to go broke; (3) if you trade less than optimal *f*, your risk decreases arithmetically but your profits decrease geometrically.

Trading at the optimal *f* is emotionally hard because it can lead to 85 percent drawdowns. It should be attempted only with true risk capital. The key point here is that if you trade more than the optimal fraction, you are certain to destroy your account. The lesson is: When in doubt, risk less.

Computerized testing of money management rules has confirmed several old-timers' rules and observations. The true measure of any system's financial risk is its biggest losing trade. A drawdown depends on the length of an adverse run, which can never be predicted. Diversification can buffer the drawdowns. You can diversify by trading different markets and using different systems. Closely related markets such as currencies offer no diversification. A small trader is forced to follow a simple rule: Put all your eggs into one basket and watch it like a hawk.

According to Vince, computer testing has proven several common money management rules: Never average down; never meet a margin call; if you must lighten up, liquidate your worst position; the first mistake is the cheapest.

Reinvesting Profits

Pay attention to what you feel when you handle profits. Many traders feel torn between a craving for a bigger and faster buck and a fear of losing. A professional trader calmly removes some money from his account, just as any other professional draws an income from his work. An amateur who fearfully grabs a profit and buys something with it before he can lose it shows little confidence in his ability to make money.

Reinvesting can turn a winning system into a losing one, but no method of reinvesting profits can turn a losing system into a winning one. Leaving profits in your account allows you to make money faster by trading more contracts or being able to establish long-term positions using wider stops. Removing some of your profits provides a cash flow. The government also wants its share in taxes.

There is no hard and fast rule for splitting your profits between reinvestment and personal use. It depends on your personality and the size of your trading account. If you start with a small account, such as $50,000, you will not want to drain profits from it. When your account is well into six figures, you may begin treating it as an income-producing business.

You will need to make important personal decisions. Do you need $30,000 or $300,000 a year to live on? Are you willing to cut spending in order to leave more in your account? The answers to these questions depend on your personality. Make sure to use your intellect and not your emotions when you make these decisions.

48. EXITING TRADES

Taking a loss can be emotionally hard, but taking a profit can be even harder. You can take a small loss automatically if you have the discipline to set a stop the moment you enter a trade. Taking a profit requires more thought. When the market moves in your favor, you need to decide whether to stay put, get out, or add to your position.

An amateur can tie his mind into a knot trying to decide what to do about a profit. He multiplies the number of ticks by their dollar value and feels a surge of greed: Let the trade run, make even more money. Then the market ticks against him, and he is hit with a jolt of fear: Grab that profit now, before it melts. A trader who acts on his emotions cannot make rational decisions.

One of the worst mistakes of traders is counting money while they have an open position. Counting money ties your mind into a knot. It interferes with your ability to trade rationally. If you catch yourself counting paper profits and thinking what you can buy with them—get rid of those thoughts! If you cannot get rid of them, get rid of your position.

If a beginner cashes out too early, he kicks himself for leaving money on the table. He decides to hang on the next time, overstays a trade, and loses money. If a beginner misses a profit because of a reversal, he grabs the first profit on the next trade and may well miss a major move. The market tugs on the amateur's emotions and he jerks in response.

A trader who responds to his feelings instead of external reality is certain to lose. He may grab a profit here and there but will eventually bust out, even if his system gives him good trades. Greed and fear destroy traders by clouding their minds. The only way to succeed in trading is to use your intellect.

Quality Before Money

The goal of a successful trader is to make the best trades. Money is secondary. If this surprises you, think how good professionals in any field operate. Good teachers, doctors, lawyers, farmers, and others make money—but they do not count it while they work. If they do, the quality of their work suffers.

If you ask your doctor how much money he earned today, he won't be able to answer (and if he can, you do not want him for a doctor). Ask your lawyer how much money he made today. He may have a general idea that he put in some billable hours, but not exactly how many dollars he made. If he counts money while he works, you do not want him for a lawyer. A real pro devotes all his energy to practicing his craft the best he can—not to counting money.

Counting money in a trade flashes a red light—a warning that you are about to lose because your emotions are kicking in and they will override your intellect. That is why it is a good idea to get out of a trade if you cannot get money off your mind.

Concentrate on quality—on finding trades that make sense and having a money management plan that puts you in control. Focus on finding good entry points and avoid gambles. Then the money will follow almost as an afterthought. You may count it later, well after a trade is over.

A good trader must focus on finding and completing good trades. A professional always studies the markets, looks for opportunities, hones his money management skills, and so on. If you ask him how much money he made on the current trade, he will have only a general idea of being a little or a lot ahead of the game, or a little behind (he can never be a lot behind because of tight stops). Like other professionals, he focuses on practicing his craft and polishing his skills. He does not count money in a trade. He knows that he will make money, as long as he does what is right in the markets.

Indicator Signals

If you use indicators for finding trades, use them also to get you out of trades. If your indicators are in gear with the market when it is time to buy or go short, use them to decide when it is time to sell or to cover.

A trader often becomes emotionally attached to a trade. Profits give people a high, but even a loss can tingle the nerves, like a scary but exciting ride on a roller coaster. When those indicator signals that flagged a trade disappear, get out of the market fast, regardless of your feelings.

For example, you may go long because a 13-week EMA has ticked up on the weekly charts while daily Stochastic fell into its buy zone. If you go long, decide in advance whether you will sell when daily Stochastic rallies and becomes overbought or when the 13-week EMA turns down. Write down your plan and keep it where you can always see it.

You may go short because weekly MACD-Histogram ticked down and daily Elder-ray gave a sell signal. Decide in advance whether you will cover when daily Elder-ray gives a buy signal or when weekly MACD-Histogram turns up. You need to decide in advance which signals you will take. There will be many signals — and the best time to decide is before you enter a trade.

Profit Targets, Elliott, and Fibonacci

Some traders try to establish profit targets. They want to sell strength when prices hit resistance or buy weakness when prices reach support. Elliott Wave theory is the main method for trying to forecast reversal points.

R. N. Elliott wrote several articles about the stock market and a book, *Nature's Law*. He believed that every movement in the stock market could be broken into waves, smaller waves, and subwaves. Those waves explained every turning point and occasionally allowed him to make correct predictions.

Those analysts who sell advisory services based on Elliott's methods always come up with so-called "alternate counts." They explain everything in hindsight but are not reliable in dealing with the future.

Fibonacci numbers and their ratios, especially 1.618, 2.618, and 4.236 express many relationships in nature. As Trudi Garland writes in her lucid book *Fascinating Fibonaccis*, these numbers express the ratios between the diameters of neighboring spirals in a seashell and in a galaxy, the number of seeds in the adjacent rows of a sunflower, and so on. Elliott was the first to point out that these relationships also apply to the financial markets.

Tony Plummer describes in his book *Forecasting Financial Markets* how he uses Fibonacci ratios to decide how far a breakout from a trading range is likely to carry. He measures the height of a trading range, trades in the direction of a breakout, and then looks for reversal targets by multiplying the height of the range by Fibonacci numbers. Experienced traders combine profit targets with other technical studies. They look for indicator signals at the projected turning points. If indicators diverge from a trend that is approaching a target, it reinforces the signal to get out. Trading on targets alone can be a tremendous ego boost, but the markets are too complex to be handled with a few simple numbers.

Setting Stops

Serious traders place stops the moment they enter a trade. As time passes, stops need to be adjusted to reduce the amount of money at risk and to protect a bigger chunk of profit. Stops should be moved only one way — in the direction of the trade. We all like to hope that a trade will succeed — and a stop is a piece of reality that prevents traders from hanging on to empty hope.

When you are long, you may keep your stops in place or raise them but never lower them. When you are short, you may keep your stops in place or lower them but never raise them. Cutting extra slack to a losing trade is a loser's game. If a trade is not working out, it shows that your analysis was flawed or the market has changed. Then it is time to run fast.

Serious traders use stops the way sailors use ratchets — to take out the slack in their sails. Losers who move stops away from the market vote in favor of fantasy and against reality.

Learning to place stops is like learning to drive defensively. Most of us learn the same techniques and we adjust them to fit our personal styles. The following are the basic rules for placing stops.

1. Stop-Loss Order

Place your stop the moment you enter a trade. Trading without a stop is like walking down Fifth Avenue in Manhattan without pants on. It can be done, I have seen people do it, but it is not worth the trouble. A stop will not protect you from a bad trading system; the best it can do is slow down the damage.

A stop-loss order limits your risk even though it does not always work. Sometimes prices gap through a stop. A stop is not a perfect tool but it is the best defensive tool we have.

When you go long, place your stop below the latest minor support level. When you go short, place a stop above the latest minor resistance (see Section 20). The Parabolic system (see Section 44) moves the stops in the direction of the trade, depending on the passage of time and changes in prices. If you use the Triple Screen trading system (see Section 43), place your stop after entering a trade at the extreme of the past two days' range.

Avoid all trades where a logical stop would expose more than 2 percent of your equity. This limit includes slippage and commissions.

2. Break-Even Order

The first few days in a trade are the hardest. You have done your home-work, found a trade, and placed an order. It has been filled, and you placed a stop-loss order. There is not much else you can do—you are like a pilot strapped into his seat for takeoff. The engines are blasting at full power, but the speed is low, and there is no room to maneuver—just sit back and trust your system.

As soon as prices start to move in your favor, move your stop to a break-even level. When the takeoff is completed, your flight is at a safer stage. Now you get to choose between keeping your money or gaining more, instead of choosing between a loss and a gain.

As a rule, prices have to move away from your entry point by more than the average daily range before you move your stop to a break-even level. It takes judgment and experience to know when to do it.

When you move a stop to a break-even level, you increase the risk of a whipsaw. Amateurs often kick themselves for "leaving money on the table." Many amateurs allow themselves only one entry into a trade. There is nothing wrong with re-entering a trade after getting stopped out. Professionals keep trying to get in until they get a good entry, using tight money management.

3. Protect—Profit Order

As prices continue to move in your favor, you have to protect your paper profits. Paper profit *is* real money—treat it with the same respect as money in your wallet. Risk only a portion of it, as the price of staying in the trade.

If you are a conservative trader, apply the 2 percent rule to your paper profits. This protect-profit order is a "money stop," protecting your equity.

Keep moving it in the direction of the trade so that no more than 2 percent of your growing equity is ever exposed.

More aggressive traders use the 50 percent rule. If you follow it, half the paper profit is yours and half belongs to the market. You can mark the highest high reached in a long trade or the lowest low reached in a short trade, and place your stop halfway between that point and your entry point. For example, if prices move 10 points in your favor, place a stop to protect 5 points of profit.

If in doubt, use the Parabolic system (see Section 44) to help you adjust your stops. When you are not sure whether to stay in a trade or not, take profits and re-evaluate the situation from the sidelines. There is nothing wrong with exiting and re-entering a trade. People think much more clearly when they have no money at risk.

After the Trade

A trade does not end when you close out your position. You must analyze it and learn from it. Many traders throw their confirmation slips into a folder and go looking for the next trade. They miss an essential part of growing to become a professional trader — review and self-analysis.

Have you identified a good trade? Which indicators were useful and which did not work? How good was your entry? Was the initial stop too far or too close? Why and by how much? Did you move your stop to a break-even level too early or too late? Were your protect-profit stops too loose or too tight? Did you recognize the signals to exit a trade? What should you have done differently? What did you feel at the various stages of the trade? This analysis is an antidote against emotional trading.

Ask yourself these and other questions and learn from your experiences. A cool, intelligent analysis does you more good than gloating about profits or wallowing in regrets.

Start keeping a "before and after" notebook. Whenever you enter a position, print out the current charts. Paste them on the left page of your notebook and jot down your main reasons for buying or shorting. Write down your plan for managing the trade.

When you exit, print the charts again and paste them on the right page of your notebook. Write down your reasons for exiting and list what you did right or wrong. You will have a pictorial record of your trades and thoughts. This notebook will help you learn from the past and discover blind spots in yyour thinking. Learn from history and profit from your experiences.

Afterword

One hot summer, in the mountains of northern Italy, I sat down to draft the first outline of this book. Two and a half years later, on a frigid January in New York City, I printed out its last chart. I wrote and rewrote this book three times, to make it clearer and to reflect my growing experience.

I have changed as a person, and my methods continue to evolve. If I could work on this manuscript for another two and a half years, it would become a different book, but it is time to let go.

Pulling the Trigger

Traders sometimes confide in me that they have trouble "pulling the trigger" — buying or selling when their methods tell them to go long or short. I had this problem once, for a very short time. My friend Lou, to whom this book is dedicated, helped me get rid of it.

One Sunday afternoon I mentioned to Lou that I saw several attractive trades but doubted I'd take any of them the following week because I had recently gotten beat up in the markets. Lou, who is usually cool and mild-mannered, suddenly began yelling. "I want you to trade at the opening on Monday!" I did not feel like trading — I was afraid of losing. "I don't give a shit whether you win or lose — trade tomorrow at the open!" I seldom trade at the open, but I could trade 10 minutes later, looking for an opening range breakout. "10 minutes is OK, but trade tomorrow!"

I thought about what had happened and realized what my problem was. I was like a skier at the top of the hill who had taken a bad spill and was afraid to go down again. Whatever my technique, if I was afraid to go downhill, I could not be a skier.

Fear of placing an order is the biggest problem that a serious trader can have. There is no way to handle this problem with ease and comfort. It has to be handled hard, by a sheer effort of will, which is why Lou yelled at me — as a friend.

You need to design a system or borrow one from this book and adapt it to your needs. Skiers do a little practice on a bunny slope, and you can paper-trade. Design a sensible money management plan, using the 2 percent rule. Limit your monthly losses to the maximum of 6 percent or 8 percent of your risk capital. At this point you are like a skier, ready at the top of the hill. Push off when your system flags you to go! Push off now!

If you do not go downhill when the flag comes down, you might as well sell your skis and take up golf or raise goldfish. In other words, forget about trading.

Now you have a system, you've learned money management rules, you know the psychological rules for cutting losses. Now you must trade. Can you? Traders try to weasel out of making this decision. They papertrade for years, buy automatic trading systems, and so on. Several traders have even asked me to hypnotize them. These games must end. It is time to make an effort of will!

Consider this book my friendly yell at you.

The Endless Trail

Markets change, new opportunities emerge, and old ones melt away. Good traders are successful but humble people — they always learn. Being a trader is a lifelong challenge.

I hope this book helps you to grow as a trader. If you have read this far, you must be serious about your work. Take this book for what it is — a description of what's on one trader's mind and how he goes about solving problems that all of us face. Take the ideas that appeal to you, and shape them to fit your style.

If you believe that being a trader is worth the effort — as I decided years ago — my best wishes to you. I continue to learn, and like any trader, I reserve the right to be smarter tomorrow than I am today.

Acknowledgments

After finishing a project of several years, I owe a sweet debt of gratitude to hundreds of persons — teachers, friends, and clients. If you do not see your name here, please forgive me, and I'll thank you in person the next time we meet.

Thanks, first of all, to all the clients of Financial Trading Seminars, Inc. Often a phone would ring and a trader would ask for "Dr. Elder's book." The book was not written yet, not advertised anywhere — but clients expected a book from me. That was terrific encouragement.

Writing a book was a hard job, but it helped me organize my thoughts and become a better trader. Two friends provided a soft push at the birth of this project. First, Tim Slater invited me to seminars in Asia, and then Martin Pring introduced me to people at WEFA, which led to a conference in Italy. Walking with Tim through Snake Alley to a smoky restaurant in Taipei and, a few months later, sitting in a cafe in Milan with Martin, I felt friendly but unmistakable pressure to organize my thoughts and start writing.

The blank screen of a word processor seemed huge and forbidding. To get the job rolling, I offered a number of seminars and taped some of them. Those transcripts helped me flesh out the ideas for this book. Thanks to all the analysts and traders in New York and Toronto, London and Singapore who came to my seminars, listened, and asked hundreds of questions. Some were experts whose comments forced me to stretch my mind farther than I expected; others were beginners whose questions served as a reminder to keep my feet on the ground. I hope you are all making money trading.

Three persons, a colleague and two patients, have opened my mind to the idea of 12 Steps — a major factor in my improvement as a trader. Thank you, Dagmar O'Connor, Jim S., and Kathy H. (Kathy died last year, after a long battle with cancer, and visiting her for months in a hospice reinforced my belief that there are values more important than money.) Thanks to the professional traders who came to consult with me as a psychiatrist and entrusted me with their confidence. You reinforced my conviction that if you get your head in order, money tends to flow in.

Great thanks to everybody who works for my company, Financial Trading Seminars, Inc. It is a unique group of people—intelligent, dynamic, and fun to be with. Each has been selected from dozens if not hundreds of applicants—you are the best. Thanks especially to our managers—Carol Keegan Kayne and Inga Boguslavsky. Carol helped me edit every chapter. We had many passionate arguments about the language, most of which Carol won, and if you have any complaints about the clarity of this book, I'll give you her number.

Once the manuscript was ready, I divided it into a dozen sections and mailed each to a top expert in the field. These busy and successful people found time to review several chapters each and suggested many improvements. In addition to the friends already mentioned, they included Gerald Appel, Stephen Briese, Ralph Cato, Mark Douglas, John Ehlers, Perry Kaufman, Tony Plummer, Fred Schutzman, Bo Thunman, Ralph Vince, and David Weis. Thank you for being so generous with your time and advice. If the market is a minus-sum game, then having friends like you is an especially big plus!

Thanks to the analysts who wrote before me. It was often hard to find who was first—there is a thicket of conflicting claims in our field. As Henry Kissinger once said, "Academic fights are so bitter because the stakes are so small." Most charts in this book were drawn using CompuTrac software on an IBM-compatible and imported into PageMaker® for the Macintosh. Thanks to Norbert Rudek for helping to set up the system and for unstinting phone support. Thanks to the editors at *Barron's, Futures, Technical Analysis of Stocks and Commodities, Futures and Options World,* and other magazines for encouraging me to write articles and book and software reviews—it was a good training for the book.

Many thanks to Stephen Reibel, M.D., a fellow psychiatrist and a former boss at St. Luke's–Roosevelt Hospital Center for covering my practice. I can go and teach all over the world knowing that my patients in New York are in good hands.

Lou Taylor, to whom this book is dedicated, has offered a treasury of superb ideas. I wish he would write a book. His wise advice made a huge difference at several important turning points. My family, especially Miriam, Nicole, and Danny, provided cheerful support and a happy diversion from business.

Finally, I want to thank my friend from way back when, Nicolai Gorbunoff. A scientist, he was destroyed by the Soviet system when I was but a teenager. In the closed, Communist party–dominated world that we lived in, he planted a simple but revolutionary idea in my mind: that the only standard for research and work was the "world class." You had to strive to be among the best in the world, or else it did not pay to try. Thank you Nicolai, and thank you, all my friends.

New York   Dr. Alexander Elder
November 1992

Sources

Angell, George. *Winning in the Futures Market* (1979) (Chicago: Probus Publishing, 1990).

Appel, Gerald. *Day-Trading with Gerald Appel* (video) (New York: Financial Trading Seminars, Inc., 1989).

Arms, Richard W., Jr. *The Arms Index* (Homewood, IL: Business One Irwin, 1988).

Babcock, Bruce, Jr. *The Dow Jones Irwin Guide to Commodity Trading Systems* (Homewood, IL: Dow Jones Irwin, 1989).

Balsara, Nauzer J. *Money Management Stategies for Future Traders* (New York: John Wiley & Sons, 1992).

Belveal, L. Dee. *Charting Commodity Market Price Behavior* (1969) (Homewood, IL: Dow Jones Irwin, 1989).

Bullish Review Newsletter, Rosemount, MN.

Club 3000 Newsletter, Augusta, MI.

CompuTrac Software Manual (1982) (New Orleans, LA: CompuTrac, 1991).

Davis, L. J. "Buffet Takes Stock," *The New York Times*, April 1, 1990.

Diamond, Barbara, and Mark Kollar. *24-Hour Trading* (New York: John Wiley & Sons, 1989).

Douglas, Mark. *The Disciplined Trader* (New York: New York Institute of Finance, 1990).

Edwards, Robert D., and John Magee. *Technical Analysis of Stock Trends* (1948) (New York: New York Institute of Finance, 1992).

Ehlers, John. *MESA and Trading Market Cycles* (New York: John Wiley & Sons, 1992) .

Elder, Alexander. *Directional System* (video) (New York: Financial Trading Seminars, Inc., 1988).

_____ . *Elder-ray* (video) (New York: Financial Trading Seminars, Inc., 1990).

_____ . *MACD & MACD-Histogram* (video) (New York: Financial Trading Seminars, Inc., 1988).

_____ . "Market Gurus," *Futures and Options World,* London, September 1990.

_____ . *Relative Strength Index* (video) (New York: Financial Trading Seminars, Inc., 1988).

_____ . *Stochastic* (video) (New York: Financial Trading Seminars, Inc., 1988).

————. *Technical Analysis in Just 52 Minutes* (video) (New York: Financial Trading Seminars, Inc., 1992).

————. "Triple Screen Trading System," *Futures* Magazine, April 1986.

————. *Triple Screen Trading System* (video) (New York: Financial Trading Seminars, Inc., 1989).

————. *Williams %R* (video) (New York: Financial Trading Seminars, Inc., 1988).

Elliott, Ralph Nelson. *Nature's Law* (1946) (Gainesville, GA: New Classics Library, 1980).

Engel, Louis. *How to Buy Stocks* (1953) (New York: Bantam Books, 1977).

Freud, Sigmund. *Group Psychology and the Analysis of the Ego* (1921) (London: Hogarth Press, 1974).

Friedman, Milton. *Essays in Positive Economics* (Chicago: The University of Chicago Press, 1953).

Frost, A. J., and R. R. Prechter, Jr. *Elliott Wave Principle* (Gainesville, GA: New Classics Library, 1978).

Gallacher, William. *Winner Takes All—A Privateer's Guide to Commodity Trading* (Toronto: Midway Publications, 1983).

Gann, W. D. *How to Make Profits in Commodities* (Chicago: W. D. Gann Holdings, 1951).

Garland, Trudi Hammel. *Fascinating Fibonaccis* (Palo Alto, CA: Dale Seymour Publications, 1987).

Granville, Joseph. *New Strategy of Daily Stock Market Timing for Maximum Profit* (Englewood Cliffs, NJ: Prentice Hall, 1976).

————. *The Book of Granville; Reflections of a Stock Market Prophet* (New York: St. Martin's Press, 1984).

Greenson, Ralph R. "On Gambling" (1947), in *Explorations in Psychoanalysis* (New York: International Universities Press, 1978).

Greising, David, and Laurie Morse. *Brokers, Bagmen & Moles* (New York: John Wiley & Sons, 1991).

Havens, Leston. *Making Contact* (Cambridge, MA: Harvard University Press, 1986).

Hurst, J. M. *The Profit Magic of Stock Transaction Timing* (Englewood Cliffs, NJ: Prentice-Hall, 1970).

Kannerman, Daniel, and Amos Tversky. "Choices, Values, and Frames," *American Psychologist*, 39(4) (April 1984), 341–350.

Kaufman, Perry. *The New Commodity Trading Systems and Methods* (New York: John Wiley & Sons, 1987).

Kleinfield, Sonny. *The Traders* (New York: Holt, Rinehart and Winston, 1983).

Lefevre, Edwin. *Reminiscences of a Stock Operator* (1923) (Greenville, SC: Traders Press, 1985).

LeBon, Gustave. *The Crowd* (1897) (Atlanta, GA: Cherokee Publishing, 1982).

Mackay, Charles. *Extraordinary Popular Delusions and the Madness of Crowds* (1841) (New York: Crown Publishers, 1980).

Murphy, John J. *Technical Analysis of the Futures Markets* (New York: New York Institute of Finance, 1986).

Neill, Humphrey B. *The Art of Contrary Thinking* (1954) (Caldwell, ID: Caxton Printers, 1985).

_____. *Tape Reading and Market Tactics* (1931) (New York: Forbes Publishing, 1931).

Nison, Steve. *Japanese Candlestick Charting Techniques* (New York: New York Institute of Finance, 1991).

Notis, Steve. "How to Gain an Edge with a Filtered Approach," *Futures* Magazine, September 1989.

Pacelli, Albert Peter. *The Speculator's Edge* (New York: John Wiley & Sons, 1989).

Paulos, John Allen. *Innumeracy. Mathematical Illiteracy and Its Consequences* (New York, Vintage Press, 1988).

Plummer, Tony. *Forecasting Financial Markets* (London: Kogan Page, 1989).

Pring, Martin J. *Technical Analysis Explained,* 3rd ed. (New York: McGraw-Hill, 1991).

Rhea, Robert. *The Dow Theory* (New York: Barron's, 1932).

Rorschach, Herman. *Psychodiagnostics* (1921) (New York: Grune & Stratton, 1942).

Schutzman, Fred G. "Smoothing Rate of Change: New Twist to Old Study," *Futures* Magazine, April 1991.

Shapiro, Roy. *Why Johnny Can't Sell Losers: Psychological Roots,* unpublished article, 1991.

Sperandeo, Victor. *Trader Vic—Methods of a Wall Street Master* (New York: John Wiley & Sons, 1991).

Steidlmayer, J. Peter, and Kevin Koy. *Markets & Market Logic* (Chicago: Porcupine Press, 1986).

Teweles, Richard J., and Frank J. Jones. *The Futures Game,* 2nd ed. (New York: McGraw-Hill, 1987).

Twelve Steps and Twelve Traditions (New York: Alcoholics Anonymous World Services, 1952).

Vince, Ralph. *Portfolio Management Formulas* (New York: John Wiley & Sons, 1990).

Wilder, J. Welles, Jr. *New Concepts in Technical Trading Systems* (Greensboro, SC: Trend Research, 1976).

Williams, Larry. *How I Made One Million Dollars* (Carmel Valley, CA: Conceptual Management, 1973).

_____. *The Secret of Selecting Stocks* (Carmel Valley, CA: Conceptual Management, 1972).

Index

About the Author

Alexander Elder, M.D., was born in Leningrad and grew up in Estonia where he entered medical school at the age of 16. At 23, while working as a ship's doctor, he jumped a Soviet ship in Africa and received political asylum in the United States. He continued to work as a psychiatrist in New York City, served as the book editor of *The Psychiatric Times,* and taught at Columbia University. After becoming involved in financial trading, Dr. Elder published dozens of articles, software, and book reveiws and spoke at many conferences. In 1988 he founded Financial Trading Seminars, Inc., an educational firm for traders. Dr. Elder consults for individuals and financial institutions and conducts seminars for traders. His firm produces videotapes on trading and supplies trading books.

Readers of *Trading for a Living* are welcome to request a current information kit by writing or calling:

Financial Trading Seminars, Inc.
PO Box 20555, Columbus Circle Station
New York, NY 10023, USA
800-458-0939 or 212-432-7630
Fax 718-639-8889